ADVENTISM

IN

Conflict

A. LEROY MOORE

REVIEW AND HERALD® PUBLISHING ASSOCIATION
HAGERSTOWN, MD 21740

Texts credited to Green's Greek Interlinear are from *The Interlinear Bible*, Jay P. Green, Sr., general editor and translator. Copyright © 1976 by the Trinitarian Bible Society.

Scripture quotations marked NASB are from the *New American Standard Bible*, © The Lockman Foundation 1960, 1962, 1963, 1968, 1971, 1972, 1973, 1975, 1977.

Texts credited to NIV are from the Holy Bible, *New International Version*. Copyright © 1973, 1978, 1984, International Bible Society. Used by permission of Zondervan Bible Publishers.

Texts credited to NKJV are from The New King James Version. Copyright © 1979, 1980, 1982, Thomas Nelson, Inc., Publishers.

Bible texts credited to NRSV are from the New Revised Standard Version of the Bible, copyright © 1989 by the Division of Christian Education of the National Council of the Churches of Christ in the U.S.A. Used by permission.

Bible texts credited to NWT are from the *New World Translation of the Holy Scriptures*. Copyright © 1950, 1953, 1955, 1957, 1958, 1960, Watchtower Bible and Tract Society.

This book was
Edited by Gerald Wheeler
Designed by Patricia S. Wegh
Cover design by Helcio Deslandes
Typeset: 11/13 Goudy

PRINTED IN U.S.A.

99 98 97 96 95   10 9 8 7 6 5 4 3 2 1

R&H Cataloging Service
Moore, A. Leroy
    Adventism in Conflict: resolving
the conflicts that divide us.

    1. Seventh-day Adventist—Doctrines.
I. Title.
                286.732

ISBN 0-8280-1033-1

Dedication

In Memory

I dedicate this book to the memory of my beloved mother. Melissa Letitia (Lettie) was, with her parents, baptized into the Seventh-day Adventist Church when she was 12. Under the influence of D. M. Canright, her father, Edwin Wheeler, left the church two or three years later and spent the rest of his life warring against it. To escape the hostile atmosphere, Mother left home at 17 to dedicate her life, and later her family, to the truths of Adventism.

As an only child without playmates, my mother dreamed of raising 12 children. After she discovered the Advent message, her vision expanded to training a family of workers for the cause of truth. Jennie, her first child, died at birth. James died suddenly as an infant. After the arrival of Myrtle and Miriam, Eugene also died in infancy. Then came Millicent and Marie.

Like Hannah of old, Mother prayed for a son to dedicate to the ministry. As the first of two sons, I briefly tell my story in chapter 2. My brother Paul also dedicated his life to the ministry. Marilyn and Marcea followed Paul. Mother never reached the dozen mark. But eight of the 11 children grew to serve the Lord in a variety of capacities.

Our parents both had serious health problems. This, together with the Depression, often left us destitute. I will never forget Mother's unyielding determination to provide for her family. I was 8 when she rose from her bed and, with yellow jaundice plainly visible on her face and arms, walked with me from farm to farm to secure a cow. At last a farmer responded to her promise that she would someday pay for it. Then and at other times the only food we had was the milk "Jersey" gave and the eggs the chickens laid. A year later my mother wrote Thanksgiving and Christmas songs to raise funds for our survival.

Both of our parents placed the highest priority upon Christian education. With our own help, they kept us in church school from grade school through college. In 1950 we moved to Deer Park near Pacific Union College. While Paul was still at home my parents dedicated the rooms on the third floor of Rose Haven, their home for the elderly, to college age young men who couldn't afford to live in the dorm. When my father died in 1959, Mother felt her life would end. Instead, she continued to serve as an extra mother to dozens of young men and several young women. Evangelist Dan Collins was the subject of her first book, *My Son Dan* (Pacific Press Publishing Association, 1978). She was then in her eighty-second year. Marilyn had brought Dan into the church, but he slipped into alcoholism. Mother helped him regain his faith.

Afterward she wrote several more books, all of them relating to her family and her extra children. The objective of each book was the same: to lift up Jesus to her own grandchildren and great-grandchildren and to inspire other fathers and mothers to commit themselves and their children to Him and to the message to which she had dedicated her life. In 1989 she completed *Miracles of God in Melissa's Family*.

"Truth" and "purity" were Mother's watchwords. Only the word "love" better characterized her. Her mother's heart was open to every young person in need. During one long trip she took with me in my Native American work I asked her how many young people she had mothered. It took time to recall; but she counted more than 100 young people of every color and from every continent.

Mother never lost her strong alto voice. Since her ninety-eighth birthday would fall on Sabbath, I asked her to sing a duet with me in her Elmshaven church. Unfortunately, a car knocked her down and backed into her on Sabbath, September 24, 1994. X-rays showed no breaks and she seemed to be doing well for a time, but eventually the pain greatly intensified. On October 22 the ball of her hip suddenly broke off. Replacement surgery seemed to be effective, but infection hindered her progress. When I arrived at her hospital bedside November 7, she, with my sisters Millie Westmoreland and Marie Anderson, was softly singing her "theme song," "Now, don't you let nobody turn you round."

During the two full days I spent with Mother she became much stronger, and her pain subsided. "Son," she said on the second day, "let's practice our song." Still determined to recover, she had lost none of her belief in miracles. So we practiced, "I come to the garden alone."

Two things, however, were even more on her mind: the publication of this book—which had passed the editorial staff but had not yet been approved by the marketing board—and my brother Paul's Life Talk Radio station, which had recently connected with the Adventist Media Center and was designed to carry the Adventist message to all of North America by satellite. As a major financial contributor, Mother's greatest burden until she fell asleep a week later was to help secure needed funds to develop Life Talk Radio further.

We all owe more than words can express to a mother who was born Thanksgiving day, November 26, 1896—Ellen White's sixty-ninth birthday. She went to her rest on November 15, 1994, just 11 days before her own ninety-eighth birthday. A lifelong thirst for knowledge was still evident only a week before when she asked me to discuss theological issues.

Mother was unable to finish grade 10. But she always eagerly listened to and carefully pondered the meaning of issues. This thirst and her deep commitment to honesty, fairness, and understanding of the views of others has had an incalculable impact upon my own vision of truth, from which this book evolved. She is now gone. But my mother's works live on through the lives of the many for whom she lived.

In Appreciation

Acknowledgments

W ere a complete list of the many who have contributed to this book possible, it would include my students and parishioners, as well as my own teachers, fellow teachers, and pastors. It would especially include the many who through the years have read my numerous manuscripts and offered helpful comments. A mere sample of these were my own conference officers, Jeri Patzer and Bryce Pascoe, neighboring pastors Steve Huey and Lee Roy Holmes, and professors Jack Provonsha, Raymond Cottrell, David Duffle, Douglas Bennet, and Norman Gully.

Robert H. Brown took time from heavy assignments to critique my manuscript. McDougal Brothers provided financial assistance at a crucial time. Richard Tooley, controller of the Review and Herald, had a special role in the process, and numerous other staff worked overtime to prepare this in time for General Conference session. Gerald Wheeler edited my manuscript despite a heavy schedule. My greatest debt is to editor Richard Coffen without whose critiques and consistent encouragement this book would not be in print, and to Woodie Whidden, who invited me to his home for a week of editing and cutting my manuscript in half.

I must express my gratitude to my siblings. Had not Milli and Richard Westmoreland invited us to live in their apartment rent-free while I wrote *Theology in Crisis*, I might never have been able to complete the doctoral dissertation for which this is a sequel. Moreover, Richard spent many hours six days a week for many months typing and retyping my nearly 400-page script. Both he and Milli provided vital critiques. Miriam and Orval Ross, Marie and Alvin Anderson, and Marilyn and Charles Sterling all helped by finances and encouragement. As eldest sister, Myrtle was a second mother when I was small and Mother was ill. She always took an interest in my work before her death in 1988. My youngest sister, Marcea Spencer, has helped by unfailing love, confidence, and encouragement. Last but not least, my brother Paul consistently urged me to get the concepts published, and his critiques and technical suggestions were invaluable.

I also owe much insight to my daughter, Leanne Harding, and to my son, David, and his wife, Debbie, and even to our nine wonderful grandchildren. Long discussions over the years with my son-in-law, Dave Harding, helped sharpen concepts, and his critiques have been helpful.

But to none do I owe more than to my wife, Pat. Without her confidence and encouragement through long years, which often seemed like widowhood, I could never have completed this book or *Theology in Crisis*, for which she typed the final draft while working full-time. Moreover, her insights have often been crucial.

Contents

Paradoxical Truth or Hostile Languages

Part One

1

Most of Us See
Only Half the F's

"Your only safety is in coming to Christ, and ceasing from sin this very moment. The sweet voice of mercy is sounding in your ears today, but who can tell if it will sound tomorrow?" (Signs of the Times, Aug. 29, 1892).

John Witcombe, a new intern in the Upper Columbia Conference, had been invited by the conference president, Jere Patzer, to give his testimony. Witcome was a founder and former leader of the LOR (the Lord Our Righteousness movement), a home church separatist movement. John quickly grabbed the attention of the elders and pastors at the 1994 retreat with a story that provides a vital key to understanding the multiplying divisions that threaten Seventh-day Adventist unity. He described how he had taught that believers could stop sinning instantly—"this very moment," to use the phrasing of the above Ellen White statement that Witcombe quoted.

"The year was 1987," he told the group. "We traveled about the country presenting our 'victory now' message in churches and rented halls.

"Some who made the decision to stop sinning would wonder why it didn't work for them. A number of my comrades felt the problem might have something to do with the leavening influence of their local churches.

"The Bible says, 'Beware ye of the leaven of the Pharisees, which is hypocrisy,'" they explained, and defined hypocrisy as believing what you don't do. So believers should beware of those who are not living what they believe. With deep conviction they concluded, 'When you see a sign saying "Beware of Dog," you better stay out of the yard.'

"As a seventh-generation Adventist, I opposed my friends' plan to tell our converts that they should stay away from their local churches if they wanted to maintain a victorious life. Nor was I about to leave what I firmly believed to be God's remnant church. Only if a javelin were thrown at me would I leave the palace, I assured them.

"That argument of David, Saul, and the javelin seemed to carry the day. But it was for only a day. The next day one of my friends reasoned with me over what constituted a javelin. What was more to be feared, physical javelins or spiritual javelins? he asked. Weren't our converts already dodging javelins of unbelief from members who had rejected our message? Hey, what could I say? From the crevice of self-deception I had already fallen into, I really couldn't see any other alternative but to separate.

"I was thrilled a few days later by an unusual statement that I believed was God's special assurance to me that He was leading in what we were doing! In the newly released four-volume collection of 1888 documents that I had just purchased, Ellen White states:

"'I was confirmed in all I had stated in Minneapolis that a reformation must go through the churches. . . . As reformers they had come out of the denominational churches, but they now act a part similar to that which the churches acted. We hoped that there would not be the necessity for another coming out' [Ellen G. White 1888 Materials, vol. 1, p. 356].

"And here we were right in the beginning of another coming out—one that she had hoped would not have been necessary. What a wonderful way for God to show us we were on track!"

John here interrupted his story to ask, "How could one who studied the Spirit of Prophesy as diligently as we did be so easily led into a deception like this? Indeed, how could the disciples, who had studied under the Master Teacher, be deceived in believing the Messiah was going to reign as a temporal king?" John Witcombe then asked the audience to count the number of F's in the following sentence, reading it only once:

> "FINISHED FILES ARE THE RE-
> SULT OF YEARS OF SCIENTIF-
> IC STUDY COMBINED WITH
> THE EXPERIENCE OF YEARS."

Most hands, including mine, went up when John inquired, "How many found three F's? Those who see all six F's," he continued, "are probably wondering why the majority are seeing only three. To you, six F's are obvious because you see the F's in the prepositions." Lights went on in minds throughout his audience as John stated the problem and applied the principle:

"Our method of reading permits most of us to see only one half the F's. So it was with the disciples. Their method of thinking permitted them to perceive only part of the truth. They saw only the Conquering King prophesies. Self-centered ambitions blinded them to the prophesies depicting the Suffering Lamb. And that pretty well describes the causative factor of many an offshoot movement. That kind of ambition along with pride of opinion has a blinding effect that permits only part of the F's to be seen. As my case illustrates, if people compile a certain category of quotations and focus upon these alone, they can sincerely conclude that God is calling them to separate from their church."

John Witcombe had himself fallen into that pattern of thinking. To most of those who knew him, John's case appeared hopeless. Fortunately, loved ones refused to give up hope and continued to pray for his restoration.

Just as had been Saul of Tarsus, John was deeply sincere and radically committed to truth. But neither commitment nor intellectual ability protected either Paul or John from spiritual blindness. Indeed, each intensely denied truth because he was oblivious to the obvious.

A method of thinking instinctive to all humanity blinded them to a vital part of truth. Their backgrounds had trained both to focus upon one side of truth. More significantly, pride and self-righteousness, traits that unconsciously resist any truth that might threaten personal ambition, as well as the self-assuring sense of being right, prevented them from realizing their predicament.

As did Saul when he became the apostle Paul, John now seeks to expose the kind of thinking that focuses on only part of the F's that compose the whole of truth. Indeed, that is the purpose of this book.

By examining the conflict created by focusing upon only one of truth's two poles, I want to shed light on why many sincere believers become imbalanced and turn judgmental. Too often we simply attribute the criticisms of the church's detractors to personality disorders. True, personality disorders do increase the likelihood of religious extremes. But all of us are to some degree imbalanced, and such imbalances become more acute at certain times than at others.

Moreover, personality disorders are often themselves triggered by spiritual and/or theological imbalances that we corporately foster when we focus upon one pole of truth—whichever it may be—to the neglect of its opposite pole. But just as an obsession with partial truth causes imbalance and may trigger disorder, there is healing power in truth when we do seek balance.

To be safe from the threat of such imbalance, we must become agents of reconciliation, seeking without compromise to fulfill the prayer of Christ just before His death that we might be one in Him.

Colleagues who have tested the principles in their own pastorates join me in testifying to their validity. I have been privileged to help many who were moving toward separatism, as well as a number who had already broken away from the church. Perhaps the best test of the validity of these principles is the fact that returning to positive fellowship with the body of Christ did not undermine their commitment to those valid concepts that had previously led them astray—concepts isolated from the divinely ordained balancing principles or concepts.

When John Witcombe and his wife moved to my district, they had already been rebaptized and had made great strides in their spiritual recovery. But they still clung to the imbalanced theology that had led them into the LOR movement. Nevertheless, their experience had left both of them eager to hear the Word in its wholeness.

How to Deal With Members Who Join Separation Movements

John's success in LOR testifies to the profound tensions that threaten Adventist unity. The church has never been as united as nostalgic memories of the past suggest, but neither has it been as greatly divided as we experience now. To illustrate the kind of issues that precipitate our growing division better, I now return to John's message to the pastors and elders with its vital insights—insights that I develop more fully in the chapters that follow.

"What can we do for members who have joined a separation movement?" Witcombe asked. "It would be nice if we could simply point out the other three F's, as Jesus did for those two disciples on the road to Emmaus.

"But notice *when it was* that Jesus was finally able to get those disciples to see the other three F's. He had to wait until everything had fallen apart for them. 'Then he said unto them, O fools, and slow of heart to believe all that the prophets have spoken' (Luke 24:25).

"Jesus had tried to explain all that to them before, but they could not see it. Likewise, apologetics had little impact on those of us in the Lord Our Righteousness movement. We had a ready answer for everything someone might throw at us.

"So what can we do for those who join a separation movement? We can pray for humbling circumstances, such as the disciples faced, that will make them able and willing to see 'all that the prophets have spoken.' Of course, it is helpful if we ourselves are not one-sided in our view of truth.

"It's a struggle to bring together the various aspects of truth on any polarized issue. Remember the quote I started with? 'Your only safety is in coming to Christ and ceasing from sin this very moment.' This beautiful truth highlights the urgency of the hour.

"But it is also true that 'day by day the mists of selfishness and sin that envelop the soul are dispelled by the bright beams of the Sun of Righteousness' [Patriarchs and Prophets, p. 134].

"If you come down on just one of those two sides, and build that one side to the neglect of the other, you may have difficulty experiencing the fullness of the gospel. But how do we connect 'ceasing from sin this very moment' to dispelling sin 'day by day'?

"It's really quite elementary. (It took me only 17 years to figure it out!) Our decision and commitment is that sin must cease in our lives today. However, the depth of our sin problem is such that it cannot be dealt with in one day. Both sides have to be brought together. Like a car battery, nothing works until we connect both the positive and negative poles.

"But what about Mrs. White's statement: 'We hoped that there would not be the necessity for another coming out'?

"We'll call that the negative pole of truth. Now notice the positive pole: 'No advice or sanction is given in the Word of God to those who believe the third angel's message to lead them to suppose that they can draw apart. This you may settle with yourselves forever' [Selected Messages, book 3, p. 21].

"Which do you prefer, the positive or the negative pole? Which terminal on your battery do you concentrate on in getting your car started? Your answer, of course, is that we must connect both. For neither without the other transmits power. Notice this negative pole of truth:

" 'Take the young men and women, and place them where they will come as little in contact with our churches as possible, that the low grade of piety which is current in this day shall not leaven their ideas of what it means to be a Christian' [Ellen G. White Manuscript Releases, vol. 12, p. 333].

"We kind of wish these quotes and those who bring them to our attention just didn't exist. However, we ought to say to them, 'Yes, that is one of my favorite quotations.' And then show them how it fits with its contrasting pole, such as:

" 'When anyone is drawing apart from the organized body of God's commandment-keeping people, . . . then you may know that God is not leading him. He is on the wrong track' [Selected Messages, book 3, p. 18].

"We sense strong tension between these poles of truth for a good reason. On one hand Mrs. White speaks of possible necessity for separation, but on the other hand she tells us to settle within yourselves forever, that there will be no drawing apart. This tension is designed to prevent us from developing a blind confidence in the institution of the church, while at the same time preventing us from jumping ship because everything on board is not in order.

"If we take just one side of truth, ignoring the other or using the one to diminish the other, we are in just as much danger of deception sitting here in the true church as are the separatists who cling to the other side of truth out there in their home churches. The wise will believe and accept both poles as true, permitting their unity to lead them into a deeper level of understanding regarding the church and their relationship to it."

DIVINE MIRACLES DO NOT PROVE ONE'S THEOLOGY!

Witcombe explained that his final decision to separate from the Seventh-day Adventist Church came after a series of weekend meetings held at the Sandpoint, Idaho, church. "Max Torkelsen, former Sandpoint pastor who, as conference communication director, was present in the audience, remembers well that weekend during which we presented our message," Witcombe commented to our group of pastors and elders. "An interesting thing happened to me that weekend," John said.

"Awaking early Sunday morning, I felt impressed to ask the Lord to heal my temporomandibular joint disorder. For years my jaw would click whenever I ate. Often it would lock shut, preventing me from even getting a fork in. It would open only with a good knock. In answer to my prayer God healed my TMJ disorder. From that time on it has never bothered me.

"Of course I interpreted that miracle as evidence that we were theologically on course. But God does answer a prayer of faith even if the petitioner is theologically off course. For this reason we cannot use God's blessings as primary evidence that we are on track.

"You'll hear reports of miraculous answers to prayer by those in the separatist movements. But there's no need to credit Satan with those miracles. Being deceived into leaving the denomination doesn't necessarily mean that those individuals have left God or that God has left them. God's tolerance and patience with those who are in error is much greater than ours.

"Before I tell you about one of the methods I used to influence many to leave the Seventh-day Adventist Church and join our movement, I can testify that it was a much easier task if the local church members were keeping up with the latest scandal in the denomination and were on the mailing list of the various watchdog publishers.

USING PARABLES TO PROCLAIM SEPARATION

"Three of Christ's best-known parables were very effective in removing people from the Adventist Church," John Witcomb explained. "I would start with the parable of the 99 sheep. Let me ask you a simple question. Where did Christ leave the 99 sheep when He went in search of the one lost? Safe in the fold, of course. And where did He bring the rescued one back to? Again you will answer, 'the fold.'

"May I point out that the text does not say that Christ left the 99 in the fold! It states that they waited in the wilderness. 'What man of you, having an hundred sheep, if he lose one of them, doth not leave the ninety and nine in the wilderness, and go after that which is lost, until he find it?' [Luke 15:4].

"And verse 6 says He took the lost sheep home rather than placing it among the 99 in the wilderness! The 99 are not in the secure position that we've always supposed. 'There is more joy in heaven over one sinner that repents than over the ninety and nine who suppose they need no repentance' [Review and Herald, July 16, 1895].

"A view of this parable that hinted at separation would prime the listeners' interest in learning something more that was new and unique. I would follow this up with a study of the harvest and the vinyard parables, both with a convincing separation twist to them. By the close of the weekend we would usually have the nucleus of a home church formed," John explained.

"For a little more than a year we traversed this country, establishing home churches. On one of our trips across country we stopped off at Andrews University to see what we might stir up there. We talked with the pastoral staff and were granted a Wednesday night speaking appointment. They knew that we were not SDAs, but the previous week they had had a Catholic priest speak to them, so why not us? That was a prayer meeting few of them will ever forget," John laughed.

"After presenting a strong case for victory over sin now, we invited those who wanted immediately to stop committing known sin to kneel with us, and those who didn't want to stop sinning now to remain seated while we prayed. Some immediately jumped to their feet and started arguing with us. Others kneeled, while some remained seated.

"The pastor wasn't sure what to do. With one knee down on the floor, he kept his seat on the chair. There was such an uproar that he had to quiet his congregation, telling them to remember that we were invited guests, and though they didn't have to agree with us, they ought to at least be courteous.

Why We Left LOR

"We had a lot going for us," Witcombe explained. "Because all our members paid their tithes and offerings, we were doing well financially. We traveled around the country in a nice motor home and received a comfortable salary, along with travel expenses. Once we even ferried our motor home over to England and spent several months traveling through Europe. So what caused us to leave LOR and rejoin the church? Let me summarize the three factors in our decision:

"First, as we began to recognize that our message produced despair in some while stimulating others to presumption, we saw increasing discrepencies between actual experience and our theory of total sinlessness.

"Contributing to this insight was the fact that family and friends were fasting and praying for our recovery. In answer to their prayers, God brought circumstances about that made it possible for us to see the other three F's regarding the Seventh-day Adventist Church.

"Finally, as the Spirit led us to reexamine the issues, we clearly saw that the church's prophetic destiny extends up through the final crisis of this world's history.

"The evidence for this is as powerful as the indication that Israel was to remain God's chosen church up through the coming of the Messiah. Despite backsliding and worldliness, an Israelite would know not to join a separatist movement because of the 70-week probationary period of Daniel 9:24 and the unconditional promise that Shiloh would come before the scepter of authority would depart from Judah (Gen. 49:10).

"As this became forcefully clear, we chose to surrender the financial security we enjoyed by resigning our position in LOR. Restudying the issues in light of this conviction, I rewrote all my position papers and, with my wife, was rebaptized into the Seventh-day Adventist Church.

"During this process we began to appreciate the tensions we found in the Bible on various issues. We did not yet know how to relate to the issues theologically. But as we started to let both sides of truth affect our understanding, providence led us to Leroy Moore's district. By sermons, manuscripts, and personal discussions, he greatly accelerated our learning process in the direction the Lord had led us.

"Until we heard Pastor Moore use *paradox* to explain the twofold nature of truth, we thought the term meant contradiction and compromise. But he clearly denied compromise. We were thrilled to see how consistently he united the two poles of truth. As this new approach to theology began to open to us, we told him, 'Pastor, you're giving us a theology to wrap around our experience.'"

NATURE OF TRUTH: MORE IMPORTANT THAN THEOLOGICAL ARGUMENT

Soon you will be able to read the entire thrilling story of John and Sharon Witcombe's journey into LOR and back. A well-known Adventist author is writing it for publication by Pacific Press Publishing Association. My purpose, meanwhile, is to examine the principles to which John refers.

Unfortunately, as John indicates, some do use paradox to refer to real contradiction, or a mix of truth and error. But I always use paradox in its primary sense. The Bible is full of paradoxes. And Jesus' teaching was paradoxical. All are familiar with such self-evident paradoxes as: "He who would save his life will lose it." Would any Adventist question that law and grace only appear contradictory but that each is essential to the other?

Nevertheless, *few have learned to think paradoxically.* Thus we continue to debate their relations. By paradoxical thinking I refer to the habitual effort, whatever the issue under consideration, to guard carefully the opposite principle—the other pole or aspect of a specific issue. A true paradox does not mix truth and error but unites converse principles of God's Word, each of which is essential to the other. Indeed, true paradoxical principles offer the only sure antidote to compromise.

But before proceding, let us ponder John's parting counsel. May its insight shape your attitude toward our church's growing conflict and prepare you to examine the prescription of the "faithful and true witness" who in love seeks to correct His children. John concluded his talk to the pastors and elders with the following observation:

"Let me share a last thought. Since there is little one can say to a person after he or she decides to join a separatist movement, prevention is a good place to put our energies. If we as a church lived out the light we've been given, if we just loved one another preferring the other member above ourselves no matter if they are to the right or to the left of where we currently are, there might not be such a problem with separation movements. Come to think of it, if we simply did that, we probably wouldn't still be here on this earth."

LOOKING AHEAD

Part One of this book demonstrates the paradoxical nature of truth in nature and society as well as in Scripture. But we must beware of counterfeits, such as the Chinese yin yang, that destroy true paradoxical principles. Scripture alone is the test of a true paradox, both principles of which are defined by divine revelation. As we shall see, conflict within Adventism stems from opposite patterns of violating the paradoxical principles of Bible truth. And I will present evidence that paradoxical thinking is the only true antidote to compromise.

Meanwhile, a biographical sketch traces my own discovery of truth's paradoxical (twofold) nature and my growing commitment to those principles that must unite for truth to remain true.

Part Two offers a history of the 1888 righteousness by faith controversy and shows how refusal to follow priesthood of believer principles in adamant resistance to paradoxical principles both precipitated our Minneapolis fiasco and formed the root of our present, intensifying conflict. (I will soon complete another manuscript that began as a part of this one that demonstrates that A. T. Jones, E. J. Waggoner, and J. H. Kellogg fell away from and almost split Adventism at the turn of the century because they too violated priesthood of believer principles and thus fractured paradoxical truth.)

Part Three examines issues such as perfection, the nature of Christ, and the atonement in a way to demonstrate how we continue to perpetuate the 1888 problem by splitting the poles of truth. At the same time it argues that we need to develop a pattern of thinking that will prepare us to unite in the power of the loud cry!

My Personal Journey

2

At 7 I thought I had committed the unpardonable sin. I was first exposed to smoking, drinking, and fighting when our family for a time became migrant workers while seeking to relocate. Though repulsed by them, still I felt one day a strong urge to try a cigarette.

The more I thought about it, the stronger the drive to experiment became. But a voice of warning also became increasingly urgent. How long the conflict lasted I don't know. I remember only its intensity. At the time I kept assuring myself that trying just one surely wasn't too bad. My real undoing, however, came from rationalizing 1 John 1:9. After all, according to this verse, I could confess what I had done afterward and everything would be all right!

Since I was surrounded by parents and five alert siblings, it was some time before I could sneak some matches. All the time I knew the Holy Spirit was urging me not to. But I kept reminding myself that "if we confess our sins, he is faithful and just to forgive us our sins."

When I finally got the matches, I chose the longest cigarette butt I could find and locked myself in an outhouse where no one could see me. I have no clear memory of the experiment itself. But I will never forget the horror when my deceptive assurance suddenly gave way to hopelessness. The thought that I could never be forgiven terrified me. After all, I knew I had deliberately resisted the Holy Spirit. And because I had planned my confession beforehand, I knew I could never honestly confess. At that moment a darkness settled upon me that I would fight in vain day after day, month after month, and year after year.

The mental voice that before had been so assuring now fairly shouted, "You have committed the unpardonable sin. There is no hope!" For days I could think of little else. During the next eight years I confessed my sin again and again, hoping for some hope. Though never forgotten, that sin ultimately became buried under many others.

The knowledge that I had been dedicated to the ministry at birth intensified my despair. I never lost the sense of calling. But I knew that if I could not be forgiven, I could not fill the call. Thus, earthly as well as heavenly prospects seemed forever sealed off. Locked in a self-imposed prison with no key, I did not even consider exposing my corruption to my parents or a spiritual leader.

Every effort to make myself worthy of God's approval seemed only to make me slip ever further from Him. In desperation I would kick myself internally. At times I even hit myself with my fists or beat my head on a plaster wall until I saw stars. But nothing brought relief. Nevertheless, I continued to hope that I might somehow become good enough for God to accept me. Yet no matter how hard I tried, I only kept getting worse.

At the age of 15 I faced a serious temptation from which I had been sheltered until then. Sensing I could not resist it and fearing I was about to pass the point of no return, I begged God for help. The answer was very clear, clearer than an audible voice: I must take an hour each morning and an hour each evening to study and pray. As I contemplated this directive, I felt impressed to study the life of Christ, so I turned to *The Desire of Ages*. Reading it twice, I found hope, victory, and joy beyond imagination.

Little did I dream that the principles I found in it relating to the nature of Christ, perfection, and atonement would soon be hotly debated in the church. Thankfully, my orientation came in seeking Him rather than through debate over doctrines about Him. Unless we view truth in relation to Him in whom all truths unite, we cannot grasp its trueness. Nor, unless we seek the whole truth, can we properly relate to Him who is truth. To resist any part of truth is to resist its Author and to distort our understanding of Him. We must never ignore any evidence that threatens our own perceptions of truth.

JEHOVAH'S WITNESSES EXPOSE MY DANGER

Having gained assurance in Christ, I now discovered an opposite danger. Several encounters with Jehovah's Witnesses pointed it out to me. Claiming that theirs was the only true religion, they charged all others with contradicting the Bible. But when faced with contrary Bible evidence, they always quickly changed the subject. Moreover, instead of Scripture, they used their own books as primary tools of indoctrination and urged their publications upon others. Yet they adamantly refused even to receive, let alone read, any other religious publications offered them.

At first their refusal to face issues honestly merely disgusted me. Then I began to sense that I too was in danger of treating truth dogmatically. At 19 I felt impressed to test prayerfully each doctrine to be sure that I did not merely have a hereditary faith. In that process I began to recognize how principles that appear to contradict each other are really part of and depend upon one another. Moreover, the very attempt to harmonize paradoxical principles resulted in deepening insight into truth.

THREE-STAGE COMMITMENT TO CLARIFY PARADOXICAL TRUTH

Soon after entering the ministry I became alarmed by early symptoms of our present conflict as each faction defended truth by diminishing, if not denying, the truth the other side defended. Since virtually all discussions involved much heat and little light, I felt I needed to deal with the issues on an academic level that might permit a more objective examination of the issues in conflict.

Convinced by the debate over perfection and the nature of Christ that the key to unity related to the nature of humanity and of sin, I first completed a master's thesis at Walla Walla College in 1966 in which I examined human nature as it relates to Creation, the Fall, and redemption. Thirteen years later I applied the principles to our intensifying theological conflict in a 1979 New York University dissertation, *Theology in Crisis*.*

In it I compared Dr. Desmond Ford's views with those of Ellen White, whom he quoted extensively and with whom he claimed agreement. Paradoxical principles that had been clearly evident in my first study I now explicitly stated as I demonstrated Ford's valid emphasis upon certain neglected principles to which Ellen White had given strong emphasis. But in each case I also demonstrated how he himself belittled and even denied converse truths that were just as fundamental to her message.

Both sides in conflict violate paradoxical principles on an expanding list of issues. But the nature of Christ, perfection, and atonement are still central. At the heart of all of them lies a universal law/grace paradox. Nor is our conflict unique. Confusion regarding how law and grace relate, lurk behind most divisions within Christendom.

It would seem that an advanced understanding of the nature of man accompanied by a commitment to both law and grace should make Seventh-day Adventists immune to such conflict. Nevertheless, the failure to grasp their unity at the Minneapolis General Conference session a century ago increasingly divides us.

This third effort to clarify paradoxical principles is very different from the two academic studies. My journey has been long and exhausting, though not without joy and assurance. I began trying to translate the concepts of *Theology in Crisis* into lay language soon after completing it in 1979. I did not know then that to plow new ground and to simplify the complex issues for lay readers would be vastly more difficult than to prepare a doctoral dissertation using precise technical language.

A number of readers of various earlier manuscripts saw in their principles a vital key to understanding and resolving our conflict. They urged me to hasten my work. But some insisted that I further simplify and illustrate. I have thus broken the ideas into smaller packages so as to cover the issues in a variety of ways. Thus if the concepts or remaining technical terms seem difficult, just keep reading. They will become increasingly clear as you view them from a variety of perspectives.

Until we see that truth by nature involves apparently contradictory principles that are actually essential to each other but that we instinctively fracture, we will remain spiritually blind and deaf. Seeing, we see not. And hearing, we hear not. Nor do we understand. Instead, we look upon those who defend the opposite principle as dishonest people who threaten to destroy the part of truth that we love.

The nature of truth and how we think is far more important than theological argument. Unless the way we reason harmonizes with the inherent nature of truth itself, our growth will be stunted. No matter how much truth we might begin with, we tend to retreat into a spiritual darkness that we foolishly and unknowingly identify as advancing light.

I claim no mastery of the subject. Instead, I simply share with you the keys to our dilemma that I have found extremely helpful. Like physicians, we are all "practicing." If you see blind spots in my reasoning, accept them as further evidence of the universal nature of the problem I address. Meanwhile, please call my attention to any such indications of "on the job" training, so that we may all benefit—you, me, and the church as a whole. Let us unite, individually and corporately, in seeking principles that will permit us to complete our heavenly journey.

REST STOPS AHEAD

To make your journey more pleasant and profitable, I took a tip from the interstate highway system and include occasional rest stops. As you relax, we will reflect on what we have seen, inject a current item of interest, or consider what lies ahead. May the One who is truth direct you by His Spirit of truth and richly reward your efforts as, in your own exploration of truth, you respond to my challenges.

---

* By mistake the outside cover bears the title *The Theology Crisis*. The correct title, *Theology in Crisis*, appears on the inside cover.

Uniting the Poles of Truth

3

When I met Dave in 1959 he felt no need for church. As a child, he had attended Sabbath school with his mother, a member of my Oroville, Washington, congregation. But now, as an apple ranch partner, he identified with his father, whose religion was the golden rule and the Democratic Party.

I saw in the Democratic Party's inclination toward increasing government control a threat to the principles that made our nation a bastion of liberty. But while emphasizing principles of freedom, I identified with Dave on social responsibility. As I explained to him how both principles meet in Christ, love for the Master began to awaken in Dave's heart. Before long he rejoined his mother in her faith, and remains a strong pillar in the church to this day.

Social responsibility, which Democrats demand, relates to the second table of the Decalogue. The individual freedoms that Republicans tend to stress relate to the first table. (Ominously, a Republican drive to legislate morality could threaten the freedom basic to true religion.) Each principle is thus vital. But we need them in unity with each other. To defend either at the expense of the other will actually jeopardize both. Moreover, if we but will, we may discover our own individual weaknesses reflected in those political parties that habitually violate one pole of a truth in their defense of the other.

As a little girl, my mother eagerly gave memorized speeches at her father's Socialist rallies. Always tenderhearted and willing to share, she little sensed the selfish realities that marred the altruism she innocently proclaimed. Egocentric and bent on seeking their own, whatever their politics, people blindly urge their own imbalanced "platforms" as a panacea for all of society's ills. The most universal political instinct seems to be "What is good for me must be also good for society."

Adventism in Conflict

Like cancer, each party fosters the growth of its own cells with no regard for that balance in principles needed to keep the whole body in health. To the degree that any principle gets promoted in isolation, society is threatened.

Radical, one-principle leaders such as Hitler and Stalin come to power in times of crisis because people look for quick-fix solutions to complex problems and welcome a single principle that appears to answer their every need. But the more intensely a society focuses on a single principle, the greater the threat it faces—whether it be an emphasis on social ends with little sensitivity for individuals, or individual ends with little concern for society's needs as a whole. Both major American political parties give lip service to the other's principle, yet each self-righteously undermines it in practice.

One law underlies all truth and governs all life. And that law has two poles. One relates to the Creator, the other to the creature. We reveal our integrity to either principle of the Decalogue by how we honor the other. Anyone who claims to love God but hates a brother or sister is a liar. But so also is anyone who disobeys God in the name of love for a fellow human being. Both violate the whole law.

Thus, whatever we promote, we must at the same time always protect an opposite principle. Nor is it enough just to acknowledge both poles of truth. Integrity in each depends on its relation to the other and on our personal response to those who may defend the other pole. Whether it be in politics or in religion, any split in truth's poles that diminishes either one will only fuel conflict and generate self-righteous enmity. Such conflict will inevitably destroy the unity Christ prayed for in John 17.

SPLIT TRUTH HAS NO POWER

A battery's power depends upon the acid that unites its negative and positive poles. Likewise, truth's power can be released only as its opposite poles unite. The power lies in the acid of the Word. But its transmission depends upon the union of the two poles.

A passive pole relates to grace; an active pole relates to law.

	TRUTH'S POWER	
GRACE (passive)	is in the WORD	LAW (active)

TRUTH IS PARADOXICAL

The promise "You will know the truth, and the truth will set you free" (John 8:32, NIV) depends upon a constant interaction between truth's active and passive poles. Without such an interaction between converse poles, truth ceases to be true because it loses its wholeness. Uniting truth's poles is impossible, however, except in reference to Christ, in whom both reside. To separate them—although it is an instinctive human reaction—causes us to lose our focus upon Him in whom they unite. Truth becomes as powerless as a dead battery. Neither principle of truth can empower us alone.

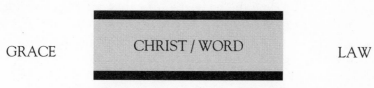

GRACE   CHRIST / WORD   LAW

"The Word of God is alive and powerful."

Internally, truth is always a perfect unity. But from the outside we may see apparent contradictions. And these seeming contradictions can lead to continual conflict over principles that are really as essential to each other as hydrogen and oxygen are to each other in the water molecule. We may try to remove the tension between the poles by denying or subordinating one of them. But when we do that, we rob truth of its wholeness and thus its trueness. For example, throughout Christian history Christians have placed law and obedience in conflict with grace and faith. Yet in reality they are not only in perfect internal harmony; they actually require each other. One simply cannot exist without the other.

Seldom do we openly reject either principle in a specific situation that seems to be contradictory. But to enforce some kind of external harmony, to eliminate the disturbing tension, we may repress or alter whatever does not fit our own particular perception of reality. By thus forcing truth to harmonize with our own viewpoint, we betray the secret of its freeing power. A power that we can find only by humbly digging beneath the surface of an issue to grasp its internal unity! We simply must accept the fact that we will never avoid the tension of external contradiction except by exercising faith in *all* of God's Word. Only as we honor each part while we seek its internal harmony can we ever discover the unity of its converse principles.

Truth is eternal, its unity absolute. But by means of paradoxical principles the Creator offers us a depth of meaning we can never fully plumb. Even uninspired proverbs suggest truth's inherently paradoxical nature:

"Look before you leap," but "he who hesitates is lost."

Adventism in Conflict

Both adages contain partial truth. Neither alone is an adequate rule for all of life. We do need to consider consequences before acting. Yet at times we must act before we can determine the potential consequences of a deed.

Life itself is thus paradoxical. The constant riddle of apparent contradiction should train us to depend upon Christ, the Source of all truth, to understand and harmonize properly the various principles we encounter.

But it is not enough to verbalize the unity of principles. Each side in our conflict does so in ways that are amazingly similar. Yet deep-seated mutual distrust prevents any real communication. Each side is so convinced that the other is misleading the body of Christ that, instead of seeking to recognize and build upon points in common, both magnify the differences in a desperate attempt to defend the issue they see as at stake. However accurately it may be stated, theory—even a paradoxical theory—will never resolve Adventism's conflict. It is one thing to verbalize the need for balance, as each side sometimes does. But it is quite another thing to transform the paradoxical principles involved in practical life.

To change us, the Holy Spirit must unite paradoxical principles in real minds and lives as He points us to the Source of all truth. Better to have no understanding of paradoxes at all than to hold such a concept perfectly while focusing upon self instead of Christ. A preoccupation with theory will foster pride and further self-deception. We may think we have achieved balance when we really haven't. Our attitudes and relations to each other deny our claims. But true balance is impossible except as we by divine grace look away from self to Him!

To Deceive, Satan Must Fracture Truth's Unity

As we have seen, truth has both active and passive poles. Law, for example, calls for active obedience, while grace requires passive reception. Depending upon the particular issues, we can also characterize truth's poles in many other ways, such as: abstract/concrete; spiritual/physical; motive/behavior; inside/outside; and unconscious/conscious.[1] On the left are *intangibles* (still another classification) that tend to relate to grace and faith while *tangibles* on the right relate to law and obedience.

We cannot deny or downgrade either pole of a truth without rupturing that truth. Nor can we unite any pair except by the Holy Spirit's aid. Without His help our focus shifts compulsively to one aspect or the other, thus giving Satan a great advantage over us.

To deceive, Satan splits the poles of truth and focuses our attention upon either one or the other. He seeks to make part-truth look like the whole of truth and cause the rest of a particular truth to seem a threat to the part we feel compelled to defend.

Truth is a unity. Both sides are so interconnected that the meaning of each depends upon its relationship to the other. But Satan splits truth by directing our attention to external differences, creating the illusion of internal conflict. Preying upon imbalanced minds (yours and mine!), he arouses pride and/or fear to stir us up to needlessly defend one pole against the other. He first established that pattern in Eden.

To separate seen from unseen realities in Eve's mind, Satan employed a talking serpent. The serpent ate visible fruit on a tangible tree to arrouse her curiosity and thus to instill unseen motives and stimulate unrecognized pride. Losing sight of unseen, eternal realities and thus believing Satan's part-truth illusion to be real, Eve concluded that she could safely eat fruit that had so "obviously" endowed the serpent with superior wisdom and even speech! Note Satan's part-truth lies:

"You will not die." Adam and Eve did not die immediately. Following sin's experiment, Eve "felt" more alive than ever. Adam lived almost twice as long as the elapsed time since Columbus sailed to America! But death was no less certain.

"You will be gods." The couple did become "gods." By denying the Creator's Word in depending upon reason and judgment to determine truth and by elevating their own will and desire above the Creator, they introduced self-worship!

"You will know good and evil." Adam and Eve came to know evil when they perverted good. They themselves, the crown of creation, became evil, but at the same time lost their capacity to know good. In part-truth, good becomes evil! And evil is perceived as good!

Before sin, Eve knew only good. Afterward she knew only evil (perverted good). Satan used God's symbol of sin, "knowledge of good and evil," to convince her that in addition to good, there was also a greatly to be desired essence called "evil." Indeed, his universal, part-truth religion rests on a concept known as dualism. Satan portrayed evil as an entity that exists independently and along with good.

But evil has no separate existence. God did not create evil. Its author, who fell through jealousy of the Creator (cf. Isa. 14:12-14), cannot even procreate (John 1:3). Until perverted by evil, everything God created "was very good" (Gen. 1:31). When He spoke of the "knowledge of good and evil," God sought to warn the first human couple against making an idol of His creation by perverting good. The result of experiencing "good and evil" is nakedness, loss of goodness (righteousness). "The eyes of them both were opened, and they knew that they were naked. . . . And [they] hid themselves from the presence of the Lord" (Gen. 3:7, 8).

31

Adventism in Conflict

By rejecting the Holy Spirit through self-exaltation, the mind's focus shifted from the Creator to self. This permanently fractured humanity's nature and produced an insanity that would forever haunt the entire human race. A mind focused upon self is a mind that imposes blindness. To hide from guilt, we hide from a holy God. But as we flee from true reality, we run away from the love that can alone heal (make whole) our shattered selves. Yet to respond to that love requires that we die to self. Unfortunately, centering upon self is as natural as breathing and as impossible to stop. Thus to perceive the unity of truth, we must continually die to our self-centered nature. But instead of dying to our fallen nature, we tend to swing from one pole of truth to the other. Indeed, it is simply impossible for us to see the unity of truth without the help of the Holy Spirit—whom our first parents drove from the body temple.

Before they expelled the Spirit, it was natural to think paradoxically. Self-sacrificing love activated every thought. But rebellion so fractured the image of God that we, Adam's children, instinctively resist the Spirit in our compulsion to defend self (Gal. 5:17). Sin now makes us uncomfortable with truth's surface tension. To eliminate the insecurity it produces, we manipulate the relations between the poles of truth in different ways to protect our self-perceptions.

The fracture is so deep that it threatens the gospel itself. Some seek security from guilt in efforts to obey. Others justify their continued practice of sin by claiming grace alone.

YIN YANG: PART-TRUTH COUNTERFEIT OF PARADOXICAL REALITY

I am often asked how the concept of paradoxical principles relates to the philosophy known as yin and yang. Chinese philosophers long ago recognized a pattern of opposites, such as: bright and dark; active and still; male and female; dry and wet; hot and cold; stimulus and response; strong and weak. (Yang is the first in each pair.) With one exception, these pairs do illustrate paradoxical realities and testify that life itself is paradoxical. Nevertheless, we must recognize significant differences between the concept of yin yang and the principles I discuss.

The Chinese philosophy deals with *facts of nature* while I proclaim the *nature of truth* as portrayed in divine revelation. Nature's pairs are real and reflect the Creator's design. But only principles governing spiritual life are worthy of being called "truth."

Moreover, natural paradoxes, such as in yin yang, are observable by even fallen human beings. But because of sin's perversion, we can discover and approach truth only by divine revelation (1 Cor. 2:14).

Yin yang's inclusion of such things as "strong and weak" suggests an even more significant difference. Nature offers many such contrasts, as between a huge elephant and a tiny mouse. But yin yang's strong and weak includes the results of sin. And any violation of the Creator's design likewise violates the paradoxical principles we have been discussing.

Unfortunately, some reject paradoxical principles out of hand because they equate them with faulty human theory rather than divine revelation. But true paradoxes are not temporary reflections of the reign of sin, such as rich and poor; sevant and master, etc. They are necessary and eternal opposites that so depend upon each other that neither could ever be complete without the other!

Yin yang theory counterfeits paradoxical truth by treating evil and its effects as an essential reality (a necessary contrast with good) rather than what it really is—a perversion of good. As with all pagan religions, this counterfeit of truth deceives by borrowing truth's external characteristics. A true paradox reflects an internal unity that external characteristics only appear to deny!

Yin yang theory counterfeits paradoxical truth by treating evil, which destroys the inner kernel of truth and leaves only an empty shell, as a complement to truth itself! It perpetuates the "good and evil" lie that the serpent used to fracture the human mind and destroy our ability to think paradoxically. By proclaiming evil a necessary opposite of good, it denies intrinsic goodness. And it hails evil as a partner to good. Neither one can be better than the other, because the theory holds that each is essential to the other.

Thus yin yang theory denies the most basic unifying principle—the Creator's design. Without His design, the creature finds itself robbed of its true identity and is forced to testify to unreality. As with all pagan religions, the yin yang counterfeit deceives by borrowing truth's external characteristics to deny its interal reality. A true paradox, by contrast, is based upon internal unity that alone can give meaning to external diversity.

Having no power to "create or destroy truth" (*Gospel Workers*, p. 281), Satan can deceive only by manipulating truth. "Error could not stand alone, and would become extinct, if it did not fasten itself like a parasite upon the tree of truth. Error draws its life from the truth of God (*The SDA Bible Commentary*, Ellen G. White Comments, vol. 5, p. 1094).

Because Satan cannot create or destroy truth, truth seen as a whole exposes every fraudulent device.

Pagan dualism, by contrast, not only sees good and evil as opposite realities existing separately from each other; it holds that a good god created one and an evil god the other. This false concept, for example, lies behind the Gnostic idea of a good spirit trapped in evil flesh. Confused by such ideas, early Christians struggled in vain to free their good spirits from the evil matter of their bodies. The concept led to asceticism of all sorts, including monasticism.

But evil is not a reality to be equated with the flesh. Evil is always and only a perversion of good. It is a temporary insanity to be eradicated by Christ's final at-one-ment.

Meanwhile, by his false dichotomy of two separated parts, Satan in opposite ways enforces imbalanced characters. Whether in pagan theory or merely in life experience, he makes evil appear to balance good, just as female is a counterpart to male. He then stimulates others to react to this delusion by repudiating paradoxical principles as themselves being evil.[2]

By countless counterfeits, Satan destroys truth in opposite ways. While the majority fall for its perversion and learn to love compromise by choosing a mix of good and evil, his supreme purpose is to trap the few who, to be faithful to God, reject all compromise at any cost. And his scheme is a startling success. To avoid compromise, many jump from the frying pan into the fire. They reject the balance the Creator built into paradoxical truth to protect us from evil.

The price for equating paradoxical truth with faulty human theory and compromise is tragically high. For only when it is whole can truth protect us against the countless perversions of good.

We are still paying for that very mistake in Adventism. Fear evoked by confusing whole truth with compromise caused Uriah Smith and George Butler to savagely attack E. J. Waggoner at the 1888 Minneapolis General Conference session. They were certain that his harmony of law and grace was a compromise of law. They opposed it because it corrected their unwitting elevation of law above grace in an effort to protect the former against antinomianism. To combat an imbalanced evangelical *language of grace*, which annuled the law, they developed an equally imbalanced *language of law*—which resisted grace.

To retain our sense of security, we unconsciously develop contrasting conceptual languages in which the vocabulary may be the same but the meanings we apply to them differ. And because we tend to be righteous in our own eyes, not only do we react to the other's error in a way to justify our own imbalance, but that very self-defense causes us to view the other as dishonest.

Paradoxical thinking, by contrast, requires a *language of truth* that provides the full expression of both inherent principles. Only this can exclude compromise. Otherwise, the more intense the effort we make to avoid compromising one principle, the more certain we will actually compromise its counterpart.

On the other hand, a full stand on both poles of every truth permits us to adopt a nonjudgmental view. For we can then honor every attempt to protect truth on both sides of the conflict. When we recognize our own impulse to defend one principle by unwittingly subverting the other, our judgmental spirit must give way to humble self-examination.

Since error can exist only by fracturing the poles of truth and pulling them apart, to exclude error we must properly unite truth to truth. By our thus reversing Satan's counterfeit, truth becomes whole, and only then has power to set us free to develop the kind of characters that will reflect the divinely ordained balance between faith and obedience.

But evil so disturbs our rational faculties that it is humanly impossible to unite truth's poles! Our fallen natures instinctively want to split truth so that we can defend our self-centered interests. Our motives and emotions automatically concentrate upon whatever part of truth makes us feel most secure.

For example, the Pharisees' concentration upon external obedience permitted them to feel self-righteous and secure even while violating more important spiritual principles. Dwelling exclusively upon love and grace gives others a sense of security while they at the same time disregard divine counsel. And we who pride ourselves on our balance face the temptation to contrast ourselves smugly with both errors! Nor is this surprising. For it takes time for even converted minds to heal of their fracture and become whole.

Two factors are vital to our healing. First is our personal response to the message to Laodicea. Do we apply that message personally? The second is that we subject ourselves to each other so that we can come to see our own imbalance. Genuine acceptance of the Laodicean message requires that each of us carefully examine the criticisms of others—even those that reflect a judgmental spirit. Only in this way can we overcome the self-deception that perpetuates the split-truth thinking that blinds everyone of us.

FOCUS UPON SECURITY PRODUCES LAODICEAN SELF-DECEPTION

Sue awakened one night with a fever. Not realizing that it was an attempt by her body to fight off the disease germs threatening her health, she went immediately to the medicine cabinet for a pill to lower it. A fever reflects the body's emergency system at work killing off an invading disease. Its discomfort and accompanying weakness also urge us to consider the cause and cooperate in its cure.

Likewise, a heightened Adventist fever, as increasingly large groups of members defend opposite principles, is actually cause for hope. It reflects the church body's increasing effort to throw off the Laodicean disease and to prod us all to cooperate in seeking a cure. As with fevers, however, we will feel worse and look more hopeless during the process of getting better. The danger is that we mistake the fever for the disease. To lower the body's temperature artificially may actually thwart its healing efforts and cause us to ignore our disease until it is too late for it to heal.

While we sometimes have to reduce life-threatening fevers, at the same time we must remember that to treat symptoms instead of the disease only allows the infection to spread. Any attempt to reduce the tensions caused by our corporate failure to unite paradoxical principles can only delay recovery. But when we properly direct our efforts to remove the disease, the fever and its disturbing symptoms will subside.

We all unwittingly bear the seeds of both liberal and conservative extremes in our minds. They only await specific circumstances to germinate and produce their deadly harvest. Nor does remaining in the middle necessarily reveal greater maturity. It may signal indifference. The True Witness declares, "I would that you were cold or hot" (Rev. 3:15, NIV). True, those at the extremes may be there because of peculiar ego problems. But many at both ends of the spectrum do seek to relate honestly to a sensitive conscience. Such tender consciences often expose issues to which others are blind or indifferent.

Indeed, Laodicean self-satisfaction within the main body of the church stirs both polar reactions. We all share responsibility for our conflict. The most innocent are guilty. And the most guilty are victims of our corporate disease. God summons all to repent! And as one extreme repents, it provides a wonderful encouragement for the other extreme to respond in the same manner.

It is easy to discern egocentricity in the opposite party. Even the born again retain natures that war against the Spirit and must be continually surrendered. We all need to recognize within ourselves a resistance to the Spirit that must be overcome by character development. It takes time to discern and triumph over selfishness's various deceptive forms. But to behold Christ is to be drawn to Him and become more and more like Him (2 Cor. 3:18).

The problem of deception lies in our self-centered attempts to find security. To rise above this requires intense focus upon Christ. As we are drawn to truth's center, we will gradually recognize our imbalances and let the Holy Spirit move within us to overcome them. But that does not mean that everyone's perspectives will be the same. They will differ considerably. If "for conscience' sake" a "weak brother" goes to extremes (Rom. 14), we must beware lest we seek to enforce behavior upon him that, however right, violates his conscience.[3]

Even the Spirit will not "control" us against our wills, but always guarantees our freedom to choose. Power of choice, the most precious gift to the first Adam, is retained by the Second Adam. He who died to guarantee that gift will never deprive us of His costly purchase. Thus as He guides our minds, the Spirit at the same time ever leaves us free. We grow only as we respond to His promptings toward those principles that we previously shied away from either because of our prejudices and desires or because of a false fear of compromise.

Either way, to resist the Spirit is to retard or halt our spiritual growth. But as we become aware of a neglected pole of truth, we face a new danger. We must beware of now resisting or rejecting the pole of truth we formerly held, thus shifting from one extreme to the other.[4]

REST STOP: RELEASE YOUR MIND BRAKE

As sharp curves loomed ahead on the steep grade, Fred's brake pedal dropped to the floorboard, and he continued to gather speed! Quickly he geared down as far as he could. But his speed hardly changed. Panic began to seize him till he remembered his hand brake. Reaching down, he pulled it, and the car began to slow. Then, shifting into low, he proceeded carefully down the hill.

Hand brakes are helpful in emergencies. But they may also create emergencies. For three years I traveled 35 miles between churches over steep, often icy, mountain roads each Sabbath. I never missed a service until I set my hand brake at a stop sign one icy morning.

Getting out, I checked my tires. Then, releasing the brake, I entered the highway. I at first attributed the car's sudden strange behavior to the slight incline and slick ice. But when, instead of picking up speed, I kept slipping over to the edge of the road, I stopped to consider the problem. When I tried again, I only slid into deep snow on the side of the road and was soon unable to go either forward or backward. The farmer who pulled me out verified a cause I had not suspected. The "released" hand brake was stuck!

Hand brakes are not the only kind that may stick without our knowing it. Pride of opinion and fear often cause mental brakes to stick—sometimes forcing us off the road. Although others may readily recognize our problem, we seldom suspect the true cause.

We will later consider how in 1888 pride and fear combined to set mind brakes, preventing denominational leaders from grasping Christ as our only righteousness. In their false attempts to protect the "old landmarks" of truth, they slid off the road—some permanently. A year later Ellen White asserted that "there is *a bracing of the mind, an opposition of the soul brought to the investigation of the Scriptures.* This leaves such souls where Satan can impress them. In Minneapolis God gave precious gems of truth to His people in new settings. This light from heaven by some was rejected with all the stubbornness the Jews manifested in rejecting Christ, and there was much talk about standing by the old landmarks . . . *Minds . . . were fixed, sealed against the entrance of light,* because they had decided it was dangerous error removing the 'old landmarks' when it was not moving a peg of the old landmarks, but they had perverted ideas of what constituted the old landmarks" (*The Ellen G. White 1888 Materials,* p. 518; italics supplied).

After enunciating the landmarks, Ellen White continued, "The men in responsible positions have disappointed Jesus. . . . Never can the heart be *stirred up with envy, with evil-surmising, with evil reports, but the intellect becomes unbalanced, and cannot decide correctly any controverted point*" (ibid., p. 519; italics supplied; cf. pp. 534, 560; 605).

As you prepare to proceed, please check your mind brake to make sure it is free.

---

[1] "The Tale of Two Trees," a manuscript that once formed the first part of this book, gives prominence to invisible/visible polar aspects of truth.

[2] In its determined effort to escape evil, the natural mind that is aware that sin is a perversion of good fears paradoxical principles because it cannot differentiate these from the dualism of good and evil underlying all paganism.

[3] The "weak brother" to whom Paul refers had an oversensitive conscience. But an underdeveloped conscience also makes a "weak brother." Of course, in either case some are not guided by conscience. But caring and understanding rather than judging is the primary principle. We must even beware of being critical of critics—who thereby identify as weak brethren.

[4] I rejoice as our corporate problem leads some in all segments of the body to seek both sides of paradoxical truth. I see increasing desire to escape Laodicean indifference by a focus upon Christ that reflects commitment to balance in truth. Many whom we consider hopeless will yet grasp and apply paradoxical principles.

Part One

Paradoxical Thinking and Character Development

4

It is dangerous to approach paradoxical issues intellectually while at the same time failing to internalize the principles involved. We must incorporate them into our daily life, how we think and act and live. The purpose of paradoxical thinking is not to philosophize, but to seek the whole of truth so as to develop character. If these principles do not correct our habits and thought patterns and shape our daily decisions, we may verbalize both polar principles but fracture their unity—and never suspect it!

Theologians have always recognized paradoxes such as grace and law, faith and works, but have continually argued and even fought over how they relate to each other. Meanwhile, the lives of uneducated believers who know nothing of paradoxical principles will often demonstrate the outworking of both poles. The key lies in a sense of their own inability as they humbly search the Word by *faith* and earnestly submit *reason* to the *Holy Spirit!*

Without humble dependence upon the *Holy Spirit* in uniting *faith* and *reason*, even the most brilliant scholars remain spiritually immature. Since they cannot unite paradoxical principles, they will not only likely engage in conflict over words, but also remain vulnerable to heresy!

Unless blended in experience, intellectual assent to paradoxical unity becomes a substitute that can sadly inoculate us against the real thing. Virtually all who speak a language of either law or grace will verbally affirm both principles. And each side thinks itself balanced even as both compulsively defend one principle at the expense of the other. They think they are balanced when their behavior demonstrates they are not.

Each false religion and every distorted experience reveals a failure to internalize paradoxical truth, to make it a part of our very being. Theorizing is easy. But to internalize requires continual battles with a self that constantly tries to hide its tailoring of truth to fit personal opinion, desire, and fear. Unless we continually resist self, we will reject the Spirit and distort the Word.

RELATIONS AMONG FAITH, REASON, AND HOLY SPIRIT

"Do not answer a fool according to his folly, or you will be like him yourself. Answer a fool according to his folly, or he will be wise in his own eyes" (Prov. 26:4, 5, NIV).

The book of Proverbs uses intentional contradiction in consecutive verses to stimulate the reader's search for internal harmony, in which *reason* and *faith* unite in dependence on the *Holy Spirit*. To do that, we must: (1) *exercise reason* in seeking to identify underlying principles; (2) *exercise faith* in the unity of revelation by subjecting reason to all of Scripture; and (3) *depend on the Spirit* to help us reconcile the polar principles involved.

Faith is based on evidence (Heb. 11:1). Thus reason must examine the evidence before faith can act. But faith must demand that reason's conclusions honor the authority of the whole Word—all that the Bible has to say on a subject. We are saved not by reason, but by faith in Christ and His Word (Eph. 2:8). Abel triumphed by faith. But God had to reject Cain because his reason assumed authority over faith (Heb. 11:3; Gen. 4).

To know the Word, upon which true faith must rest, we must diligently exercise reason. But unless tethered to faith, reason attempts to remove what it sees as external tension by adjusting truth to our perverted comprehension. When faith thus surrenders to reason rather than to the Word, it is debased to (ir)rational presumption!

TRUTH REQUIRES CHARACTER DEVELOPMENT

To think paradoxically thus not only results in character development, but actually demands character development. Every division within Christendom reflects a breakdown in those character processes that God intended these internal/external conflicts to produce. As we defend truth that we feel others need, God wants us at the same time to honor that truth that they may also hold. But this can happen only as we learn to think and live in harmony with truth's paradoxical principles.

Truth sets us free only as, under the Spirit, we let faith and reason unite in humble submission to the Word of God. Only as faith activates the will to cherish all of God's revelation despite its apparent or surface contradiction, will reason, whose function is to make sense of things, be able to accept both principles as true. Faith will then instruct reason to retain the tension while continuing to seek reconciling principles. When faith thus depends upon Him who alone can unite paradoxical principles in mind and life, only then can spiritual growth and character development occur.

But if faith does not focus upon Him who is truth, it degenerates into presumption and can produce only warped characters. In the name of faith, presumption surrenders to the natural human instinct to remove paradoxical tension by employing a logic that is blind to spiritual principles. We concentrate on what fits into our own perspective and ignore what doesn't—or at best, subordinate it so it won't disturb us as much. This reduces the tension we feel and deceives us into concluding that we are being honest even while we are still denying one pole of truth.

The problem is universal and as old as time. And all have become enmeshed in it. For example, because of a false fear of legalism, Luther unwittingly denied Bible authority by labeling the book of James an Epistle of straw. Why? Because reason could not resolve its apparent contradiction to Paul. Paul's "For we maintain that a man is justified by faith apart from observing the law" (Rom. 3:28, NIV) is difficult to reconcile to James's "You see that a person is justified by what he does and not by faith alone" (James 2:24, NIV).

Yet Paul and James harmonize perfectly. They merely address opposite problems. To counter legalism, Paul insists that obedient behavior does not add merit to divine grace, which we simply receive by faith. While to meet antinomianism (that which is "against the authority of law"), James insists that true faith responds actively as well as passively to divine justification. Otherwise it is merely presumption. Paul provides the key to unity between himself and James by describing an active/passive harmony of faith, reason, and the Spirit: "Work out your own salvation with fear and trembling; for it is God who works in you both to will and to do for His good pleasure" (Phil. 2:12, 13, NKJV).

Only the Holy Spirit can integrate converse principles within the finite human mind. The choice is now ours to grow symmetrically in truth by actively exercising reason that is by faith subject to the Spirit. Otherwise our natural instincts will attempt to tailor the Word to our own particular blindness.

The Spirit will never violate our freedom to deceive ourselves. To truly surrender to and to genuinely cherish God's Word requires that we continuously make faith choices. Choices that will resist those distortions that result when we depend upon either feeling or reason rather than a Spirit-interpreted Word.

But such faith choices are contrary to fallen human nature. We must have help in choosing His will. Only the Holy Spirit can stimulate and empower our obedient response. Unless He frees us to unite our will with

Christ's by His motivating presence, it is impossible for us to resist our instinctive tendency to split truth into apparently contrary fragments.

FREE TO DECEIVE OURSELVES

When we receive it internally in balanced fullness, truth always sets us free (John 8:32). But when it deviates from the balance of principles set forth by its Author, truth ceases to be true, because we have distorted it, making it incomplete and in a very real sense a lie. A lie is a partial truth. The only way we can avoid threatening the integrity of truth is to permit the Spirit both to direct and to correct us so that we see all of a truth.

But how does the Spirit correct us? He who guarantees our freedom never interferes with our reason. Nor does He prevent us from tailoring reality to our own perceptions. Instead He allows this to happen to expose our split-truth problems. By permitting the consequent confusion and conflict, He seeks to correct and teach us not to trust our own perceptions but to actively submit our own reason to revelation.

Jesus dramatized this freedom by patiently dealing with Judaistic prejudices. For three and a half years He by precept and example repudiated His people's separatist attitudes. To expose their problem and to demonstrate how to relate to Gentiles, He led His disciples to the borders of Tyre and Sidon. But He left each disciple free to apply the lesson in his own way. None of them clearly grasped it at the time. The one who came closest to seeing the key of humility repudiated its purpose and betrayed His Master instead.

God had cautioned the Jews to remain separate from the pagan world around them for their own protection. He wanted them to be a divinely ordained priesthood that would represent Him and evangelize the world. It took a long time for them to see that they must avoid pagan idolatry. They had to go into exile to grasp this fact. But when they did focus their worship only on the God of Israel, pride entered the picture. Seeing themselves as heaven's favorites, they sought to retain their status by exclusivism, thus short-circuiting what God had created them as a people for in the first place.

Christ could have removed much of the confusion by opening Scripture to His disciples. But they were blinded by unconscious pride and ambition—something they could recognize and overcome only as they learned to distrust self and seek the Spirit's aid in penetrating their hidden motives.

Christ's death—or even the experience of Pentecost—did not fully remove the blindness. God had to repeat the vision of the sheet let down from heaven three times before Peter began to grasp that the Gentiles were not to be considered unclean (Acts 10; 11). Indeed, years later he had to face public rebuke from Paul for still equivocating on the same principle (Gal. 2:11, 21).

Moreover, even Paul had to overcome certain character-inhibiting blindness. He was right when he said missionaries must not run away because of obstacles and homesickness. But he resisted Barnabas' balancing principle. Paul's conflict with Barnabas over young Mark was so intense that they parted company. Meanwhile, God did not reject the apostle, but compassionately used his faulty judgment to bring additional missionaries into His service. Moreover, Paul eventually came to treat Mark as a son in ministry, as the young man's later faithfulness helped deepen his own grasp of paradoxical principles.

Consider now the greatest paradox of all, a twofold paradox that underlies all others: the living/written Word. Every truth about Christ (the Source of all truth) and about His written Word (the basis for our understanding of truth) is endlessly alive with paradoxical insight.

PARADOX OF ALL PARADOXES

Christ Himself embodies and exhibits truth's paradoxical nature: fully divine, yet fully human; eternal, yet begotten. He who set worlds in space and sustains all life was a helpless babe. The All-Powerful could do nothing in His own strength.

Moreover, He, the Fount of all knowledge, depended upon the Spirit to tutor Him through nature, experience, and Scripture. He who ruled the waves and drove out demons with a word spent whole nights pleading for strength to meet His enemy.

Even the noun "Word" is paradoxical. It refers to divine revelation through the prophets. But its supreme meaning is Christ Himself, who could speak whole worlds into existence. Yet when on earth, He repeatedly bowed to the authority of the written Word that He Himself had inspired!

What we have said about the living Word also relates to the written Word. Nor is the written Word merely a logical combination of words. It is the voice of Christ and conveys His personal presence. Yet again, paradoxically, that presence and voice is conveyed by the Holy Spirit.

The great I Am (John 8:58), the self-existent One, dependent upon no one, upholding the universe by His power (Col. 1:15-17), took the nature of fallen humanity to become utterly dependent upon the Spirit. Likewise, the written Word, bearing the power of re-creation (1 Peter 1:23), conveys Christ's infallible messages through fallible human beings in the imperfect language of the human race. Moreover, the power of the written Word is subject to our dependence upon the Spirit as we compare one passage with another while seeking to grasp and assimilate its principles. We reveal our attitude toward and dependence upon the living Word by our attitude toward and dependence upon the written Word.

Human beings have always struggled with the divine-human paradox. During His life on earth people thought Christ to be only human. Even Peter could confess His divinity only by divine illumination (Matt. 16:13-17). After He ascended, a battle began between those who said He was an ordinary man with extraordinary powers (or that He became the Son of God only at His baptism) and those who, to protect His divinity, argued that He only appeared to have real human flesh (or that God adopted the human body of Jesus but that the two natures were not really one).

John warns that to split the divine/human nature of Christ (fully God, fully human; John 1:1-3, 14) is a mark of antichrist (John 1:1-3, 14; 2 John 7-9). Yet through the centuries Christ's own assertions of dependence upon His Father have led countless sincere Christians to confess Jesus' divinity but deny His eternity and equality with God.

As far as we know, the majority of the pioneers of the Seventh-day Adventist Church, including James White himself, held either an Arian or semi-Arian view. Until Ellen White clarified that "in Him was life, original, unborrowed, underived," we as a church considered Christ as less than the Father. Perhaps the most significant factor in changing our attitude toward the divinity of Christ was Ellen White's *Desire of Ages*. Its third sentence puts the issue straight: "From the days of eternity the Lord Jesus Christ was one with the Father" (p. 19).

Few Adventists would now question Christ's eternal divinity or knowingly undermine the reality of His humanity. Nevertheless, we find ourselves seriously divided over His human nature. In Part Three I show that the same paradoxical principals that resolve the tension over His divine/human nature will help unravel the relationship between His fallen human nature and His sinlessness.

If history teaches anything, we have the right to be optimistic that we will yet unite on Christ's humanity. How often have you met an Adventist Arian? The few I have met are of very recent origin and on the fringes of Adventism. Yet a century ago almost all Adventist were Arian!

All Adventists currently affirm both the full divinity and complete humanity of Christ. But as we seek to grasp this mystery, many of us shift to the side of truth regarding the human nature in opposition to others who overstress the divine nature. An experience with what Jehovah's Witnesses have done with the humanity of Christ first made me aware of our own mishandling of the twofold nature of the living/written Word.

MY SECOND LESSON FROM JEHOVAH'S WITNESSES

I will never forget an encounter I had in Fairbanks, Alaska, nearly 40 years ago with the sharpest Jehovah's Witness I ever met. Possibly a former Seventh-day Adventist, he seemed to know every Bible reference to Christ's human limitations, such as "I can of mine own self do nothing" (John 5:30). But he also quoted early Adventist statements and skillfully misconstrued Ellen White comments to support his insistence that "Christ is totally and only a man."

That incident launched me upon an intense study of the nature of Christ that lasted for months. He used a filtered list of texts representing one pole of truth to nullify equally valid scriptural testimony to the truth of His divinity. My task was to assure that I did not use an opposite list of texts in a manner that did not fully respect the passages that he emphasized.

My study made me more acutely aware of our own manipulation of revelation in dealing with compilations regarding the fallen nature of Christ and His absolute sinlessness. More than anything else, it confirmed my growing conviction regarding the paradoxical nature of truth. In addition, knowing personally and respecting the integrity of champions on both sides of the nature of Christ issue helped me become less critical of the gross infractions of the Jehovah's Witnesses.

Jehovah's Witnesses no doubt seek to be honest. But, having split the most fundamental of all paradoxes—God took upon His infinite, all-powerful, divine nature our finite, dependent, human nature—they really do not know how to interpret such passages as "I can of my own self do nothing." Rejecting the paradoxical key of Christ's voluntary surrender of the exercise of His innate divine powers (Heb. 10:5-7; cf. Heb. 1:2, 6-10), they go to unusual extremes to deny passages such as:

"In the beginning was the Word, and the Word was with God, and the Word was God. The same was in the beginning with God. All things were made by him; and without him was not any thing made that was made. In him was life; and the life was the light of men" (John 1:1-4).

To deny the living Word, they manipulate the written Word in their own translation, the New World Translation. Please note the NWT brackets in their attempt to correct the divinity "error":

"In [the] beginning the Word was, and the Word was with God, and the Word was a god. This one was in [the] beginning with God. All things came into existence through him, and apart from him not even one thing came into existence. What has come into existence by means of him was life, and the life was the light of men" (John 1:1-4, NWT; all brackets are theirs).

But positing more than one God is sheer polytheism! They contrast Christ, "a god" (sub-god?), to the God He was with. The higher God is held to have created a lower being and endowed him with creative power, thus installing him as "a god." But what a price they pay when they wrest Scripture in this manner!

Rejecting Christ's divinity, which they cannot relate to His human dependency, they deny the very admonition their theology rests upon: "Hear, O Israel: The Lord our God is one Lord" (Deut. 6:4). This Jehovah's Witnesses key text denies multiple pagan gods possessing differing powers—and often opposed to each other. Years before, Moses had asked God whom he should say sent him. God answered "I AM THAT I AM," or "I AM hath sent me unto you" (Ex. 3:14).

Moreover, the very Gospel of John, whose declaration of the divine Word is at stake, quotes Jesus as claiming to be the I AM. In response the Jews tried to stone him for blasphemy (John 8:58, 59). Jehovah's Witnesses obviously fracture the poles of truth. But consider what they must do in the process.

To appear consistent when they insert the indefinite article where there is no definite article in Greek, the NWT authors twice bracket the definite article when it is unnecessary. Each language has its own rules of grammar. Translators must convey the meaning of the first (Greek)—not the exact words—in the second (English). The definite article is often either required in English where it is absent in Greek, or it is required in Greek when absent in English.*

Thus, "in [the] beginning" needs no brackets. Nor does the absence of the article in Greek require the indefinite English article "a god." (Can you image an "a" before every noun in the New Testament that has no definite article before it?) Both context and harmony of Scripture require "the word was God."

After reading my Jehovah's Witness account, Review and Herald Publishing Association editor Richard Coffen wrote me regarding an amusing incident of his own. Knowing he was not a Greek expert, Richard was somewhat uneasy when some Jehovah's Witnesses asked for his Greek New Testament so they could prove to him that John 1:1, 2 speaks of two very different gods. But he smiled and relaxed when they pointed to what they believed was the distinction between the two Greek nouns. The following was their rendering (see Greek in brackets): "In the beginning the Word was, and the Word was with [the] God [Theon] and the Word was a god [theos]."

They ignored an elementary principle of noun declension. The n to s change is required by the noun's function in the sentence—but it makes no difference whatsoever in English.

But that is not all the doctoring necessary to deny the divinity of the Word. The succeeding verses identifying Him as "the light" and the very source of "life" strongly imply divinity. Jehovah's Witnesses manipulate John 1:4 to read: "What has come into existence by means of him was life, and the life was the light of men."

Thus do Jehovah's Witnesses continue their mutilation of a grand, complex theme: the Word is the Creator, the very source of life and the light of all humanity. To deny Christ's divinity, they must defuse this, the central theme of John's Gospel. They must treat Him not only as an inferior god, but also as a mere secondary source of life and light.

But once again, their translation, "what has come into existence by means of him," threatens the principle underlying their own insistance upon one God! For it exalts a mere created man to divinity, attributing our very life and light to him! (Contrast John 1:9, 10; 2:19; 5:24; 6:35, 47-63; 7:37-39; 8:12, 53; 9:5; 10:10, 18; 11:25, 26.)

Far from ridiculing Jehovah's Witnesses, however, my purpose is to illustrate an obvious violation of paradoxical principles that reflects the very kind of thinking that, on a much more refined scale, characterizes the accelerating conflict within Adventism. My desire is to awaken within ourselves a commitment to examine our own relationship to paradoxes—including those regarding the living/written Word.

In Part Three we will examine our nature of Christ theology, but meanwhile, I repeat that the common denominator of most if not all of our multiplying conflicts—just as at Minneapolis—relates to passive/active faith. Satan can mislead us only by splitting those poles in a manner to make us think they still remain united!

REST STOP: CHECKING MIND BRAKES

"But to this one I will look, To him who is humble and contrite of spirit, and who trembles at My word" (Isa. 66:2, NASB).

Is paradoxical thinking still illusive? If so, you might want to check your mind brake. A sticking mind brake makes understanding very difficult, if not impossible. Two opposite things to check for are hidden pride of opinion, and the fear of betraying truth by error.

Adventism in Conflict

We must always fear pride. But we must trust God's promises to protect and direct in truth the humble, who tremble at His Word. May we fully grasp, as we prepare for the history and theology parts, that it is not by intellectual might or power, but by the Spirit of God, that we will triumph. And also remember that He leads us only as faith and reason unite under His direction in an earnest search for truth.

It seems appropriate, however, before moving into historical and theological issues in Parts Two and Three, that I include my own confession and testimony in chapter 6, along with a final discussion of the nature of truth and an explanation of why I use the terms liberal and conservative. The testimony and explanations relate to chapter 5 and the necessity of practicing priesthood of believers principles, which I describe by the terms vertical (believer to God) and horizontal (individual believer to Christ's body of believers).

My confession upholds a *flexible* commitment to the horizontal principle: a humble acknowledgment of weakness and genuine desire for help from others is the key to being part of the priesthood of believers. At the same time I follow an *inflexible* commitment to the vertical principle. Being in the priesthood of believers requires a full surrender to Christ and a refusal to compromise His Word. But we must combine it with a distrust of self—which will permit Him to discipline and correct us directly through His Word and indirectly through His earthly body, the church.

I see many young men and women who grasp this first, vertical principle of priesthood of believers, but whose usefulness is in serious question. We all long to see such young men and women rise to carry the torch of truth. Few realize, however, that in the absence of a clear grasp of paradoxical principles, such commitment may lead to extremes that threaten to separate them entirely from Adventism! Indeed, that is now happening on an unprecedented scale, both on our right and on our left!

John and Sharon Witcombe are not the only ones whose zeal for truth has led to serious extremes. Many zealous reformers whom God has ordained to have a part in finishing His mission on earth must first be rescued from split-truth thinking.

If we want them balanced, let us bring those who appear imbalanced into the full priesthood of believers by honoring their commitment to the first principle. Then we may have the privilege of demonstrating the second principle by listening attentively and respectfully as well as exhorting. We need to search the Word patiently with them, showing them how to unite balancing principles.

Paradoxical Thinking and Character Development

Let us link arms as we together climb the mountain of truth. And let us, with them, scale its heights to plant the pure standard upon its summit of paradoxical principles!

---

* The *New World Translation*'s authors were obviously aware of this principle. They not only placed [the] twice before the word "beginning," but omitted the article entirely before *Theon* while imposing the indefinite article before *theos* immediately thereafter! Thus they demonstrate that there is absolutely no grammatical reason for using the indefinite article, "a" god!

Part One

Where the Rubber Meets the Road

5

Warning! This chapter may tax your mental faculties and faith perceptions. But it could set you free. Free to be spiritual without being self-righteous and judgmental. Free to show genuine compassion and understanding to those who violate or reject the principles that you earnestly defend—without breaking your own commitment to those principles. Free to seek unity without compromise. In it I show why what I call priesthood principles are essential to paradoxical thinking. At the same time I also explain why a true priesthood of believers is impossible without paradoxical thinking.

Here the rubber meets the road. Your decision regarding paradoxical principles will likely be determined by whether you clearly see that each must and does pass the test imposed by the other.

We pride ourselves on seeking the whole truth. Yet our conflicts testify that we split truth without realizing that we are doing it. We opt for one side of an issue over the other without suspecting that we do so. During the 1888 crisis Ellen White repeatedly urged a priesthood of believers concept that would have produced unity upon the issues in conflict, the relationship between grace and law, and the nature of the old and new covenants. (See Part Two.)

Ellen White did not, however, use the expression *priesthood of believers*. The sixteenth-century Reformers employed it to identify their third Reformation pillar. All agreed that the concepts or principles of *sola scriptura*, justification by faith, and the priesthood of believers stand or fall together. Unfortunately, the latter term lost its meaning and fell into disuse as the Reformers and their successors neglected one of two primary principles in truths they wrestled with.

This ultimately emptied *sola scriptura* of its meaning—that Scripture is the sole source of authority for all doctrine or practice. By this first pillar the Reformers had boldly denied any authority to church or tradition, except as they faithfully conveyed the ultimate authority of Scripture. And in so doing, they had rescued truth from a mass of false doctrines, ceremonies, and superstitions. But it was the priesthood of believers pillar that proved the fatal blow to the Papacy. It united the people with the Reformers in rejecting heretical doctrines and practices.

The subsequent failure of the Reformers to uphold the third pillar not only subverted *sola scriptura*, but it also produced confusion over the second pillar, justification (or righteousness) by faith, upon which the Reformers were in complete agreement. That doctrine had needed only to be refined by the corporate body in applying it to practical issues as well as to other key doctrines the Reformers had not yet recovered. But a neglect of the third pillar of the Protestant Reformation blocked that recovery and prevented the application. Thus, instead of deepening unity, multiplied conflicts over justification by faith have continually convulsed the Protestant world—and now threaten Adventism.

But the conflicts are not a result of scriptural ambiguity. They reflect, rather, the failure of the Reformers to maintain the paradoxical principles of their third pillar, by which they threw off the papal yoke.

VERTICAL PRIVILEGE AND HORIZONTAL RESPONSIBILITY

The proclamation that all individuals serve as their own priest to go directly to Christ and to decide truth for himself restored the vertical privileges that the papal system had stolen. It caused the power of priestcraft to collapse.

When vertical privilege unites with horizontal responsibility, the principles of the priesthood of believers will always empower God's people and advance them in their search for truth. But when we focus upon one principle to the neglect of the other, *sola scriptura* and claims to faith become meaningless. Unless we practice both the vertical and the horizontal, we remain under human authority.

The vertical requirement is obvious. Without personal dependence upon Christ we either avert scriptural authority or reduce it to a legalism that subverts faith. Yet Scripture and faith both depend on the horizontal pole as well. Unless we observe the horizontal principle of the priesthood of believers, the vertical principle will also collapse. And *sola scriptura* will become a delusion that leads to anarchy in a chaos of beliefs. Authority figures will inevitably rise to control doctrine and religious practice under illusions of scriptural authority. It has happened again and again within Protestantism.

Rather than continuing to combine personal and corporate study, in which each listens to and shares with all others without coercion and without respect to status, each faction in the various theological conflicts rallied behind a favored Reformer and unwittingly submitted to that Reformer's theological authority. This not only dwarfed the powers of the individual believer, but it educated the Reformation leadership to usurp to themselves authority that resided within the Word itself and was available only as all—both those whom God called to proclaim His message and those who heard—joined together in studying the Word and testing in union all doctrine.

The Reformers, though divinely called individuals, dramatized our own present-day plight. They obstructed the very principles they had so powerfully proclaimed. Instead of leading the people in continued, corporate search to know the Word of God for themselves, each Reformer anathematized anyone who dared to present a different view.

Unwittingly reflecting the papal viewpoint of the Lord's Supper, for example, Luther insisted that Christ's words "This is my body" can only mean that we chew the literal body of Christ with our physical teeth. Because Zwingli interpreted this as a spiritual eating, Luther opposed him and treated him as an agent of the devil. Only with great reluctance did he finally agree to discussions with Zwingli, but even then Luther would not listen to his arguments, and refused him the hand of fellowship at the close.

Meantime, Luther had recovered the truth that the dead are asleep and thus cannot suffer in purgatory. But only two years after Luther's 1532 commentary *Ecclesiastes*, John Calvin responded, in his famous *Psychopannychia*, that the soul was fully conscious. Just as Luther did to Zwingli, Calvin now accused those holding this doctrine of manipulating Scripture. He even charged them with "insanity." Directing his attack at Anabaptists, he berated them as "bablers, madmen, dreamers, drunkards" (L. E. Froom, *The Conditionalist Faith of Our Fathers*, Vol. II, pp. 116-118).

The doctrine of *sola scriptura* is not a doctrine of theological infallibility. Rather, it is a testimony to human fallibility. Although we must settle all issues by Scripture, it requires that we follow the horizontal practice of calmly coming together in humility to seek to know all that the Word says regarding the issue in dispute. Anything short of this is either *sola theologica* or *sola ecclesia*. Why did Luther not humbly approach Zwingli to search

Scripture prayerfully with him? Was it not because he refused to examine his biblical evidence? He did not want to become "confused."

But this is *sola theologica,* not *sola scriptura.* And why did not Calvin come to his older colleague, to whom he owed much, and both share his Bible evidence and listen to Luther's evidence? Such failure always signals a waning of confidence in God's Word. Instead of allowing Scripture to prevail, Calvin set the specific pattern for Protestant rejection of soul sleep. His arguments have prevailed to this day. And the pattern he reflected spread to many other issues of truth.

However sincere one is in believing his or her position scriptural, any attempt to enforce a personal view is to usurp the authority of Scripture. In this age none can exercise authority as did Calvin. But on every hand we still see the spirit of intolerance behind the saddest chapter of his life. Under Calvin's direction, Servetus, who, seeking to escape death at Roman Catholic hands, had fled for protection to Geneva, was imprisoned, tried, and burned at the stake on a threefold charge of "heresy." His heresy: denial of the Trinity, denunciation of infant baptism, and belief in soul sleep. In each case he simply rejected what he perceived to be papal error. And our pioneers agreed with all three positions, including the first! Can we ask for greater testimony to the urgency of our need to practice the priesthood of believers?

It is right to study diligently and teach others what we have learned. And it is proper to defend truth. But it is equally imperative that both theologians and laity continually insist that their word not be taken as authority but that each must test every principle to assure a "Thus saith the Lord."

Indeed, we must teach others to think for themselves by training ourselves to listen courteously and thoughtfully to the convictions expressed by even the humblest and least educated. We need to honor their conscience by encouraging them to retain their beliefs, even if wrong, till they have a biblical base for changing. Instead of exhibiting an authoritarian posture that seems to say "I am right because I am a scholar or an administrator," we must learn the art of humility in standing with all others meekly before the Word, carefully considering their expressions as well as sharing our own. Note the implications of the following familiar passage: "Out of the mouth of babes and sucklings hast thou ordained strength because of thine enemies, that thou mightest still the enemy" (Ps. 8:2).

The greatest of all enemies is our own ego. When we learn to honor the spiritual babes in our midst, the Lord will use them to provide additional insights. But the greatest aid to spiritual victory will be in the very humility and respect we show, not merely to the individuals, but to God's priesthood method of correcting, disciplining, and refining us.

In every generation since Luther and Calvin new leaders have risen in the name of *sola scriptura*. But few have honored the horizontal principle of subjection one to another. And without this, *sola scriptura* has no real validity.

The verticle pole unites us with Christ, our head, by means of His Word. Through it we test doctrinal truth and practice. The horizontal pole incorporates us in His body. By it our Head tests our balance in truth and practice. Personal union with Christ requires humility as we loathe our selfish spiritual rags and claim His robe of righteousness. But repentance, which must deepen every day if we are to remain in Him (*Christ's Object Lessons*, pp. 159-163), is tested by our corporate subjection to each other.

But you ask: Does the Bible teach a vertical/horizontal priesthood of believers? That is a vital question in view of the sad history of Protestantism, which, in violating priesthood of believer principles, belied its claim to *sola scriptura* and thus destroyed its unity on justification by faith.

ORIGIN OF PRIESTHOOD OF BELIEVERS PRINCIPLE

"Now the Lord had said unto Abram, Get thee out of thy country, and from thy kindred . . . and in thee shall all families of the earth be blessed" (Gen. 12:1, 2).

The first clear intimation of a divine priesthood of believers occurs in Abram's summons to go from Mesopotamia to Palestine. God called him and his family out of one center of world civilization to train them as missionaries to the whole world. But when in Egypt, also a primary center of world civilization, Abram's descendants forgot their high destiny and became slaves to the god of this world. After rescuing them from slavery but before returning them to Palestine, God clearly revealed His purpose for them by a priestly covenant: "Now therefore, if ye will obey my voice indeed, and keep my covenant, then ye shall be a peculiar treasure unto me above all people: for all the earth is mine: and ye shall be unto me a kingdom of priests, and an holy nation" (Ex. 19:5, 6).

Of the two dimensions of the priesthood, the vertical one of privileged personal relations with God must always remain first in priority. Its central feature was the writing of His law in every heart (Eze. 36:24-29). The supreme covenant requirement was love. And love is a very personal response to a loving Creator. Every Isrealite child was to be carefully instructed in covenant principles, as epitomized in the Decalogue (Deut. 6:

4-15). Indeed, God identified the Ten Commandments as the "covenant" (Deut. 5:3-21) and had them placed within the sacred chest that symbolized His throne, thus its name "the ark of the testimony" (Ex. 25:16).

But from the beginning that priestly covenant also had a horizontal, corporate dimension of mutual responsibility and accountability between believers. A striking lesson took place immediately after Israel's return in which God enforced the horizontal principle and sought to prepare His people for their priestly ministry.

When Achan sinned, all Israel felt divine displeasure. The defeat at the little town of Ai immediately followed the great victory at Jericho. In holding the entire nation responsible, God provided a dramatic lesson for us (*Patriarchs and Prophets*, pp. 494-497; *The SDA Bible Commentary*, Ellen G. White Comments, vol. 2, p. 996). Whether laity, pastors, or administrators, all are to be subject one to another within the body, being both accountable to and responsible for each other.

But the response of the 10 tribes to Reuben and Gad when they built an altar on the east side of the Jordan warns of wrong methods of fulfilling our priesthood responsibilities. The 10 tribes rightly accepted responsibility to see that God's people did not practice idolatry. But their grievous error in how they approached that responsibility could have been deadly. The horizontal principle does not permit authoritarian, harsh, or judgmental treatment of erring members:

"How often serious difficulties arise from a simple misunderstanding, even among those who are actuated by the worthiest of motives; and without the exercise of courtesy and forbearance, what serious and even fatal results may follow. The ten tribes remembered how, in Achan's case, God had rebuked the lack of vigilance to discover the sins existing among them. Now they resolved to act promptly and earnestly; but in seeking to shun their first error, they had gone to the opposite extreme. Instead of making courteous inquiry to learn the facts in the case, they had met their brethren with censure and condemnation" (*Patriarchs and Prophets*, p. 519).

Fortunately, the other two tribes gave a good example of how any who may be mistreated by the body or its leaders should respond. "Had the men of Gad and Reuben retorted in the same spirit, war would have been the result. While it is important on the one hand that laxness in dealing with sin be avoided, it is equally important on the other hand to shun harsh judgment and groundless suspicion" (*ibid.*).

We too often go to war with each other. When we do, the fault lies not in the priesthood principles themselves, but in our abuse of them. Moreover, misusing the horizontal principle also violates our individual relationship to the Head of the body, who gave His life for each of us and requires that we as His body reveal His character by acting in His Spirit.

The vertical principle of the priestly covenant appears throughout the New Testament. The book of Hebrews not only emphasizes the necessity of the law written in the heart, but identifies the Word of God as its base. And it does this to announce that Israel's failure did not cancel God's plan, but that He transferred His priesthood covenant to the church (Heb. 8). And James identifies this vertical principle as the basis for Christian warfare (James 4:7, 8).

After quoting the Old Testament to apply its priestly covenant to the church, Peter also enunciates its horizontal principle. To this he then joins the vertical, even linking humble subjection to one another with submission to God.

"But ye are a chosen generation, a royal priesthood, an holy nation, a peculiar people."

"Yea, all of you be *subject one to another*, and be clothed with *humility: for God resisteth the proud, and giveth grace to the humble. Humble yourselves* therefore *under the mighty hand of God*, that he may exalt you in due time" (1 Peter 2:9; 5:5, 6).

Three times in two short verses, Peter underlines the supreme key to both principles. He twice identifies humility as a horizontal condition. But by humility he also introduces the vertical principle.

Largely because of pride, which Peter declares that God always resists, church history reveals far more violation than application of priesthood principles in every generation. But the exceptions inspire faith. The first and no doubt most perfect example of its practice, occuring right after Pentecost, is a type for our day: "And they, continuing daily with one accord in the temple, and breaking bread from house to house, did eat their meat with gladness and singleness of heart, praising God, and having favour with all the people. And the Lord added to the church daily such as should be saved" (Acts 2:46, 47).

When social and religious experience combine in a true priesthood of believers, the result is gladness and joy. Self-sacrificing love elicits favor with others and causes growth in Christ's body. The ultimate result will be the loud cry of the latter rain.

No Manipulation or Control

The church is Christ's body, not His head. By calling for mutual subjection within the body, He more fully subjects us to His own authority. For not only is Scripture the authority for the verticle principle of the priesthood of believers, it is also the sole authority on the horizontal level.

Knowing that each one of us sees only part of truth and that we are blind to truth that others clearly perceive, He places us in corporate, mutual subjection. While helping to expose imbalances in others, we are at the same time to let them correct our own imbalance. By listening attentively to others amplify the Word, whatever their office or status, each of us thus more clearly hears and more fully surrenders to its truth and authority.

But as we respond to counsel within the body, we are still responsible for our own decisions. Yet at the same time a proper decision always honors the body even when we might reject some counsel that does not seem to honor the Word. Thus we are neither independent of nor dependent upon each other. We depend on the Word in interdependence within the body, as we ever seek harmony while simultaneously honoring the freedom and responsibility of each to act with integrity to his or her own conscience.

Either to control someone else or to surrender to another's manipulation is to deny the authority of our Head—who Himself will never manipulate or coerce.

I Have Never Been Able—Nor Am I Now Able

I confess. I have never known how to unite these two principles properly. And I am not now able to do so. But because God's Word presents these paradoxical principles, I do believe them. Moreover, by God's grace I am learning to understand and practice them.

Part Two of this book provides many examples of how Ellen White urged such priesthood of believer principles. A July 23, 1895, *Review and Herald* article gives several warnings against violating these principles. Note the following:

"Let man be warned; be careful how you treat the Lord's 'peculiar treasure.' All discourtesy, all pain, all neglect, which these souls suffer at your hands, is charged against you as inflicted upon Jesus Christ. They are not to be treated in a lordly, commanding manner."

Ellen White here exposes the violation of the horizontal principle by church leaders who, as officers of the Lord's army, go beyond their delegated authority and oppress the soldiers on the lines. This serious usurpation of the heavenly General's authority to give direct guidance by His Spirit, sets aside the vertical principle. Church officers have a vital role. But they must take care not to interfere with the role of the Holy Spirit. No one can be faithful to Christ while surrendering his or her conscience to someone else's control.

The warning applies to all leaders—independent as well as conference or local leaders. All, in whatever category, face the same temptation either to control others or to neglect their responsibilities to give counsel and direction. And they may even be guilty of both mistakes simultaneously and not be aware of either violation.

But the divine Head does indeed give responsibility to human officers of His earthly body. The "Holy Spirit [Himself] has made [some] overseers" (Acts 20:28). And "he that ruleth" God commands to do so "with all diligence" (Rom. 12:8). Failure to honor the overseer's responsibility to rule "with all diligence" thus also usurps the Holy Spirit's role in dividing the gifts. Indeed, it defies His command and prevents His own ministry in maintaining the unity of Christ's body (1 Cor. 12:6-31). Whether officer or soldier, we must "remember that the church of believers constitutes the body of Christ, and 'that there should be no schism in the body' (1 Cor. 12:25)" (*Ellen G. White Manuscript Releases*, vol. 11, p. 275).

But what do you do when you think the Lord directs one way and an officer commands in a different way? It is not a question of which principle to uphold—the vertical or the horizontal—but how to honor both. For our General mandates both. But that faces us with a human impossibility. Neither the Lord nor the human "overlord" will accept compromise.

Then what is the solution? First and most important, appeal in faith to the only One who knows your heart as well as that of the human leader. Meanwhile, we must keep certain biblical principles in mind. Both David's experience with Saul and Paul's response to the high priest when unjustly tried by him teach us that we must honor any legitimate position of authority even when its occupant dishonors it. If the authority is not legitimate, however, remove yourself from it at once! Either way, remember that God permitted the condition both to develop your character and to seek to rescue the offender.

That indicates our need to search our own hearts rather than the other person's so that we can understand the corrections and/or lessons God intends for us. He has a thousand ways to resolve our problems—just when He knows they need to be resolved—of which we know nothing. Thus, let us pray in faith that He who has promised will, in His own time and way, give us the needed wisdom and strength (*The Desire of Ages*, p. 668; James 1:1-5).

Finally, He expects us to put Him first, not merely in the issue that may be in conflict, but in our entire attitude and spirit in relating to the conflict. Whatever else, that will mean setting an example in humility. God alone knows whether He wants us to comply with the human directive until He changes our circumstances. He may direct us to wait for further developments. But note:

"Laws and rules are being made at the centers of the work that will soon be broken into atoms. Men are not to dictate. . . . Let each work in the line which God may indicate to him by the Holy Spirit. The soul is accountable to God alone" (*Review and Herald,* July 23, 1895).

At some time we might "be stirred by the Spirit" to step out from under that humanly abused authority:

"If the cords are drawn much tigher, if the rules are made much finer, if men continue to bind their fellow-laborers closer and closer to the commandments of men, many will be stirred by the Spirit of God to break every shackle, and assert their liberty in Christ Jesus" (*ibid.*).

But before considering such a step, we must know first that we have fully surrendered everything to Christ, our head, including our pride and reputation. Also we must recognize that another spirit will cause us to chafe and experience an indignation that feels righteous, but that is as evil as the wrong imposed upon us. A good test to make of our response is to ask ourselves whether our actions and attitudes harmonize with the spirit of Jesus when He faced injustice from those He had come to save. Do our hearts truly cry out, "Father, forgive, for this person knows not what he or she is doing"?

Consider the fact that Ellen White speaks to a widespread problem. "Laws and rules are being made at the *centers* of the work that will soon be broken into atoms. Men are not to dictate" (*ibid.*; italics supplied). It was not just at Battle Creek or some other center that injustice prevailed, but at *"the centers"*—apparently everywhere in the church.

Also consider that those she addressed were not bad people seeking to exploit others, but good ones seeking to be responsible. She spoke to "leading workers" whom she honored. But she was in love forced to rebuke (Rev. 3:19) their unwitting "rule or ruin" mentality (*ibid.*).

Their problem is also ours. The pioneers were sincere but too confident in their own opinions and methods. And they had too little confidence in the Holy Spirit's direction of others in ways that differed from theirs.

Is it surprising that similar circumstances exist today? Such problems and conditions have haunted God's work from its beginning. But the fact that they clearly surface is essential to the future of the church. For this deep-seated and universal human problem can never be overcome until it is exposed. Yet seeing it exposed in others, I can become judgmental of them if I am at the same time hiding from that same weakness in myself. If I am to be purified, God will eventually have to expose that same problem in me. I will have to apply personally the straight testimony to Laodicea to myself. And the sooner the better.

Adventism in Conflict

Our problem is self-righteousness as reflected in self-justification (Rev. 3:17). We unconsciously resist the Spirit's attempt to expose our imbalance, thinking it an enemy attack. Thus after a century and a half, the True Witness must continue to plead for His people to respond (verses 19, 20). To force us to recognize our problem against our will would violate His character and prevent the development of our own. But His twofold priesthood plan offers whole truth—which alone has the power to free us from our unwitting self-righteousness.

Adventism was born of priesthood of believer principles. But a Laodicean condition of self-righteousness, against which Ellen White warned us as early as 1852, soon caused a falling away from the third pillar of the Reformation—just as happened during the first generation of Protestants. Having rejected the Minneapolis appeal, we still waver between the two principles without ever actually fusing them. While some try to enforce the horizontal in a way that threatens the vertical, others despise the horizontal principle in seeking to enforce the vertical.

But we cannot truly accept Christ's vertical authority without at the same time subjecting ourselves to each other in a way that God designed should expose our self-centered thinking. Failure to learn and to practice the principles of mutual submission is thus a sure sign of independence from Christ—an independence that we mistakenly identify as loyalty to Him!

Indeed, our violation of the horizontal principle is largely responsible for the Laodicean indictment itself (verses 15-17). The genuine practice of priesthood of believer principles, in which submission to God accompanies humble mutual subjection to each other—in the Lord and through His Word—would quickly remove our dangerous self-satisfaction. Meanwhile, as we continue to compare ourselves with each other, the weaknesses in others that should arouse us to examine ourselves instead foster a false comparative sense of righteousness.

But how can we remain *individually* responsible to God and His *perfect Word*, yet be *corporately* (as a body) subject to each other within an *erring* church under divine rebuke (verses 14-22)?

We dare evade this question no longer. The Word reveals both principles. And God never demands the impossible. Yet no one can seriously attempt faithfulness to both without experiencing an intense inner tension. But we have no option. For to cling to the first principle and diminish the second is to compromise truth as surely as to grasp the second and diminish the first!

No Choice but to Seek Unity

Few would deny either principle. But we undermine them both in opposite ways. Many of us resolve the tension and seek a sense of security by submitting to accepted norms and/or by leaning on theological opinion without determining truth for ourselves. On the other hand, those who deplore any violation of the first principle too often disregard the second and compulsively foster an independence that Ellen White—whose statements they use in their defense—repeatedly deplored as very wrong.

From the human standpoint, full commitment to both principles is impossible. Nevertheless, our spiritual growth and the destiny of the church rest upon uniting *individual* responsibility to the Head of the body and *corporate* responsibility within His body—both through His Word. True believers in every age have accomplished this to some degree. But except for brief moments in history, the emphasis has constantly shifted from one pole of truth to the other in a way that has always retarded spiritual growth.

Significantly, after rebuking church administrators in 1895, Ellen White concluded her article with a sharp focus upon Christ's prayer of John 17 that we, the body, might become one in Him, the head. She pleads: "Come to the gospel feast; the supper is prepared, come. The weak must not now trust in finite men if they would be as David, and David as the angel of the Lord. . . . *God calls the church* to arise and clothe herself with the garments of Christ's righteousness" (*Review and Herald*, July 23, 1895; italics supplied).

Note that she makes this horizontal appeal to the church, not simply to private individuals whose sole focus on vertical relations tends to reinforce their egocentric tendencies. She calls the church itself to the wedding feast. But to come, that church must first unite by a humble mutual subjection among all the members of the body. In her transition from her reproof to leaders for their "rule or ruin" approach to administration to her discussion of Christ's prayer for unity, Ellen White emphatically declares: "But under the guidance of the Holy Spirit, *unity must and will be preserved*" (*ibid.*; italics supplied).

Before that unity can prevail, however, we will have to learn to unite consistently the passive and active principles that so often precipitate conflict. This will demand more than individual effort. It will require an honest, corporate wrestling and sharing together as we seek to adhere to both priesthood principles. But to avoid the ditch of legalism, we must simultaneously rest in Jesus. His own rest/strive plea illustrates the *passive* and *active* unity that was at stake at Minneapolis, the fracture of which continues even now to divide us. Christ's classic paradox offers insight into the kind of inner tension within truth that we must consistently honor as we faithfully seek to unite in our lives and relationships both poles of the pillar of the priesthood of all believers.

STRIVE TO REST, BUT REST WHILE STRIVING

Christ first invites: *"Come unto me . . . , and I will give you rest."*
But He immediately commands: *"Take my yoke"* (Matt. 11:28, 29).
Though externally contradictory, Christ's paradox is internally harmonious. Only by taking His yoke of labor can we enter into His rest. He Himself explains the paradox: "For my yoke is easy, and my burden is light" (verse 30).
The promise precedes the command and motivates obedience. But to experience His promised rest, we must choose to bear His burden. Though appearing heavy, His yoke proves so light as to lift us! Yet if we try to bear His burden before first coming to Him, His command becomes a grievous burden—whether we evade it or attempt to obey.
Hebrews 4:11 conveys the same paradox: "Let us labour therefore to enter into that rest." The mind in tune to the Spirit strives as though salvation depends upon its effort. But it rests implicitly in Jesus, knowing that human effort is worthless in meriting or achieving heaven.
Unfortunately, we abuse this truth in opposite ways. Some emphasize striving and obedience. Others stress rest and faith. Each verbally acknowledges both poles and assumes he or she integrates them. But any focus upon one pole that diminishes the other only fractures truth's internal unity and robs it of its power. The result is either an immediate burden of legalism or its delayed burden via disobedience.
On the other hand, as abstract faith obediently springs into concrete action in response to divine authority, rest and effort unite in mind and life to preclude both legalism and disobedience.
Thus we strive to rest. And by resting in Him, we work out our salvation by permitting Him to work in us to will and to do His will (Phil. 2:12, 13). But we can realize each principle only in light of and in relation to the other. For neither truth remains true when separated from its counterpart.
Abstract/passive principles (such as rest) give life only when translated by concrete action (such as labor). Moreover, unless *concrete/active* principles of obedience are based upon unseen provisions of grace that we

cannot produce but only receive, the result is spiritual death in legalistic bondage. Again, when not properly united, each truth becomes invalid. Indeed, when not whole and in balance, the very truth designed to free and to empower us to reveal Christ's purity and self-sacrificing love actually disables our Christian experience.

But to achieve that balance, we must put forth our greatest efforts to unite the vertical and horizontal poles of the priesthood of believers because all else depends upon the practice of this third pillar of the Reformation. By it alone can we honor the first principle of sola Scriptura and realize in our lives the experience of the second, justification by faith.

Thus, when not whole and in balance, the very truth designed to set us free and empower us actually disables our Christian experience.

REST STOP: YOU'VE GOT IT MADE

You've got it made now! Your wrinkled brow sometimes caused me concern. But I was heartened by sudden expressions of relief as the sun occasionally peeked through the clouds. You still have questions, some of which I am sure we will answer in the next chapter. But you have climbed the steepest grade. This chapter is so crucial that you may want to return to it for an occasional review.

Probably you still can't see how priesthood of believer principles can work in a worldly church. I can't either. Its a matter of faith in the Word that they actually can. But my attempts to test it are also reassuring to me. God's Word continually demands the impossible. But He surrounds every command by promises that it can and will be fulfilled. And He takes full responsibility for effecting each command in those who truly rest in Him. So rest in Him, assured that "he which hath begun a good work in you will perform it until the day of Jesus Christ" (Phil. 1:6).

Remember, meantime, that inner humility—something neither you nor I possess of ourselves—must precede unity. And humility is a gift of the Spirit that He gives by exposing our pride and independence. The very worldliness of the church thus becomes an opportunity to understand ourselves. It is a standing call to experience more deeply the repentance and humility our spiritual brothers and sisters so clearly need. As they see repentance and humility in our lives, others will be led to seek and receive this most precious gift themselves.

Do you decry the sins of the church, wish you could correct them but, in hopelessness, feel the impulse to withdraw? And is it possible that some you might consider hopeless are conscious of your own violation of principles and thus withdraw from you because they feel your case is hopeless? Do you castigate each other and feel mutually justified in view of the un-Christlike spirit of the other?

But don't go yet. I must share a message from Nora Hackett. Nora learned to paint when 70 and taught painting till she became too blind to continue, near the century mark. That beautiful saint often exclaimed in sorrow: "Pastor Moore, I'm nothing but an old sinner." She meant it. But her life never revealed it. I never knew her to speak an impatient word or to violate principle knowingly. In the four years she lived with us, caring for our children, I saw nothing but joy and humility.

Nora often expressed appreciation for my sermons. But, reminding me of a principle from the writings of Ellen White, she also warned me not to get too far ahead of the "brethren"! Both the Bible and Ellen White testify to God's patience in dealing with His people. As a faithful shepherd, He slows His pace so as not to overdrive His sheep. His plan for preparing His people for the loud cry of the latter rain is to plead, wait, and allow circumstances to amplify His voice—but never to force.

Character development requires a readiness to respond that cannot be imposed from the outside. It must arise from an inner sense of need. We only delay this process by human pressure. Truth must be set forth. But let us follow Christ's pattern in considering time, place, and circumstances for appeal.

Part One

Preparing to Examine History and Theology 6

Too often we use the labels liberal and conservative in contempt. Nor can we even define them in a way to satisfy everyone. Conservatives are considered liberal by those far to their right. Liberals are thought to be conservative by those to their left. Moreover, a lifestyle conservative may be liberal in theology, while lifestyle liberals may be theologically conservative.

Indeed, most liberals have some conservative characteristics, and most conservatives are in some ways liberal. We are all somewhere on a continuum from ultraliberal on the left to ultraconservative on the right. Virtually all of us reflect some of both traits. Fortunately, few fit either category completely.

Why then do I use labels that describe no one adequately and are likely to be misunderstood? The poles are real, and polarization and conflict require that we examine their cause and effect. To see how and why we fracture truth by our conflicting languages, we need reference points of some kind.

But please keep in mind throughout this book that my purpose is to understand ourselves, not to label or to judge any person or group. My concern is not "them" but "us." I will seldom mention the great majority that lie between the liberal/conservative poles. But I am not ignoring them. In warning against split-truth thinking I address all—left, right, and center. And non-Adventist as well as Adventist. We are all caught in the cross fire, and in some ways and to varying degrees we all reflect the imbalance of one or both patterns.

The conflict is not peculiar to Adventism. The problem is universal. Every person has split-truth instincts that affect business, politics, and social life, as well as theology. And all need an understanding of paradoxical principles, to heal not only the soul but also relationships.

LIBERAL AND CONSERVATIVE TERMS RELATE TO AUTHORITY

By "conservative" I refer not so much to lifestyle as to a consistent desire and priority to protect the authority of divine revelation against any apparent rational threat. By "liberal" I identify a compulsion to defend reason against real and/or apparent irrational perversion of that authority.

Conservatives accuse liberals of exalting reason above revelation while liberals charge conservatives with denying revelation by refusing to probe its principles. The key conservative question is: "What does the Word say?" Liberals ask, "What does it mean?" Both questions are vital.

Nevertheless, first things first. What the Word says must precede its meaning. Unless we know what it says and are committed to its message, we can never know its meaning—however diligent our search! And unless God's written Word is our authority, our search can lead only to delusion. Human reason must bow low before divine revelation, or it will set us adrift upon an intangible sea of human speculation and rationalization.

Reason is vital, however, and faces constant threat from dogmatism that does not honor truth. A rigid focus on behavior fails to probe the principles that should govern that behavior. Thus too often we treat Scripture and the writings of Ellen G. White as codes of law to be enforced, rather than as instructors and enablers.

In contrast, by undue focus upon progressive revelation, reason robs God's Word of its authority. Dwelling upon progressive revelation can reduce enduring principles to temporary expressions of developing maturity—or of culture. But in reaction, many virtually deny the place of culture and progressive revelation. While they admit that messages rather than words are inspired, their focus upon words too often obscures the principles of revelation. When we ignore time and circumstances of writing and fail to pay adequate attention to context and/or related divine counsel, we are liable to deny truth's message by treating part-truth as its full essence.*

The very urgency pervading our conflict over divine authority makes communication almost impossible. Each side so intensely defends one set of principles that it precludes any objective examination of the other. No issue is more urgent or poses greater peril than revelation. Conservatives proclaim its divine authority, but tend to breed authoritarianism. In attacking such authoritarian perversion, liberals threaten divine authority itself.

God, our supreme authority, is not authoritarian. Instead of stifling mental processes, He seeks to prod them into action. He will not do our thinking for us, but guides our thought processes. There is freedom in authority only when we grasp and act upon the principles involved in revelation. But we rob ourselves of truth's freedom when we dogmatically apply to our present circumstances specific counsel given by revelation for past issues. The two may indeed be parallel. But we cannot know this without considering the undergirding principles of the specific counsel, which may now actually apply in a different way to the new mix of circumstances.

Authoritarianism creates many problems for the whole issue of revelation. We forget that the authority is God's, not ours. But His commitment to human freedom is so great that He died on the cross rather than manipulate or force our thinking. Indeed, He leaves us truly free to decide what is truth and how to relate to it. By contrast, we instinctively tend to take His authority into our own hands and to impose our perceptions of revelation upon others.

Virtually all would agree that unless God's written Word is our authority, our search can lead only to delusion. Yet we remain hopelessly divided because some focus upon faith at the expense of reason, while others concentrate upon reason at the expense of faith. Our conflict is not over whether they must relate, but over *how* they relate.

Liberals do not deny faith. And conservatives would never reject reason. But one makes faith subservient to reason while the other subjects reason to faith. In the process we subvert the proper role of each. And subservience of either to the other destroys the function of both.

To elevate reason above revelation—even to a par with revelation—presumptuously transfers the latter's authority to a rational self whose wisdom is foolishness (1 Cor. 1:19-25). Nevertheless, for us to grasp the message of revelation reason is absolutely essential. Thus to diminish reason in the name of faith is to debase faith to presumption. It is to assume that we can trust our own perceptions of truth without testing them by careful examination of the Word itself.

Indeed, reason's vital function is to establish faith's integrity by deciphering the meaning of revelation. The Creator designed that we should exercise reason, judgment, and will (the highest human faculties) to the fullest. But reason reaches its greatest height as it bows *with* faith before revelation. Each is effective only as God's Word directs them *together*.

To truly hear the Word of the Lord, faith must not only permit reason to assure its integrity to the *content* of God's Word, but it, in turn, must protect reason's integrity by enforcing its submission to the *message* of that Word.

To try to grasp revelation by faith without the diligent exercise of reason presumptuously transfers authority to our irrational self! But to impose reason over faith also shifts authority to self! That we still focus upon one pole of truth or the other a century after the 1888 conflict is a symptom of the Laodicean self-justification we have contracted from the world from within as well as from around us. It also testifies to the faithfulness and accuracy of the True Witness in His diagnosis and prescription for our spiritual condition (Rev 3:14-21).

TRUTH: AN ARROW OR A WHEEL?

To what shall we compare truth? Is it like an arrow, which points in only one direction? Or is it like a wheel, which circles a central point? The opposition to Waggoner at Minneapolis in 1888 demonstrates how viewing truth as a straight line extending in a single, "right" direction blinds us to the reality of truth and perpetuates our alienation toward each other (see Part Two).

If we view truth as pointing in one straight direction, we are liable either to go to extremes or to stop short and cease growing for fear of going to extremes. Upon reaching what we presume to be *the truth,* we feel we must maintain a holding pattern or we will move away from truth.

The sixteenth-century Protestant Reformation demonstrates that it is no better to stagnate than actually to depart from truth. To stop growing in truth is to die. Fearing extremism, each reform group creedally established its own truth boundaries. Insisting that all come to its "truth," and viewing any movement beyond that position as heresy, each group of Reformers attempted to enforce upon all others its partial truth with its artificially imposed, human limitations. The result of such straight-line truth-perception was not only stagnation but also persecution and war.

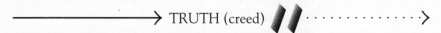

The blocked line illustrates the fate of Protestantism. Straight-line thinking left only a name to testify to the vitality of the vigorous life with which the Reformation began.

Instead, truth is like a wheel. Understanding results from revolving around and moving ever closer to Christ, its great center. This suggests endless growth in unity. Bound by a rim of revelation, truth's spokes point to and unite us in Christ, the hub. The rim holds all truths together and marks the boundary set by the Creator Himself, a boundary beyond which everything becomes mere human speculation (Deut. 29:29).

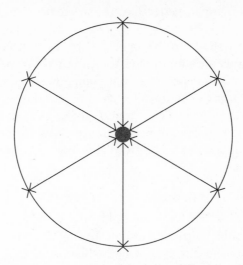

The rim forms a continuous series of arcs intersected by truth's spokes. Each arc points in opposite directions to adjacent truths. They in turn direct us back to the initial truth as well as on to converse truth on the other side of the Hub.

Our primary danger, then, is in spiritual death resulting from a straight-line thinking that causes us either to cease to seek truth or to move beyond the rim of truth.

In Christ opposite spokes unite as one. But just as all spokes must converge to form a single wheel, even so, to reveal the Creator, all principles must come together in a single wheel of truth.

Nevertheless, every spoke is unique in meaning and has a specific function in relation to the great Hub from which it emerges and to the rim that sets its bounds. But the meaning of each individual spoke relates not only to Christ and His Word but also to other spokes of truth. For all truths are thus interdependent. And each principle in various ways points toward all others. However, for primary support, the spoke on top depends upon its paradoxical counterpart, the bottom spoke. Meanwhile, since the Word always points to Christ, to move from any truth to another is inevitably to move toward Him, toward the converse truth, and thus toward one another!

By way of contrast, to resist any paradoxical spoke of truth in favor of another is to distance ourselves from the Source from which all truth radiates and to threaten His body with schism. Such split-truth thinking shattered our movement in 1888. It now threatens Adventism in battles over the nature of Christ, perfection, the atonement, and a host of other issues.

Those who do not see truth's opposite spokes as necessary for mutual support and integrity are sure to view the concept of paradoxical principles as nothing more than compromise. But compromise never unites truth. It instead imposes error by diminishing one or the other of those principles that, when united, will exclude error and protect us from needless conflict. Nor is there balance in compromise. Balance exists only within the rim of revelation and through the Hub. Truth thus not only unites in Christ but is defined by Him.

SHOULD LIBERALS AND CONSERVATIVES UNITE?

Liberals and conservatives both hold vital principles that must come together if we would be true to either. To violate either pole of truth is actually to destroy the integrity of both. Neither is true unless joined to its counterbalancing truth. Converse principles are internally as united as are the left and right arms of the body. From opposite sides they move in converse directions but function as one. So also, paradoxical principles function as one. Each is as essential to the other as are opposite rafters on a house. In meeting they form one strong supporting unit.

But focusing upon what seems to be external contradiction will only blind us to internal harmony. Failure to grasp the paradoxical nature of truth has repeatedly marred the history of the Christian church and shattered its harmony. The result has been either conflict or compromise.

What then? Should liberals and conservatives unite? What do you say? Absolutely not? Most certainly? Neither response alone is correct. Liberals and conservatives could not unite without mutually compromising their integrity. God judges us not simply by truth itself, but by our integrity in relating to what we see as truth. This requires not only commitment to truth as we now perceive it, but also to the authority of God's Word to correct and redirect us as we mature and advance. Any failure either to maintain our own integrity or to honor the other's faithfulness to present convictions will violate the principles of spiritual growth.

The result will be deepening apostasy, and God will permit multiplying heresies in His attempt to prepare us for true unity. Only God-ordained unity can remove our Laodicean self-confidence. The simple merger of parties would thus be disastrous for truth. In appearing to resolve our confusion, a liberal/conservative compromise could only abort God's purpose to help us find the principles and understandings that will really enable us to make sense of our problem.

Truth's triumph awaits a fusion of true principles within each perspective. But only defeat of both as self-conscious parties can produce the long-awaited victory of truth in righteousness by faith that humbles the glory of each in the dust!

"You shall know the truth, and the truth shall make you free" (John 8: 32, NASB). But part-truth can never free us from the constraining influences of the world by which mystical Babylon intoxicates, confuses, and thus perpetuates both heresy and apostasy (Rev. 14:8; 17:1-5; 18:1-4).

I challenge you to "buy the truth, and sell it not" (Prov. 23:23). Pay any price for truth, including painful separation from those misconceptions you have long held as truth. Yet never surrender one hemisphere of truth for another. All heresy is based upon part-truth that has become severed from its balancing truth. Only as truth links with truth is it truly whole and thus true. This alone can protect us from heresy!

COMPROMISE ANYTHING BUT PRINCIPLE

I hope it is now unquestionably clear that I do not call for compromise of principle but a refusal to compromise either biblical principle that may be in tension. Indeed, compromise avoids tension by sacrificing one or both of the elements in tension. Compromising any principle will never lead to any true or lasting unity. To compromise principle is to subvert the freeing power of truth.

Yet there is plenty that we can honestly compromise in our search for unity. We can and should compromise our self-assurance. It is instinctive to confuse our opinions with ultimate truth. Thus we can always afford to compromise our rigidity and false dignity by humbly and courteously coming close to those who differ with us. All of us need to compromise the pride that drives us to enforce our own concept of right in the name of righteousness. And we must compromise our suspicion of and judgmental attitudes toward those who may oppose our views.

But never should we compromise conscience. However, since it is impossible to be certain we are properly distinguishing between the Holy Spirit's guidance and the arrogance of pride that assures us we are right, we must learn to live with tension, seeking to compromise opinions but never the balancing principles of the divine Word. For to diminish either principle is to pervert both.

God's Word—the whole Word—must guide in the process. God designed the balancing principles of that Word both to test and to develop our integrity. Until we fully commit ourselves to each principle, we will never realize the assurance that "all His biddings are enablings" (*Christ's*

Object Lessons, p. 333). Meanwhile, to maintain the tension, refusing to compromise either pole of truth, requires an intense heart-searching and pleading for divine illumination.

REST STOP: CLARIFICATION AND PERSONAL CONFESSION

I sense your frustration. You want to "buy the truth, and sell it not." But you still fear I am asking you to sell some truth you hold dear. You want to know more exactly what I mean by liberal and conservative. You have a right to know. But it is impossible for me to so clarify terms that you could unerringly locate your own position on my scale. For I use no scale, but deal with patterns that probably won't seem to fit your individual case. You no doubt identify with one category in some ways and the other in other ways and may even differ from both classifications part of the time. Most of us assume we are near the center.

I trust you do truly represent the growing number who seek to unite both poles of truth in Christ crucified. Unfortunately, those who don't will tend to confuse my efforts with Laodicean compromise, that condition which spawned the reactionary extremes on both sides in the first case!

Paradoxical thinking is not easy. Our innermost selves are compulsively driven to split truth. I invite you to join me in identifying within yourself the weaknesses of both poles and also of a Laodicean center. In different ways all three positions reflect the same principles of resistance to truth.

The same compulsion for security that pushes one person left drives another right, but also demands that still another stay "in the middle of the road." Those on the ends, however, tend to be more ideological. Both fear any truth that seems to threaten their peculiar perception of truth. Those in the center tend to be more pragmatic, but less concerned about truth's purity.

I confess! I have always considered myself conservative. My first priority is, by faith, ever to submit reason's exercise to the authority of God's Word. I also confess that I believe the writings of Ellen White speak for their divine Author, the living Word. Scripture alone is always the final test as to when and by whom Christ speaks. By repeatedly testing the messages conveyed by Ellen White with Scripture, I find in them His signature. Thus I accept them as His voice, His testimony, His Word to me.

Earlier I said that truth's triumph demands the defeat of both parties. I now commend a *liberal-conservative stance.* I say stance, not party. Stance testifies to our stand on issues that demand a ringing testimony in uniting both principles of truth. Parties represent our identity within groups who usually can not hear one another. Each group sees in the other only an enemy of truth. In a Week of Prayer reading immediately after Minneapolis, Ellen White twice warned against a "party spirit," declaring it "a work of the enemy to create a party spirit, and to have party feelings" (*Ellen G. White 1888 Materials*, p. 199).

I also say liberal-conservative, not conservative-liberal; to me there is a vital difference. The authority of God's Word, to which reason must submit, is the most urgent issue we face. If we surrender His authority to reason (or experience, theology, science, etc.), we will surely fall.

The Word of God—neither science, experience, nor emotion—is alive and powerful (Heb. 4:12) and fully able to sustain us. To grasp the truth that alone sets us free, we must exercise our reason to the full. But reason must submit to God's Word in faith—even when it seems on the surface to be contradictory!

My deepest grief is not over corruption in the church. Anguishing as that is, God permits it to stimulate us to repentance. Rather, my grief is in my own slow progress in reflecting Christ's character. Honesty in facing this fact may at first seem to leave but a step between me and those who deny this goal. Take that further step, they demand, and simply claim His unmerited favor.

The latter I ever seek to do. But to deny the goal would surrender revelation to reason and experience—a step I cannot take. To superimpose experience-based reason over His Word would expose me as a liar in the judgment (Rom. 3:4). I thus find myself between a rock and a hard place—just where my Lord wants me!

Paradoxically, Christ wants us all to recognize our absolute inability ever to achieve the standard He places before us. He challenges us to seek that goal in faith, knowing we have no power to achieve it. And each time we fail He urges, "Try again."

My liberal friends cry in horror, "Legalistic nonsense! Don't try! Just trust!"

Trust we certainly must. But any genuine trust will try again. Why? Because if I refuse to try, I ignore His command and deny His authority over my life. Faith is *acting* upon His Word because it is His Word.

Only by seeking in vain to reach the goal He sets before us can we truly learn the vital lesson underlying trust: we can of ourselves do nothing! Until we learn this in the paradoxical defeat that prepares for victory, we will never grasp the assurance that "with God all things are possible."

Our own success, meanwhile, is ruinous failure. For our success would preclude *His* victory. We will succeed only as we recognize and face our failure. As we despair of our most intense efforts and depend solely upon

Adventism in Conflict

His righteousness, our defeat will prepare us for the victory that has long awaited the proper exercise of faith. To receive full at-one-ment and be prepared for the final conflict, our faith must be purified of every element of self-confidence.

---

* Opposite statements by Paul and James offer a classic example of the need to transcend words by examining context and circumstances and to search the whole of God's Word for interpretive principles (see chapter 4).

Facing Ourselves in History

Part Two

The Purpose of History Is to Understand Ourselves

7

"When the history of our cause and work reveals that men who have occupied positions of sacred trust, who have been teachers of the truth to others, are found unfaithful . . . , what carefulness should it lead us to! What distrust of self! How it should strip us of self-sufficiency and spiritual pride! What humble views we should have of our wisdom and our own insufficiency! How we should sense the fact that we are kept by the power of God through faith!" (Ellen G. White 1888 Materials, p. 262).

Has it ever bothered you that the Bible exposes the sins of its heroes? It did me until I began to grasp the importance of this to me. Human nature makes us want to see the participants in the struggle for truth as either nearly faultless heros or as villains. But if we deny the reality of their flawed experience, we also deceive ourselves about our own. We instinctively identify with the presumed goodness of the hero while using the villain as a scapegoat to hide our own weaknesses.

As I probe the failings of leaders of the past, I neither praise nor blame. Instead, I seek understanding. When we avoid glamorizing history, it may help us see ourselves as does the True Witness to Laodicea, who recognizes that we are all hiding our flaws from ourselves. To prepare ourselves for the heavenly Canaan, we must know why our predecessors failed to enter it (Heb. 3; 4). Their weaknesses are always ready to spring to life in our own lives.

1950: A CHALLENGE BY TWO YOUNG MISSIONARIES

Two delegates from Africa to the 1950 General Conference session lit a fuse of controversy that even now continues to intensify. Researching E. J. Waggoner's Minneapolis message, Robert Wieland and Donald Short became alarmed by a recent denominational history and two seminary theses that painted as a great victory an episode that Ellen White repeatedly had identified as a terrible defeat in which denominational leaders had resisted Christ Himself! They were appalled when—under the theme "Christ-centered Preaching"—a number of the 1950 presession ministerial institute speakers also proclaimed Minneapolis a glorious triumph.

Moreover, contrary to Waggoner, who had exalted the law while proclaiming grace, Wieland and Short perceived in the 1950 emphasis a subtle undermining of law and obedience, the very thing that denominational leaders had falsely charged Waggoner with in 1888. Seeing in this a serious blindness to the nature of Waggoner's Christ-centered proclamation, Wieland and Short felt compelled to warn of the danger of a false christ.

To denominational leaders who meant only to turn attention from the law to Christ our justifier, the claim by Wieland and Short seemed grossly unfair. As did Waggoner, the 1950 leaders saw the "schoolmaster" as the moral law, which cannot save but only enforces guilt. They also held that obedience contributes nothing to justification. Justification, they emphasized, can be received only by faith, "without the deeds of the law."

With Waggoner, they insisted that all true obedience results from beholding Christ crucified. Apart from Him and His merits, human obedience yields only condemnation. Thus the 1950 leadership assumed that their Christ-centered theme magnified the law in the same way that Waggoner had done. But by relating spiritual effort to legalism, they had unwittingly muted his active principle of faith—that we must take the cross in unmodified commitment to obedience.

To receive Christ's righteousness, faith must grasp two poles: one passive and the other active. Any one-sided focus on truth always precipitates an opposite reactionary swing. Thus the 1888 General Conference session's fear that Waggoner's "faith principle" threatened the law gave way at the 1950 General Conference session to an oversimplified view of legalism that produced in many an automatic fear of all spiritual effort. Just as some leaders resisted Waggoner's proclamation of grace in 1888 because they thought it endangered the law and Sabbath doctrines, so in 1950 some neutralized his active principle of obedience by emphasizing a concept of grace that contained the fear that efforts to obey fathered legalism.

THE LANGUAGE OF LAW STIMULATES A LANGUAGE OF GRACE

A strong passive emphasis, when not fused with the active principle, will engender antinomian tendencies.[1] Either by itself will pervert faith. Unless it rests upon grace, obedience does breed legalism. But when not claimed by active faith that harnesses one's efforts to obey, the claim to grace will in turn breed presumption. *Both principles must unite—each in its own fullness—if we would represent Christ. To resist either of them can only distort truth and misrepresent its Author,* who personally glorifies and heightens the meaning of both law and grace by joining them in Himself.[2]

Waggoner and fellow editor A. T. Jones actually triggered the Minneapolis conflict three or four years before the 1888 session. Feeling the urgency of their message and fearing that others would mute it, they disregarded principles of church unity and pushed ahead regardless of the controversy they might stir up. Not only did they teach their controversial view at Healdsburg College without consulting other church leaders; they heralded it in the missionary organ *Signs of the Times.*

In response, the General Conference president and the *Review and Herald* editor together declared theological war against them. Not only did George Butler and Uriah Smith fear antinomianism; they were stinging from what they felt was the disrespect of the young editors. Ellen White shared Butler and Smith's dismay. Soundly rebuking the young men, she called for private discussion with denominational leaders who should carefully study their views.

Humbly accepting the rebuke, Waggoner and Jones quit agitating the subject. But when the older men continued their opposition, Ellen White insisted that in fairness Waggoner should receive an opportunity to present his ideas. This he did at the 1888 session.

Choosing J. H. Morrison to defend their side, certain conservative leaders challenged Waggoner to debate the issue. He declined, so they presented their opposing views separately. But this did not relieve the animosity, especially since the atmosphere had already been charged by Jones's presession debate with Uriah Smith over the horns of Daniel 7's fourth beast. Jones's derision of Smith (author of *Daniel and the Revelation,* recognized authority on prophecy, and the church's unofficial dean of theology) further stoked the fires of mistrust and hostility. Resentment and anger were thus already boiling over as Waggoner, Jones's editorial associate, began his series on the law in the book of Galatians.

Those opponents who did not leave the church later confessed their wrong in opposing Waggoner and Jones. But numerous Ellen White references to Minneapolis testify to a continued hostility years after the confessions. With scores of such references in hand, Wieland and Short insisted that to restore the Minneapolis loud cry message, which is to lead to the latter rain, we must acknowledge our rejection and repent of our continuing resistance or always remain vulnerable to the deception of a false latter rain.

I first heard about the 1888 debate right after the 1950 General Conference session from Felix Lorenz, a Madison College Bible teacher. I recognized that to receive righteousness strictly by faith and not by works harmonized with *The Desire of Ages*. But I did not know what to think of the key issue: Did we reject the message in 1888? And do we even now represent it?

My focus, however, was not upon Minneapolis, but upon the paradoxical nature of truth. When I did read Waggoner and Jones two and a half decades later, however, I was amazed to find that those who opposed them did so precisely because of the paradoxical way they united law and grace.

For years Ellen White had warned about a language of law that focused primarily upon faith's active obedience. Church leaders responded to her concerns by carefully presenting the law with reference to Christ the law-giver and insisting that His Spirit must empower our obedience.

But by proclaiming grace primarily to enforce law, they overlooked its primary passive dimension and intensified their active focus upon faith and obedience. Alarmed at their subordination of the cross to law and obedience, Waggoner shifted the spotlight from our obedience to Christ our righteousness and powerfully proclaimed faith's passive role. We receive His righteousness only as a free gift, and meet the law's demands, he insisted, only by virtue of His justifying sacrifice.

That sounded ominous to Smith and others. To defend those pillars of truth that they thought Waggoner now threatened, they described his "passive truth" as cheap grace and the destroyer of law and obedience. In opposing passive faith in defense of "security by active faith," they unwittingly denied Christ Himself as our only righteousness. Within a few years most of Waggoner's opponents acknowledged their error. But this did not resolve our problem, as Ellen White testified 13 years later.

"I feel a special interest in the movements and decisions that shall be made at this conference regarding the things that should have been done years ago, and especially ten years ago, when we were assembled in conference [1891?]. . . . The brethren assented to the light God had given, but there were those connected with our institutions, especially with the Review and Herald office and the [General] Conference, who brought in elements of unbelief, so that the light given was not acted upon. It was assented to, but no special change was made to bring about such a condition of things that the power of God could be revealed among His people" (*Ellen G. White 1888 Materials*, p. 1743).

Obviously the church body had not "assented to" Waggoner's message in 1888. By 1891 ("ten years ago" in 1901) many had confessed their error in opposing him. Some joyfully accepted the message of righteousness by faith. Others (including Smith) acknowledged that their spirit was wrong in resisting it, but remained blind to the vital importance of the passive principle Waggoner proclaimed. "Elements of unbelief" still prevented any real action upon the light, so that even by 1901 "no special change was made." Meanwhile, two years after the 1891 session, Ellen White wrote:

"The opposition in our own ranks has imposed upon the Lord's messengers [Waggoner, Jones, and herself] a laborious and soul trying task. . . .

"It is not the opposition of the world that we have to fear; but it is the elements that work among ourselves that have hindered the message. . . . Love and confidence [in the messengers] constitute a moral force that would have united our churches, and insured harmony of action; but coldness and distrust have brought disunion that has shorn us of our strength. . . .

"The influence that grew out of the *resistance of light and truth at Minneapolis tended to make of no effect* the light God had given to His people through *the Testimonies*. . . .

"The *dullness* of some *and* the *opposition* of others have confined our strength and means largely among those who know the truth, but do not practice its principles" (Ellen G. White letter to the GC session, *General Conference Daily Bulletin*, Feb. 28, 1893, p. 4; italics supplied).

The "dullness of some and the opposition of others" blocked the loud cry message from going to the world. "Resistance of light and truth at Minneapolis tended to make of no effect the light God had given . . . through the Testimonies." As a result, four and a half years later she said it still required vast "strength and means" to deal with the church's resulting internal problems.

Indeed, for six decades an imbalanced focus upon law continued because we identified righteousness by faith exclusively with: (a) justification for past sins, and (b) obedience by the power of His Spirit. But by the mid-twentieth century certain leaders began an attempt to correct this by shifting the focus to passive faith. Unfortunately, however, by confusing active faith with legalism, which it is not, they introduced an opposite distorted language, one centered exclusively on grace.

Whether it be a language of law or of grace, the problem is universal: a concern for our own salvation and security eclipses our concern for Christ's glory. Thus the 1950 reaction sought security by passive faith. By diminishing obedience, it also resisted Christ. Whether we relate perfection to salvation on one hand or downplay its importance on the other, we still deny grace and undermine law. Either way, an obsessive concern for our security supersedes Christ and the cross! We place more value on our own security than on the glory of Him who is our security!

Obedience is not meant to ensure our salvation, but to honor and glorify Christ. Thus perfection relates neither to salvation nor to assurance—but to His glory. To make perfection our theme—instead of Him—produces a neurotic, self-centered focus that denies the cross.

Yet to minimize obedience and oppose perfection because some make them the basis of their salvation reflects the same error—in reverse. To minimize character development by confusing active faith with legalism undermines the cross (the essence of His glory) as surely as does legalism.

To uplift Christ, we must unite Waggoner's twofold "passive/active" principle by focusing upon Him rather than upon our security by either law or grace!

In 1888 church leaders sought security in an obedience that unwittingly competed with the cross because it wasn't properly rooted in Christ and wrapped in grace. By 1950 some sought their security in a concept of grace that also dishonored Him. Although seemingly rooted in Christ, it wasn't properly wrapped in obedience. Again it depicted the human obsession with salvation itself instead of with Christ the source of salvation.

Prior to 1950 our theologians recognized a continuing legalism, which they sought to cure by refocusing the Minneapolis message. But in reacting to certain claims that we had rejected the 1888 message, our denominational historians argued that we had indeed accepted it and in fact continued to proclaim it. By strangely echoing this defense, the 1950 ministerial institute speakers betrayed their real cause.

How could they restore a message that had never been lost? If it was largely lost, how could they deny this while trying to evaluate and restore it properly? Not only did their denial unwittingly justify our 1888 resistance to Christ; it obscured the nature of the language of law they sought to correct. Misdirected attempts to counter legalism thus actually undermined active faith and threatened law and obedience.

WALTER MARTIN AND *QUESTIONS ON DOCTRINE*

Our confusion about the relationship between law and grace would soon plague our discussions with Walter Martin, who, in connection with Donald Barnhouse, editor of *Eternity* magazine, intended to expose Adventism as a legalistic cult.

Certain of our legalism but desiring to represent us correctly, Martin contacted the General Conference with a long list of questions. Our sharp focus upon Christ in response to those questions surprised and troubled him. If he simply reported his findings, Evangelicals who could cite endless examples of our language of law would simply dismiss whatever he said out of hand. Martin thus asked the church leadership to publish an official reply to which he could refer in his writings.

Questions on Doctrine (*QOD*) came out during the latter part of 1957. Martin's *The Truth About Seventh-day Adventism* (1960), which used *QOD* as its primary reference, defended Adventists as Christians but opposed Adventism's unique beliefs and echoed Barnhouse, who ridiculed the idea that Christ entered the Most Holy Place in 1844 as nothing more than "a face-saving device." Feeling betrayed, many Adventists entered into open conflict with those leaders whom they felt had sold the faith for a mess of apostate Protestant pottage.[3]

As the conflict intensifies, each of our languages (law and grace) defends one Waggoner principle against the other, which nevertheless we acknowledge as also true! Proponents of each charge the other with an imbalance that threatens truth. But neither side can recognize its own imbalance. Indeed, seeing the integrity of Adventism at stake, each seeks to enforce its own imbalance as the essence of balance! Thus the True Witness continues His call to us all to repent. Meanwhile, let me share with you how this controversy touched my own personal history.

LETTIE WHEELER'S DECISION WAS FINAL

"Come back home, Lettie! Please come back home," Eugene Wheeler pleaded with his daughter. "I'll go away and find work if you'll just come back home."

Lettie might have avoided this dreaded parting, but she had decided to bid a neighbor goodbye. As she pulled the rented horse and buggy that she used to haul her trunk to the train station back onto the road, her father ran frantically toward her.

The bonds of affection were unusually strong between the daughter and her father, who when she was only 3 had watched helplessly as his young wife lost her battle with tuberculosis. Nine years later, and midway (1908) between Ellen White's 1901 lament about the failure of the 1891 session and her 1915 death, Lettie and her father became Seventh-day Adventists.

But tears now ran freely down both faces as 17-year-old Lettie, carrying her few belongings, rode determinedly away from home, never to return.

If parting brought both such grief, why did Lettie refuse to reconsider her decision? She had not been abused. Nor was she going away to school or to an early marriage. Indeed, she had no idea of where she was going. She simply knew she could stay no longer in an atmosphere of unbelief.

Isolated as they were, the Wheelers rarely had opportunity to attend church. As Gene's first love for the Seventh-day Adventist message had faded, he had become increasingly discouraged with himself and critical of others. While in a depressed state about two years after his baptism, he read a book that confirmed his spiritual and emotional darkness and brought never-ending discord and unhappiness into his home.

D. M. Canright's representation of Adventism and Ellen White in *Adventism Renounced* seemed irrefutable. Who could know the situation better than a former leading minister who had worked closely and even lived with the Whites for a time? Eugene now concluded that Ellen White's legalistic writings had been the cause of his present confusion and darkness. A. F. Ballenger's books soon confirmed that conviction.

Wheeler, who soon became expert at spotting Ellen White's "heresy" for himself, began printing his own tracts. With much zeal but little joy he went from one Adventist community to another. Urgently he implored everyone who would listen to escape Adventism.

Lettie's confidence in her father's integrity never wavered. Even before professing to be a Christian, he had always prized honesty and purity. But seeing the gross distortion in his arguments, she refused his constant urging that she attend his meetings and read his Scripture texts for him. Much as she loved him she could not, even by her presence, lend her influence against truths that meant so much to her.

The father's demands that she cooperate or leave home eventually led to the daughter's decision to depart. Nor could his tears now dissuade her. Coming to the turn that would take her forever out of sight, she, with aching heart, looked back. There stood her father, transfixed as he gazed helplessly after her. The impulse to return and comfort him was almost overpowering. But knowing the comfort he sought was the surrender of her faith in God's message and her confidence in His messenger, she drove resolutely on to loneliness and unknown trials—but to a life of faith.

Had Adventists responded to Minneapolis's twofold, Christ-centered principle, the church might have rescued Canright himself. Only humble, dependent focus upon Christ—which that message portrayed—could save one whose unbelief resulted from making self the center. As with Smith and Butler, Canright's language of law was both the cause and effect of a focus upon self rather than upon Christ (*Testimonies*, vol. 3, pp. 308, 309; *Selected Messages*, book 2, p. 163). When he switched to a language of grace, it reflected the same problem. Nothing really changed. His discovery of grace was theoretical. He had not integrated it into his life by personally receiving Christ crucified—the strongest argument in favor of the law and the greatest motivator of obedience. To focus truly upon Christ is to see in Him the union of law and grace.

"Christ was both the law and the gospel. The angel that proclaims the everlasting gospel proclaims the law of God; for the gospel of salvation brings man to obedience of the law, whereby their characters are formed after the divine similitude" (*Ellen G. White Manuscript Releases*, vol. 1, pp. 44, 45).

Moreover, had Waggoner and Jones practiced the principle of the priesthood of all believers, which underlies their message, they and Ballenger might not later have fallen away. Even then, however, had we grasped the lesson of their fall and proclaimed the Minneapolis message, Eugene (who came in soon after they had left) might not have lost his faith or his family. Paradoxical truth might have filled the deep longings of his heart and reconciled the apparent contradiction in the writings of Ellen White. Had we seized the two sides of Bible truth needed to set him free from guilt and pride, the message designed to prepare us to withstand last-day split-truth deceptions might have given him joy and confidence instead of the bitterness and frustration with which he was left to struggle in vain.

I say might, for Eugene would have had to internalize those principles—something that Canright never did and Jones and Waggoner ceased to do. As is true of others who received God's message and then opposed it, an unresolved independence and pride precipitated his life of bitter opposition.

All of us are infected by a deadly virus that we must overcome, or it will destroy us. To recognize pride in our critics should only invite pity for them and repentance in ourselves—not reciprocal antagonism. Our healing, as well as theirs, requires massive doses of humility that comes from claiming Christ as our only righteousness. Unless we consistently apply this prescription, any superiority we have in faith or practice—indeed, our very doctrines, true as they are—will actually threaten our spiritual health.

Our dependence must shift from an assurance of having the truth to an assurance in Him who is the truth. When our only defense is Christ our righteousness, we will then be prepared to help those hurting individuals who in their pain lash out against church administration.

LeRoy Froom Gave Me My Name

When Lettie arrived in Boise, Idaho, to look for work a quarter century after Canright's defection and only a few years after Ballenger's departure,

Adventism in Conflict

Dr. John E. Froom became a spiritual father to her. Nineteen years later I received the name, Leroy, after his son, a young minister whom my mother admired for his strength of character and commitment to God's message. Lettie continues to prize that message more than life itself.

My mother saw LeRoy only a few times. But her impression of a man of unusual drive, ability, and commitment proved true. His massive four-volume *Prophetic Faith of Our Fathers* and the two-volume *Conditionalist Faith of Our Fathers* are a monumental defense of two of Adventism's pillars of faith. Tracing through the centuries the developing understanding of the day/year time prophecies of Daniel that point to 1798 and 1844, he demonstrated how divine providence throughout history prepared for the Advent movement. He likewise showed how even during times of great apostasy faithful individuals continued to preserve a knowledge of the nonimmortality of the soul.

But in his attempt to resolve it once and for all, Froom also perpetuated and intensified the debate over what had happened at Minneapolis. He mistakenly led us to assume that those later confessions of error from those who had opposed the Minneapolis message were proof of our understanding and actual acceptance of it.

The man who could have been especially qualified to affirm the Wieland-Short concern thus became the one most influential in denying its validity. *Questions on Doctrine*'s primary writer, Froom climaxed 21 years of opposition by his book *Movement of Destiny* (1971). It may be argued that Froom was at least partially right. Most of the 1888 opponents did confess their error in fighting Waggoner. Nor did the church ever take an official action against the Minneapolis message. But one may be technically correct and yet very wrong. We will later see how technical correctness confirmed Smith and Butler in serious error. Corporate rejection of truth always precedes any vote and is no less real even if a vote is prevented, as at Minneapolis by Ellen White's insistence and W. C. White's vigilance.

Of Wieland and Short's claim Froom demanded that "if true, there should surely be some clear-cut *historical* evidence to definitely establish its validity.... But if it is merely personal opinion, or impression, or conjecture, it should be discounted and denied" (*Movement of Destiny*, p. 358).

When I received a prerelease copy of Froom's book while in Africa, I was amazed at his call for "explicit confession." Froom himself provided the very "*historical* evidence" he demanded! But like Smith and Butler, his own perceptions blinded him. We all find it hard to recognize what we already assume cannot exist—especially if it contradicts conclusions we hold dear.

The Purpose of History Is to Understand Ourselves

Breaking a 22-year silence they had imposed upon themselves, Wieland and Short used Froom's own words, "An Explicit Confession . . . Due the Church" (November 1972), in their response to him:

"We said in 1950 that there is a neglected but essential preparation to make before the final outpouring of the Holy Spirit in the latter rain can possibly come to enable the church to finish God's work on earth. That most necessary preparation is recognition of and repentance for the misunderstanding and rejecting the 'beginning' of . . . the loud cry. . . . According to Ellen G. White, [this] was . . . brought by two young ministers to the 1888 General Conference session. Nearly one hundred times in her writings she endorses this message and the messengers in language never used at any time about any other message or messengers.

"For us now as a people to beg Heaven to give us the latter rain without recognizing this obvious fact is just as unreasonable as for the Jews to keep begging the Lord to send them the Messiah without recognizing how He kept His promise and did send Him two thousand years ago.

"Below are two typical Ellen G. White endorsements of Jones's and Waggoner's message:

"The Lord in His great mercy sent a most precious message to His people through Elders Waggoner and Jones. This message was to bring more prominently before the world the uplifted Saviour, the sacrifice for the sins of the whole world. . . . It is the third angel's message, which is to be proclaimed with a loud voice, and attended with the outpouring of His Spirit in a large measure" (*Testimonies to Ministers*, pp. 91, 92).

"The time of test is just upon us, for the loud cry of the third angel has already begun in the revelation of the righteousness of Christ, the sin-pardoning Redeemer. This is the beginning of the light of the angel whose glory shall fill the whole earth" (*Review and Herald*, Nov. 22, 1892).

How could Froom hold 83 years later that we had accepted and continued to proclaim the loud cry message that was quickly to finish the work in latter rain power? Happily, during the two decades since he wrote *Movement of Destiny* a number of prominent leaders have acknowledged our failure to receive the 1888 message.

Until we grasp the paradoxical nature of the Minneapolis truth and see how we in opposite ways still resist it, we are doomed to go on to ever greater extremes in our responses to Minneapolis.

REST STOP: LAODICEA RESISTS THE INVITATION

The Minneapolis message, that of the third angel, and the Laodicean message are all really one and the same message. When by receiving

Christ's long-offered wedding raiment Laodicea accepts the intimate fellowship proclaimed at Minneapolis and described by Scripture through the symbolism of the marriage supper of the Lamb (Rev. 3:18-20), God will then quickly and joyously send forth His heralds with the announcement "Let us be glad and rejoice and give Him glory, for the marriage of the Lamb has come, and His wife has made herself ready" (Rev. 19:7, NKJV).

Notice how the passage integrates both the active and the passive: The bride "has made herself ready" indicates active cooperation with the Groom as she prepared for the wedding after an almost endless delay in receiving the garment He "granted" (verse 8, NKJV) that she should "be clothed" with by Him (passive). Both active and passive elements are also reflected in the plea "I counsel you to buy . . . white garments, that you may be clothed" (Rev. 3:18, NKJV). We must *buy* His wedding garment. Yet the only currency Heaven accepts is a dependent faith that allows Christ the privilege of clothing us.

However, dependence upon Christ, who must both furnish and clothe us in His bridal garment, is itself active as well as passive. It involves character transformation in which "righteous acts" are attributed to the bride (saints). Though received from Him, righteousness is acted out by her and becomes her own. Thus eternal loyalty to the groom is guaranteed on the part of a once reluctant, fickle bride, one so self-righteous as previously to consider her own clothing suitable for the banquet and wedding.

Christ thus awaits our response to the Minneapolis/Laodicean call for a divine-human relationship. A relationship that will permit Him to begin a marriage long delayed by a reluctant, self-righteous bride who cannot yet after the passing of another century distinguish her rags from His robe (cf. Matt. 22:1-14; Rev. 3:18-22; 19:7-9).

We all share responsibility for the delay. By an excessive focus on human preparation, conservatives rejected Christ's 1888 plea that we accept and proclaim His wedding invitation to the world. Failing to unite both poles of that message properly, Froom and his colleagues focused upon the divine responsibility for our preparation in a way that threatened human cooperation.

Chapter 8 illustrates our corporate blindness by the way we use the writings of Ellen White to delay the marriage. Our problem dates back to Minneapolis. Butler and Smith turned a blind eye and a deaf ear to testimonies of reproof to themselves that might have brought joy and light if they had only responded to them. And they did this while using the testimonies as a primary argument against Waggoner.

The Purpose of History Is to Understand Ourselves

[1] Some but by no means all Evangelicals are antinomian. But many urge obedience to the moral law. Those with antinomian reactions to legalism would generally consider the charge unfair. And they may be as honest as we feel we are. Providence now permits our law/grace conflict to help us understand those who see Sabbath observance as legalistic. But many of us are too busy turning judgmental guns upon each other to grasp this fact. When we learn to nonjudgmentally proclaim Christ our righteousness, honest Evangelicals will actually see in the Sabbath an antidote to legalism. And the resulting latter rain power will precipitate the final collapse of mystical Babylon.

[2] Although Christ repeatedly challenged legalism, at the same time He, by precept and example, honored the law. He portrayed its inner principle by reflecting its self-sacrificing love, revealing law as the necessary context of grace and making perfect obedience—*in relation to Himself*—an honorable life goal.

[3] To judge the motives of the church leadership in their relationship to Martin and Barnhouse not only violates Christ's express command; it also precludes an understanding of both the issues involved and ourselves. The leaders who dialogued with Martin and Barnhouse believed our only hope lay in the passive element of faith, which Waggoner proclaimed. I do not deny that they were also motivated by a desire to project a positive understanding of Adventism toward Evangelicals. That in itself was appropriate. The issue and willingness to downplay something relates to motives that He who alone knows the heart forbids us to judge. To judge only identifies our own mixed motives and hinders our own self-examination!

Part Two

Response to Divine Reproof: The Key to Minneapolis 8

O ctober 22, 1844, came and went. But Christ did not come. Disappointment beyond expression mingled with ridicule from every hand. Moreover, this time of terrible trial posed yet another problem. Assurance of Christ's immediate coming had held Advent believers together despite their wide diversity in other beliefs. Now their unity was breaking up.

Disillusioned and embarrassed, many repudiated their faith. Some set new dates. But a few clung to an 1844 termination of Daniel 8:14, confident that the Lord had indeed inspired the "midnight cry." The prophecy, they concluded, pointed not to His return to earth, but to a special work of judgment in the Most Holy Place of the heavenly sanctuary.

Some of them saw in Ellen Harmon's visions, which confirmed Christ's transition in ministry, the fulfillment of Scripture's divine promises to restore the gift of prophecy in the last days. Others discovered that the remnant would keep all of God's commandments, including the seventh-day Sabbath. As these convictions converged, all decided that their study of Daniel's "little book" had fulfilled the prophecy of Revelation 10. It had indeed been sweet in the mouth but bitter in their belly.

In the command of verse 11 to proclaim again the 2300-day/year prophecy of Daniel 8 they recognized a commission to preach the third angel's message of Revelation 14. This meant presenting the Sabbath in the context of a judgment based upon God's law. According to the Day of Atonement typology, this had commenced in the heavenly sanctuary on October 22, 1844.

But to fulfill this commission would require greater unity. In true priesthood of believers fashion, they met in various places to confirm their agreement and to seek unity on those many issues of disagreement. With fasting and prayer they submitted to each other as they intensely studied the Word. By 1849 they had bonded together in agreement upon a number of doctrinal pillars. The unusual way in which the visions confirmed these points of agreement provided an additional source of union.

But proclaiming the Sabbath and a heavenly judgment based upon the moral law aroused strong opposition. Many Evangelicals used Galatians 3 to argue that the Ten Commandments were only temporary, designed for the Jews and done away by the cross:

"Why *the Law* then? It *was added [at Sinai] because of transgressions.* . . . But before faith came, we were kept in custody under the law, being shut up to the faith which was later to be revealed. Therefore the *Law has become our tutor* to lead us to Christ, that we may be justified by faith. *But now that faith has come we are no longer under a tutor*" (Gal. 3:19-25, NASB).

Such antinomian "proof" faded before the idea of two kinds of laws in the Bible: the eternal, moral law of the Ten Commandments, placed inside the ark, the symbol of God's judgment throne; and the temporary ceremonial and civil regulations, put outside the ark. It then evaporated like the morning dew in the clear light of the literary and historical context of Galatians. The primary issue, Adventists insisted, was not the moral law, but circumcision as a pledge to keep the ceremonial law.

A message resting not so much upon particular doctrines as upon their harmonious integration seemed impervious to arguments. But this introduced a more sinister danger. With each debate against our critics and opponents we became more self-confident. A growing love for confrontation and a spirit of pride and self-sufficiency demanded divine reproof. Thus on June 10, 1852, Ellen White applied to the *Review and Herald* readers the Laodicean message they had previously regarded as speaking of their opponents.

In this setting J. H. Waggoner reexamined Galatians and concluded that there was indeed some substance to the charge of legalism. In his 1854 book *The Law of God* he argued that Paul did mean the moral law. Imagine the consternation of Adventist evangelists when one of their own leaders repudiated a finely tuned argument that Adventism's opponents had tried in vain to meet.

Waggoner's message needed to be heard. But two serious mistakes sabotaged his purpose. The most deadly was his violation of the principles of the priesthood of believers[1] in going public without careful, prior consultation with denominational thought leaders. Nor would he honor the efforts of those attempting to remove the confusion precipitated by his untimely action.

Adventism in Conflict

In 1856 Stephen Pierce arranged to study the issue with the leadership in Battle Creek. But rather than participate in the discussion, Waggoner left town (*Manuscripts and Memories of Minneapolis*, p. 305). Such a disregard for the principle of the priesthood of believers permitted the kind of intellectual pendulum swing that too often accompanies new discoveries. Waggoner repudiated the contextual-historical realities relating to the ritual law in Galatians, which, as he feared, the leadership in Battle Creek had unanimously confirmed. But despite his refusal to join them, they validated his moral law principle by declaring for the entire law system (*ibid.*).

What does this ancient history have to do with our present conflict? Much in every way! The tragedies and triumphs of truth in the history of our interpretation of the law in Galatians suggest how we must proceed today. A review of our debate during those years highlights three crucial principles: (1) the importance of the priesthood of believers, (2) the relationship of law and gospel, and (3) the need to practice paradoxical thinking to grasp Bible truth in its wholeness, not just its isolated parts.

E. J. Waggoner's Discovery, Error, and Repentance

While listening to an Ellen White camp meeting message in 1882, Ellet J. Waggoner suddenly found himself lost to his surroundings in a vision of Jesus upon the cross, an experience he compared to Paul's Damascus road encounter (E. J. Waggoner, "Confession of Faith," p. 6; cf. Emmett K. Vande Vere, *Rugged Heart*, p. 83). The incident caused him to approach Scripture from a Christ crucified focus. Soon he began to sense that often Adventists did not really proclaim Jesus, but merely referred to Him in passing as they defended the law.

As he probed the book of Galatians, Waggoner saw an indictment in Paul's warning about putting law where Jesus should be and placing obedience in competition with the cross. So radical was the shift in his thinking that, just as did his father, Waggoner lost sight of the context and argued that Paul was speaking of the moral law *rather than* the ceremonial law.[2]

Moreover, E. J. Waggoner repeated his father's more serious error. He failed to consult his fellow believers. He no doubt feared they would reject the principle he felt was too important to remain silent upon. Thus he denied himself the help from them that would have aided him in keeping both realities in focus.

Perhaps most galling in the minds of Adventist leaders was the publishing of his views in the missionary periodical *Signs of the Times*. Moreover, he and A. T. Jones had the temerity to teach their "heresy" to impressionable college students at Healdsberg. Nor would either young man listen to any cautions from older leaders.

The price for violating the principles that had given birth to Adventism in the first place would prove to be high. Indeed, the heavy mortgage payments the controversy imposed upon the church have yet to be met.

General Conference president George I. Butler, *Review* editor Uriah Smith, and evangelist D. M. Canright were determined to meet Waggoner's deadly "heresy" head-on. Butler himself wrote an 85-page rebuttal to Waggoner's moral law position, *The Law in the Book of Galatians*, which he gave to every delegate to the 1886 General Conference session. This and a nine-member committee, including Butler himself, were intended to silence Waggoner once and for all.

Meanwhile, in Europe Ellen White waited in vain for a response from Waggoner to her letter of reproof. Not having received it, however, Waggoner proceeded to do battle with the conservative leadership. Following the 1886 session, he immediately began a reply to *The Law in the Book of Galatians*. Only a few weeks later he mailed the General Conference president a preliminary copy of *The Gospel in the Book of Galatians*. Just then, however, a second long and urgent letter from Ellen White halted him:

"You have departed from the positive directions God has given upon this matter, and only harm will be the result. This is not in God's order" (*Ellen G. White 1888 Materials*, p. 22).[3]

In deep repentance Waggoner put his manuscript aside until the Minneapolis session. But permanent damage had already resulted. Ellen White told him, "You have now set the example for others to do as you have done, to feel at liberty to put in their various ideas and theories and bring them before the public. . . . We must keep before the world a united front. Satan will triumph to see differences among Seventh-day Adventists" (*ibid.*).

In fulfillment of her prophecy, many now confidently appeal to Waggoner's example to justify their own violation of the concept of the priesthood of believers. The entire 11-page document from Ellen White bore the following burden:

"My husband had some ideas . . . differing from . . . his brethren. I was shown that however true his views were, God did not call for him to put them in front before his brethren and create differences of ideas. While he might hold these views subordinate himself, once they are made public, minds would seize [upon them], and . . . make these differences the whole burden of the message, and get up contention and variance" (*ibid.*, p. 24).

If James White was not to advocate his ideas, "however true," and if both the Waggoners and Jones received censure for proclaiming a message that proved to be inspired by God without consulting with the church's thought leaders, what about those on the right and left who now concentrate in public upon concepts known to be divisive? Earlier Ellen White declared:

"If you, my brethren, had the experience that my husband and myself have had in regard to these known differences being published in articles in our papers, you would never have pursued the course you have" (ibid., pp. 21, 22)

We are to proclaim the straight testimony. But that testimony to Laodicea, which the Minneapolis message represents, reproves the independent spirit against which Ellen White warned both factions. When we humbly follow the priesthood of believers approach, Christ will open the way for every vital truth—even if He must remove leaders from office to do so. But He must wait until the Holy Spirit has prepared others to take their places, individuals who will not repeat their errors.

By taking things into our own hands, we create problems Heaven did not ordain. Little do we grasp the harm done by a pride that prompts us to violate priesthood principles by assuming responsibilities the Lord does not lay upon us.[4] Nor are administrators free to violate the principles when dealing with those who do. Concerning the 1886 session, where General Conference president Butler attempted to silence the erring Waggoner, Ellen White declared prophetically:

"I do not think that years will wipe out the impressions made at our last conference. . . . We must have more of Jesus and less of self. If there is a difference upon . . . Scripture, then do not be with pen or voice making your differences apparent and making a breach when there is no need of this" (ibid., p. 26).

To proclaim Christ our righteousness with power, Waggoner and Jones had to set self aside and humble themselves in a personal focus upon Christ and His atoning sacrifice:

"Elder [J. H.] Waggoner has loved discussions and contention. I fear that E. J. Waggoner has cultivated a love for the same. We need now good, humble religion. E. J. Waggoner needs humility, meekness, and Brother Jones can be a power for good if he will constantly cultivate practical godliness, that he may teach this to the people" (ibid., p. 25).

Ellen White spoke of the serious loss that had resulted during the sixteenth century because each Reformer violated the principles of the priesthood of believers.[5] Two years before Minneapolis she had prophetically declared:

Response to Divine Reproof: The Key to Minneapolis

"There has been a door thrown open for variance and strife and contention and differences which none of you can see but God. His eye traces the beginning to the end. And the magnitude of mischief God alone knows. The *bitterness*, the wrath, the resentment, the *jealousies*, the heart burnings *provoked by* controversies of *both sides of the question causes the loss of many souls*. . . .

"Oh, if the hearts were only subdued by the Spirit of God! If the eye was single to God's glory, what a flood of heavenly light would pour upon the soul" (*ibid.*, pp. 26; italics supplied).

Humble acceptance of this reproof prepared E. J. Waggoner to present his message as a true Christian gentleman at Minneapolis. His task was not so much to inform as to reveal his message in attitude and spirit. Ellen White was thrilled by his proclamation of Christ crucified. As predicted, nevertheless, his former course would long bear its evil fruit. Meanwhile, her 1887 reproof to Smith and Butler was a repeat of her rebuke to Waggoner and Jones:

"I wish that finite minds could see and sense the great love of the infinite God, His great self-denial, His self-sacrifice, in assuming humanity. God humbled Himself and became man and humbled Himself to die. . . . Oh, that we might see the need of humility, of walking humbly with God, and guarding ourselves on every point" (*ibid.*, p. 29).[6]

Waggoner's response to the reproof for speaking vital truth without seeking unity should set an example to others who follow his independent pattern:

"I have read the testimony several times very carefully, and the more I read it, the more convinced I am that it was timely and is needed. I have been able to *see some things in my heart of which I was unconscious. I thought that I was actuated by nothing but pure motives and love for the truth,* in what I have said and written. But I can see plainly that there has been very much love of self mixed in" (*Manuscripts and Memories of Minneapolis*, p. 71; E. J. Waggoner to Ellen G. White, Apr. 1, 1887; italics supplied).

Without divine aid, Waggoner could not have recognized Ellen White's words as valid. In thanking "God for the testimony of His Spirit," Waggoner declared: "The strongest proof to me of their genuineness is that they have revealed to me my heart to an extent that it could not possibly be known by anyone besides God. *I have nothing to say in self-justification*" (*ibid.*).

If such a response was necessary from someone God had chosen to present a special message to the church, how much more from those who today violate those same principles of the priesthood of believers? Indeed, to reject such counsel is to deny one's own calling! Oh, that all violators would testify: *"I can see that I really hindered the advancement of the truth, when I thought I was helping it" (ibid.).*[7]

BUTLER'S ACCUSATIVE SELF-DEFENSE

The penitent response to reproof for violating priesthood principles by men divinely commissioned with a vital message stands in stark contrast to that of Smith and Butler, who opposed that message. Having repeatedly sought Ellen White's support and having become increasingly agitated over her failure to comply, they now seized upon her reproof to Waggoner to put him in his place. Butler's prior defensive-accusative response to Ellen White (Dec. 15, 1886) is revealing of his whole attitude toward the situation:

"Possibly you will not care to hear it. . . . I have written you on this subject heretofore, to which you have never made reply. Very likely you do not sympathize with what I have said. . . .

"We have been waiting for years to hear from you on the subject, knowing that its agitation would end only in debate" (*Manuscripts and Memories of Minneapolis,* pp. 42, 43; italics supplied).

Thus for years Butler and Smith took a position of total self-justification. They placed all blame for the conflict upon Waggoner and Jones. When rebuked for abusing the letter of reproof Ellen White had sent Waggoner, they felt completely misjudged. Her rebuke came as a crushing blow. They were unable even to consider that their attitudes and methods might be wrong. Butler's long-delayed reply (it came only shortly before the 1888 session) exuded strong self-pity as he ascribed to that letter all his subsequent ills.[8]

But his confusion was not wholly without cause. Waggoner not only violated the principles of the priesthood of believers, he refused to acknowledge other self-evident truth in Galatians. Yet Butler's real problem was unsurrendered pride. God intends His reproofs as expressions of love seeking to heal. If we resist them, we will mistakenly view them as unfair blows from an enemy. We either humble ourselves and rejoice in His justification or impose upon ourselves the pain of attempting to maintain our self-assurance by condemning others for our own plight.

Both 1888 and a 1901-1904 crisis that precipitated the withdrawal of Jones, Waggoner, and John Harvey Kellogg testify to the urgency of uniting both the horizontal and the vertical principles of the priesthood of believers. Until we submit "one to another in the fear of God" (Eph. 5:21) so as to truly hear one another, the Lord will permit us to retain the spiritual and theological darkness we protect as light. Such a reaction can only put out the light of any specific truth by denying one or the other of its paradoxical principles.

In a further attempt at self-justification, Butler spoke of the "little pamphlet" (an 85-page book!) he gave to the 1886 delegates:

"And now *you censure me for having written a little pamphlet* on the . . . law in Galatians. My writing that pamphlet you say makes it necessary to have a public discussion . . . [to] give Dr. Waggoner the same liberty that I have taken myself. . . .

"I had pleaded with you for advice three different times, however, before venturing this, but could get no reply. And then after all this, would you say, Sister White, that it was duty while I was president of the General Conference . . . to sit still and not say one word? *Do you call that fairness? If so, let me have no fairness.* . . . What did I do even after he had taken such a defiant course and published his views to so many? *I simply wrote a little pamphlet,* and circulated it to perhaps 180 persons" (*ibid.*, pp. 98, 99; italics supplied).[9]

His pride and independence prompted repeated appeals to "the testimonies" against their author, Ellen White, for misjudging and supporting one he knew to be in "error." The faith that Butler and Smith thought they had in Christ and the writings of Ellen White was really only misplaced confidence in their own opinions.

SMITH'S RATIONAL IRRATIONALITY

Shortly before his death Smith was still justifying his opposition to the moral law in Galatians. "The brethren in Vermont . . . sent Eld. Stephen Pierce on here to Battle Creek in 1856 to have a study on the question of the law in Galatians. J. H. Waggoner was then here . . . [but] . . . would not stay to the examination. . . . Brother Waggoner took the position . . . that the law in Galatians was the moral law. *Bro. Pierce argued that it was the law system,* 'including the ceremonial law.' . . . *Sr. White shortly after this had a vision in which this law question was shown her, and she immediately wrote J. H. Waggoner that his position on the law was wrong,* and Bro. Pierce was right" (U. Smith to W. A. McCutchen, Aug. 8, 1901; *Manuscripts and Memories of Minneapolis,* p. 305; italics supplied).

Did Ellen White declare that J. H. Waggoner's *position* on the moral law was wrong? Or did she instead reprove his violation of the principle of the priesthood of believers, his running ahead of the community of faith? The latter was cause enough for reproof. Moreover, persistent refusal to harmonize his book with the consensus the thought leaders of the church had arrived at was sufficient cause for James White to refuse to allow its republication.

Smith wrote further:

"Brother Waggoner would not attend the discussion, and would not yield a particle. A few days afterward, Sr. White had a vision . . . and wrote to J. H. Waggoner, 'I saw that your position was wrong.' . . . But now a great many do not know that Sr. White has ever seen anything on this question, and she has lost what she has written" (*Manuscripts and Memories of Minneapolis*, p. 304; U. Smith to H. J. Adams, Oct. 30, 1900; *Manuscripts and Memories of Minneapolis*, p. 16).

Suppose Smith was right that Ellen White did declare Waggoner wrong in his theology, not just in his attitude. This could only have been for denying the ceremonial context of Galatians. Smith's own testimony that she agreed with the eventual consensus ("whole law system") still affirms Waggoner's moral law application! The same type of logic that Smith used is still prevalent among us—and is humanly impossible to cure. That Smith carried his confusion to the grave the following passage attests:[10]

"I have never seen occasion to change my position since 1856. Brother J. H. Waggoner . . . took the position that the law in Galatians 3:19 referred to the moral law. . . . Meetings were held some three days studying the subject, in which we all became satisfied that the position of Eld. Pierce was correct . . . the whole law system; and *the law system was the moral law as a rule of life, and the ceremonial law* as a means of recovery from sin" (*ibid.*).[11]

Here we see a classic illustration of our problem. Smith clearly acknowledges a role to the moral law. He even describes its function as "a rule of life." But he then hastens to illustrate part-truth blindness in defending one pole of truth by resisting the other—*even while claiming to accept both!* "*According to this, the law that was 'added,' and that was 'our schoolmaster' was the ceremonial, or remedial law*" (*ibid.*; italics supplied). This is like declaring that "water is made up of hydrogen and oxygen" and then insisting, "According to this, water is made up of hydrogen," thus deliberately excluding oxygen!

What Smith refused to change was not Pierce's unified view, but his own moral law exclusion. To defend the historical context, he denied its spiritual principle.

But what could so blind a mental giant like Smith? Except for divine grace, one cannot see what one already "knows" should not exist, especially when pride is at stake. But nothing confirms intellectual blindness in brilliant minds like a conspiracy mentality.

Response to Divine Reproof: The Key to Minneapolis

THE DEADLY CONSPIRACY MENTALITY

As a participant in the Pierce examination, Smith considered his position irrefutable. He "knew" E. J. Waggoner was wrong. Ellen White had written a letter to Waggoner's father that put the issue beyond question—indeed, so far beyond question that he could not trust her present testimony sent to Smith himself. It had "obviously" been influenced by her son W. C. White, whom he "knew" to be under Waggoner's control.

Meanwhile, only months prior to his own reproof Butler had declared, "I am perfectly willing our brethren should cherish their views on the subject, and claim the same privilege myself, till God shall speak. Then I promise to listen and *if my views are condemned, I can at least close my mouth*" (G. I. Butler to E. G. White; Dec. 16, 1886; *Manuscripts and Memories of Minneapolis*, pp. 42, 43; italics supplied).

But the offer to close his mouth if God should condemn him was irrelevant. Butler would honor nothing as from the Lord that did not confirm his memory of the lost J. H. Waggoner testimony, which hung upon a fragile, three-decade-old thread. Indeed, he would soon deny any validity or fairness to her current testimony to himself and would boldly defend his own theology, attitudes, and behavior.

An upbeat March 31, 1887, response to her Waggoner/Jones rebuke reveals the confusion of Butler's own opinions:

"The copy of the letter you wrote to Dr. Waggoner and A. T. Jones afforded me great relief. I have been in great perplexity over this matter. Views were being taught by them which I CANNOT believe to be the truth. *If those views were to be sustained, I confess I shall never know what to believe and I think it would close up my ever trying to write anything on doctrine, as I . . . could have no confidence in . . . knowing the leading of the Spirit*" (G. I. Butler to E. G. White, Mar. 31, 1887; *Manuscripts and Memories of Minneapolis*, p. 68).

Taking part-truth perception as truth itself, Butler, who adamantly denied any hard feelings toward Waggoner—even while expressing them—soon charged W. C. White with manipulating his mother's letters that declared Butler's spirit satanic (see *Theology in Crisis*, p. 322)! Far more confident in himself than in Ellen White's integrity, and seeing himself a martyr, fully innocent in all things rebuked, he accused her of "unjust" reproofs.

"*I claim that I did everything that a man could do to keep the peace,* and followed the directions, customs, and teachings of the testimonies relative to those controverted questions. . . . Here was a question that I believed in my soul was wrong, and which had been condemned by the testimonies" (*Manuscripts and Memories of Minneapolis*, pp. 94, 95).

Butler repeatedly blames her for rebuking him for merely doing his duty. He then has the temerity to imply his conspiracy theory. He and Smith now "know" beyond question that her son controls what she writes! "I have believed and do to the present time that *your son W. C. White is more responsible for it than any other man*" (George I. Butler to Ellen G. White, Oct. 1, 1888; *Manuscripts and Memories of Minneapolis*, pp. 94, 95; italics supplied).

Ironically, the conspiracy-manipulation theory actually resulted from Ellen White's refusal to be manipulated—Butler's manipulation! For at least two years Butler sought her support to silence Waggoner. But having no instruction except that neither side was wholly correct, she refused to comply. Precisely because she faithfully remained neutral she came under grave suspicion.

The ultimate conspiracy "proof" was W. C. White's alleged "secret" weekend meeting with Waggoner and Jones to coordinate their conspiracy. But Butler and Smith were wrong regarding both conspiracy[12] and Ellen White's doctrinal sympathies. She not only declared Waggoner in some respects wrong, but she actually leaned toward Smith and Butler until Minneapolis.

Ellen White knew by divine instruction that both sides were partly wrong. And she was open to any truth Waggoner might hold. But her own printed positions harmonized with that of Smith and Butler. True, she had reproved them for violating priesthood principles. But not until she saw their satanic spirit more fully revealed at Minneapolis—in their self-righteous war upon one who had deeply repented of his own violation—did she have her first intimation that the two church leaders might be theologically wrong.

Meanwhile, the Minneapolis message was perfectly designed to correct a universal weakness revealed in each of the men—and that is present in us all. Its purpose was to cleanse pride and independence from Waggoner and Jones as well as Butler and Smith (and each of us).

REST STOP: FRIENDS OR ENEMIES?

"With friends like that, who needs enemies?"

Friends or enemies? Good or bad? Righteous or unrighteous? The answer is yes! Butler and Smith were like Peter, an ardent friend whose self-confidence led him to betray Jesus. Nevertheless, after losing confidence in himself, he faithfully demonstrated love and loyalty. The most devout of Christ's followers will surely betray Him unless they learn to distrust self.

Response to Divine Reproof: The Key to Minneapolis

Meanwhile, each position needed to be corrected and supplemented by the other. Both pairs, Smith and Butler and Waggoner and Jones, defended truth.[13] The central message of the younger men relating to Christ crucified as the only basis of salvation was not only correct but most vital. On the ceremonial law, however, the older men were right and the young men wrong. The Smith-Butler concern, moreover, was not simply the law and the Sabbath. They stood in defense of the integrity of Scripture, whose ceremonial law context Waggoner (with Jones) disavowed—as did his father.

---

[1] Some, including James White, saw merit in his concepts, according to Milton R. Hook (*Towards Righteousness by Faith: 1888 in Retrospect,* p. 27).

[2] J. H. Waggoner "took the controversial stance that 'not a single declaration' in Galatians 'referred to the ceremonial or Levitical law'" (Arthur L. White, *Ellen G. White: The Lonely Years,* p. 387).

[3] Perhaps the most vital lesson is that no matter how urgent we feel over an issue, nor how sure we are that we have a message from God—as was Waggoner—"only harm will . . . result" unless we follow "God's order" and follow priesthood of believer principles!

[4] Christ Himself set us the right example. "[He] did not reveal many things that were truth, because it would create a difference of opinion and get up disputations" (*ibid.,* p. 24).

[5] *"The Reformation was greatly retarded by making prominent differences* on some points of faith and each party holding tenaciously to those things where they differed. . . . To present your views in decided opposition to the faith or truth as it has been taught by us as a people is a mistake, and will result in harm, and only harm, as in the days of Martin Luther. *Begin to draw apart and feel at liberty to express your ideas without reference to the views of your brethren, and a state of things will be introduced that you do not dream of "* (*ibid.,* pp. 23, 24; italics supplied).

[6] Ellen White continued: "I know that Satan's work will be to set brethren at variance. Were it not that I know [that] the Captain of our salvation stands at the helm to guide the gospel ship into the harbor, I should say, Let me rest in the grave.

"Our Redeemer liveth to make intercession for us, and now if we will daily . . . cherish the lessons He will teach us in meekness and lowliness of heart, we shall have so large a measure of the Spirit of Jesus that self will not be interwoven into anything we may do or say. . . . We need to make special efforts to answer the prayer of Christ that we may be one" (*ibid.*).

[7] Jones had already responded: "I thank the Lord for . . . showing me where I have gone wrong, and *shall try earnestly to profit by the testimony. I am sorry indeed that I have had any part in anything that would create division"* (*Manuscripts and Memories of Minneapolis,* p. 66; A. T. Jones to Ellen G. White, Mar. 13, 1887).

[8] Had E. J. Waggoner and A. T. Jones not humbly repented, they would have responded to reproof in the same way Butler did. (They later did!) And had Butler responded to their rebuke as they did, he would have received none. But further excerpts from his letter portray outraged, self-justifying blindness that felt no need for anything but commendation!

"The first point I shall mention is this matter of the law in Galatians. I am well satisfied that it is the way that this matter has been pushed and urged by responsible men in the cause, and by your seeming attitude also which has brought me to my present [breakdown]" (George I. Butler to Ellen G. White, Oct. 10, 1888; *Manuscripts and Memories of Minneapolis,*p.80).

"But with the attitude in which you place my efforts in this matter I cannot see the justice. I think that I have not been too sharp with Dr. Waggoner, and that every word that I have said is true and much of the truth has not been told" (*ibid.,* p. 85).

"I have tried to follow the things which make for peace. . . . But these things in my judgment are wrong, and I cannot and will not sustain what I think is wrong for anyone" (*ibid.,* p. 91).

"A more bare-faced and defiant course . . . I never saw. . . . One would suppose in view of the principles heretofore taught by the testimonies and by long custom of this body that controverted points should not be introduced without being brought before leading brethren. . . . And if you are prepared, my dear sister White, to treat the highest officer in this body thus, and that is your policy you wish to introduce and sustain, I wish you to tell me. . . . One would hardly suppose . . . that a person holding the position of president . . . was obliged to keep his mouth shut while persistent efforts were being made to bring up a silent controverted point before the public" (*ibid.,* pp. 92, 93).

[9] Butler continued: "*My only regret, Sister White, [is that from the first] . . . Elder Smith and I did not just wade into them and show them up in the widest channels possible. . . .* I have got about tired of this policy that young fledglings who have just fairly got seated in the editorial chair can attack any point of faith without the least hesitation no matter how long it has been settled and spread their views out broadcast no matter how much it may conflict with the views of the oldest pioneers in the work. If there is any justice or propriety in it, I am mistaken. This is plain language, Sister White, I know; but before God I believe it is true. . . .

"I am happy to say that one whom he had been trying to work upon has strongly settled on the right side of this question. And he will never be able to move him no matter how cunning his efforts may be. . . . *And after the positions that the testimonies have taken concerning them, do you suppose that such a man as Eld. Uriah Smith . . . will ever be changed by anything that such a man as Dr. Waggoner could produce?*" (*ibid.,* pp. 100, 101; italics supplied).

[10] Specifically referring to Smith more than a year after he had confessed to Jones of hard feelings that he had previously denied, Ellen White declared: "The conference at Minneapolis was the golden opportunity for all present to humble the heart before God and to welcome Jesus as the great Instructor, but the stand taken by some at that meeting proved their ruin. They have never seen clearly since, and they never will, for they persistently cherish the spirit that prevailed there, a wicked, criticizing, denunciatory spirit" (Arthur L. White, *Ellen G. White: The Australian Years,* p. 65).

[11] Smith's memory is technically right (see *The Acts of the Apostles,* pp. 385-387). His duty was to show E. J. Waggoner that it also referred to the ceremonial law. This might not have been difficult after Waggoner's humble response to Ellen White's rebuke for violating the priesthood of believers principles. Had Smith only affirmed Waggoner's moral law burden, as Pierce permits, his ceremonial evidence might have been accepted as the proper context for the deeper spiritual principle.

[12] Confused over the issues, W. C. White did meet with E. J. Waggoner and A. T. Jones to try to better understand their position. Upon hearing of this meeting, Pastor W. M. Healy, a Butler/Smith supporter who shared their conspiracy fears, urgently fired a warning letter to Butler. Thus the "California conspiracy" theory that Waggoner, Jones, and W. C.

Response to Divine Reproof: The Key to Minneapolis

White conspired to change Adventist doctrine and to seize administrative control from Battle Creek now seemed an indisputable "fact."

[13] No wonder W. C. and Ellen White were confused. Both arguments were partly right. But each excluded the other's truth! As the thought leadership had concluded in 1856, the "law" Paul refers to is the entire law system, with the moral law as its foundation!

Conflict Over the Law in Galatians

9

To really understand the 1888 debate, one must bear in mind that it did not center upon righteousness by faith (Waggoner's primary theme), but upon two technical points: Paul's covenant concept and what law he referred to in the book of Galatians. (Part Three relates to the covenants.)

Waggoner and Jones claimed it was the moral law.[1] Butler and Smith insisted that Paul was speaking about the ceremonial law. Ellen White identified with the young men in their focus upon Jesus but refused to affirm their position in the debate over what law was referred to in Galatians. The Holy Spirit only showed her that Jones and Waggoner were not without error. Even when she declared years later that Paul had both laws in mind, her burden continued to focus on the kind of attitude those involved in the dispute had. It was most urgent that they truly hear and honor one another by studying the Scriptures together in humility.

WHAT GALATIANS SAYS: BUTLER WAS RIGHT

The conflict began about 1884 but first came to a head late in 1886. Butler determined to silence Waggoner at the General Conference session by a nine-member committee and his book *The Law in the Book of Galatians*. Contextual evidence for the ritual law, he believed, was overwhelming. Paul concludes Galatians by declaring: "Those who desire to make a good showing in the flesh try to compel you to be circumcised, simply that they may not be persecuted for the cross of Christ. . . . For neither is circumcision anything, nor uncircumcision, but a new creation" (Gal. 6: 12-15, NASB).

How could Waggoner honestly fail to acknowledge that the text, in both its literary and historical context, relates specifically to the ceremonial or ritual law, for which circumcision was both symbol and entry rite? He was well aware of the facts. He simply could not hold them in focus because they seemed to threaten the message he must protect at all costs! That he did not sense his violence to context we can understand only in light of the universal difficulty of thinking paradoxically when the principles held dear are threatened. Indeed, Paul inserts his ritual law key in his very introduction of the Galatian problem:

"But neither Titus, who was with me, being a Greek, was compelled to be circumcised. . . . But when Peter came to Antioch, I withstood him to the face, because he was to be blamed. For before that certain came from James, did eat with the Gentiles; but when they were come, he withdrew and separated himself, fearing them which were of the circumcision" (Gal. 2:3-12).

Peter, who had testified that the Holy Spirit had declared uncircumcised Gentiles ritually clean, both ate with them and baptized them (Acts 10, 11). But under pressure at Antioch he surrendered to Judaizers who insisted that Gentiles be circumcised before any social contact with them was lawful. Clearly the ritual law is the very context in which Paul introduces justification!

"Nevertheless knowing that a man is not justified by the works of the Law but through faith in Christ Jesus, even we have believed in Christ Jesus, that we may be justified by faith in Christ, and not by the works of the Law; since by the works of the Law shall no flesh be justified" (Gal. 2:16, NASB).

This declaration and its subsequent explanation introduce chapter 3—the heart of Paul's solar plexus blow to any law-based salvation. Thus the circumcision issue is specific to Paul's negation of law/works:

"You foolish Galatians, who has bewitched you, before whose eyes Jesus Christ was publicly portrayed as crucified? This is the only thing I want to find out from you: did you receive the Spirit by the works of the Law, or by hearing with faith? Are you so foolish? Having begun by the Spirit, are you now being perfected by the flesh [circumcision]? . . .

"And the Scripture, foreseeing that God would justify the Gentiles by faith, preached the gospel beforehand to Abraham, saying, 'All the nations shall be blessed in you.' . . .

"For as many as are of the works of the Law are under a curse. . . . Now that no one is justified by the Law before God is evident; for, 'The righteous man shall live by faith'" (Gal. 3:1-11, NASB).

In condemning "works," Paul directly denies circumcision as an additional condition of salvation. His crucial chapter concludes by making it clear: faith in Jesus supersedes New Testament Judaism. And baptism takes the place of circumcision.

"For all of you who were baptized into Christ have clothed yourselves with Christ. There is neither Jew nor Greek. . . . And if you belong to Christ, then you are Abraham's offspring, heirs according to promise" (verses 27-29, NASB).

But though Butler was right concerning the historical context, he was amazingly blind to Paul's underlying principle, which Waggoner proclaimed: *no kind of law or obedience can substitute for or add to justification by faith in our only source of righteousness—Christ crucified!*

WHAT GALATIANS DOES NOT SAY: WAGGONER WAS RIGHT

Waggoner's accusers were guilty of the same thing they charged him with. While identifying him as a heretic for echoing antinomian claims, they themselves had become subverted by the antinomian claim that the law in Galatians was abolished at the cross! Their sole defense against this erroneous assumption was that the "schoolmaster" law was ceremonial and not the moral law. They could hardly have done otherwise, since they did not see that they had unwittingly surrendered to the Evangelical error of reading Galatians as talking about the cessation of some law. *Actually, Galatians says nothing about any law being abolished—at the cross or at any other time!* What, then, does it declare?

"Is the law then against the promises of God? Certainly not! For if there had been a law given which could have given life, truly righteousness would have been by the law. But the Scripture has confined all under sin, that the promise by faith in Jesus Christ might be given to those who believe" (verses 21, 22, NKJV).

The subject here is not a nullified law, but the relationship between all law and promise. Both are vital. But it is imperative that we grasp the unique, cooperative function of each. The law cannot fulfill the promise. Yet, by instilling guilt it does enforce a sense of need that brings us to One who died that through Him we might receive the promise of eternal life. Salvation comes not by obedience to the law, which can only bring us under universal guilt and bondage, but by faith in One who promises freedom and life:

"But before faith came, we were kept under guard by the law, kept for the faith which would afterward be revealed. Therefore the law was our tutor to bring us to Christ, that we might be justified by faith. But after faith has come, we are no longer under a tutor [*paidagōgos*]" (verses 23-25, NKJV).

Neither text nor context says that faith annuls the law. Nor does Paul say the law ceases when *Christ* has come. Rather, he declares that the *paidagōgos* function of the law ends "after *faith* has come"! When faith in Christ crucified removes alienation, guilt, and fear of judgment, the mature child no longer needs its guilt-directed discipline.[2]

There was, indeed, a corporate transition at Christ's death in A.D. 31 when type met antitype. But Paul's message also relates to an individual coming of age in our personal faith-acceptance of the promise certified by His death. We enter His school of grace by claiming His promise to write in us His law (Deut. 5:29; Jer. 24:7; 29:13; Heb. 8:7-13).

According to Waggoner, *Paul does not contrast law* before Christ's coming *with promise* afterward. Rather he contrasts the jurisdiction of a guilt-inducing law with that of the Holy Spirit. The Spirit frees us from the burden of sin and guilt imposed by the law, writing its principles in the mind (understanding) and on the heart (affections and will). Paul sharply questions those "foolish Galatians" who would submit to circumcision:

"Did you receive the Spirit by observing the law, or by believing what you heard? Are you so foolish? After beginning with the Spirit, are you now trying to attain your goal by human effort? . . . Does God give you his Spirit . . . because you observe the law, or because you believe what you heard?" (Gal. 3:2-5, NIV).

Again we see that the conservative thought leaders were right: the context is clearly the ritual law. But they were also very wrong. The issue is not, Which law? but, What jurisdiction?—Law or Spirit? Galatians 3 does deny Levitical jurisdiction (circumcision) as a necessary or required entry rite into Christ. *Paul does not, however, say the law in question was done away with! Faith in the promise simply transfers the believer from custodial bondage under a condemning law to freedom in the Spirit's custody based upon promise and sealed by Christ's blood.*

But does not Hebrews say Christ's death annulled the ritual law? Yes, it does. Hebrew Christians who still observed ceremonial feast days needed help in relating to the Temple's destruction and the crisis of faith that involved. That was no problem to Galatian believers. Paul's argument in Galatians is universal, applying as surely to the moral as to the ritual law, which Judaizers sought to impose. All attempts to assure salvation by any kind of obedience deny that the promise of life is only through Christ.

Both laws direct us to Christ. The moral law drives us to Him as our only righteousness. Every ritual points us to Him and dramatizes how He saves by His own righteousness. The moral law announces eternal death as the result of sin, while the ceremonial law portrays His death and depicts

His transfer of our guilt to Himself, the innocent victim. Neither law has any power to save. But each in its own way directs us to Christ and His promise of life.

Circumcision would not only rob Gentiles of their freedom in Christ; it would impose additional bondage! Left under the guilt of the moral law, they must also fulfill the demands of the entire ceremonial system or incur further guilt. Nor could they attain the righteousness they pursued:

"What shall we say then? That Gentiles, who did not pursue righteousness, have attained to righteousness, even the righteousness of faith; but Israel, pursuing the law of righteousness, has not attained to the law of righteousness. Why? Because they did not seek it by faith, but as it were, by the works of the law. . . .

"For they being ignorant of God's righteousness, and seeking to establish their own righteousness, have not submitted to the righteousness of God. For Christ is the end of the law [both of types and the moral law] for righteousness to everyone who believes" (Rom. 9:30-10:3, NKJV).

To seek either righteousness or assurance by proving our obedience is to remain in bondage to the *paidagōgos* who must awaken an ever keener sense of guilt to convince us that we are not truly obedient—no matter how hard we try to obey. Relief and assurance come only by faith in Christ our righteousness. His Spirit heals our wounded conscience as we behold His substitutionary obedience and loving sacrifice that will meet every demand of His broken law.

CANRIGHT: MINNEAPOLIS'S FIRST CASUALTY

Dudley Marvin Canright, the denomination's foremost debater, was a natural champion against Waggoner. For years his booklet *Two Laws* had been the church's primary weapon against arguments that the moral law had been annulled at the cross. To refute Waggoner, he expanded its treatment of the book of Galatians from a mere six to 24 pages.

With this mighty giant on his committee of nine, called to condemn and muzzle Waggoner, together with the *Two Laws* and his own *Law in the Book of Galatians*, Butler sought to put the moral law theory forever to rest at the 1886 session. But the committee failed. And the books were not conclusive. Moreover, Canright proved to be a Goliath rather than a David in the theological struggle.

Struck by Waggoner's theological arrows, he left the conference to ponder whether Adventism had arisen in heresy. If the law referred to in Galatians was not the ceremonial, he reasoned, then the commandments, including the Sabbath, had indeed been done away with at the cross! A number of weeks later, in February 1887, he turned in his credentials and asked that his membership be withdrawn.

Also in February Waggoner mailed Butler a prepublication copy of *The Gospel in the Book of Galatians* in reply to *The Law in the Book of Galatians.*[3] And Ellen White mailed her second reproof to Waggoner—the only one he received.

Also during that month Butler wrote Ellen White that Canright was a casualty of the "law question." Again on March 1 he stated that *Canright thought "we were exalting the law above Christ."* In declaring it "astonishing to us all how he could change so quickly and radically," Butler was wholly unaware that he and Smith teetered upon the same precipice.

THREEFOLD RESPONSIBILITY FOR CANRIGHT'S FALL

In seeing Canright's sudden fall as triggered by Waggoner's "heresy," Butler was not entirely without reason. The danger always exists that a sudden grasp of an opposite principle of truth (i.e., grace) may cause resistance to the former truth (i.e., law). Waggoner did not himself turn against the moral law. But he intensified that danger to others by demanding that they choose between the two interpretations of Galatians, both of which were valid.

That choice posed a serious problem to fellow leaders who had been unwittingly influenced by Evangelical arguments. Canright, Smith, and Butler all accepted at face value the antinomian claim that *if* the *paidagōgos* ("schoolmaster") was the moral law, *then* the Ten Commandments were, indeed, done away with. Thus the only issue they could consider was What is the *paidagōgos*? So intent were they to answer this false question by proving it was the ceremonial law that they gave no ear to Waggoner's proper question: What is the function of the *paidagōgos*?

Convicted of a legalism that only the moral law view offered to resolve, Canright saw himself with but two options: cling to legalism, or repudiate the moral law. This posed no problem to Waggoner because he rejected the Evangelical claim that the law in question had been done away with in the first place.

Because they held the same misconception as Canright, Butler and Smith also faced the same two options: follow Canright in his antinomian plunge and repudiate the moral law, or intensify their legalistic defense of the part-truth ceremonial position. The identical pride that had prompted Canright to leave the church now forced Butler and Smith to intensify their defense.

They were, in fact, far more responsible for Canright's defection than was Waggoner, who, despite his denial of the context, did offer Canright the solution to his legalism. By rejecting a Christ-centered focus as the only valid cure, Smith and Butler confirmed Canright in his egocentric tendencies. And by leaving him spiritually barren, they prompted a sudden, antinomian shift when he discovered in himself a legalism that resisted grace. Lacking Waggoner's union of law and grace in a focus upon Christ rather than upon obedience, Canright thought to remove legalism by fighting the law. This he did with the same zeal that had characterized his former defense of the law.

Butler and Smith, meanwhile, did not mean to deny grace. *Indeed, they too attributed all obedience to grace.* But their law/grace equation was so inaccurate and out of focus as to deliver to obedience the supreme place of Christ crucified! Thus they found themselves driven to defend the language of law that Waggoner was trying to correct. Smith "held this position until his death," says Knight, who portrays the fear that drove the church's leadership to the right even as Canright went left:

"Smith was one in heart and mind with Butler. For him, 'next to the death of Brother White, the greatest calamity that ever befell our cause was when Dr. Waggoner put his articles on the book of Galatians through the *Signs*.' If the denomination ever changed its position on Galatians, he flatly stated, 'they may count me out,' because 'I am not yet prepared to renounce Seventh-day Adventism'" (George Knight, *Angry Saints*, p. 24).

To understand Smith and today's activists we must honor their desperate attempt to preserve Adventism and the writings of Ellen White. But sincerity assures neither right concepts nor pure motives! The question is: Do they apply Ellen White's reproofs to their own concepts, attitudes, methods, and motives? Knight again affirms the results of misguided sincerity:

"The *Review* editor could see no possible reconciliation between the beliefs of Adventism and a ten-commandment interpretation of the law in Galatians. Such a position, he held in concurrence with Butler, 'overthrows the Testimonies and the Sabbath'" (*ibid.*).

Part-truth thinking misled all three. To defend grace, Canright repudiated the law, while to defend law, Smith and Butler resisted grace. Confident in their opinion of Scripture, they all walked in the steps of Jews who, to protect the Sabbath, murdered its Maker (Mark 2:27, 28). Contextual accuracy encouraged a spiritual pride (Rev. 3:17) that prevented an objective examination of Waggoner's principles. Thus, to protect the Sabbath, they too exalted the law above its Creator!

Was Canright, then, more noble in reexamining Galatians? Not at all. He was already on the verge of leaving for a fifth and final time (Vande Vere, *Rugged Heart*, pp. 79, 80) because he saw Adventism as impeding "false and ambitious hopes" of greatness (*Testimonies*, vol. 5, p. 621). Following his 1884 defection he had identified his problem as pride, admitting:

"When Butler, White, Andrews, Haskel, or others have said something that wounded my feelings, I have let that destroy my confidence in the truth. . . . I believe that if I ever go back from this I am lost" (Vande Vere, pp. 79, 80).

Sadly, Canright did go back. His new paradigm, that Christ annulled the law, permitted him to jettison Ellen White and Adventism. But he also had to repudiate the insistence of the author of Galatians that faith does not void, but establishes, the law (Rom. 3:31).

Presuming to turn from legalism to Christ, Canright thus rejected his Creator, whose sign of loyalty is the Sabbath, in favor of an antinomian christ against whose deceptions Paul had already warned (2 Thess. 2:3-8). In opposing the law, Canright only buried his legalism. Removing it from sight, he enforced its perpetual, manic-depressive cycle of exaltation and depression.

Together the three men blocked the gospel renewal the Spirit had sought to bring at Minneapolis.

Key: Not Doctrinal but Practical

Ellen White's key to the conflict was not doctrinal so much as practical. Her consistent refusal either to endorse or to deny the various claims about the book of Galatians accompanied her insistence that doctrinal pillars were not at stake. Although she said Waggoner's theology contained error, she did not clarify its nature. Why? The urgent need of church leaders, as she repeatedly declared, was to humble themselves one to another and to seek the Word together. Nor was technical agreement necessary to unity:

"Many commit the error of trying to define minutely the fine points of distinction. . . . All cannot see in the same line of vision. You are in danger of making a world of an atom, and an atom of a world" (*Ellen G. White 1888 Materials*, pp. 897, 898).

The "atom" made into a "world" was the law in Galatians and technical definitions of justification. Christ and His righteousness in contrast to self-righteousness was the "world" that the squabbling men had reduced to an "atom." The Smith-Butler alliance acknowledged its truth but charged that Waggoner threatened obedience by overstressing self-evident truth that all Adventists already believed anyway.

Ellen White considered it impossible to overstress Christ our righteousness when the focus is upon Him instead of a theory about Him. For in Him all truth resides. Indeed, in 1888 Christ, the mountain to fill the whole earth (Dan. 2:35), was Himself reduced to an "atom"!

To any degree that law and obedience—or even accurate theological statements about justification—supersede a focus upon Him, to that degree we reduce the "world" of truth to an "atom" even as we exalt an "atom" to an idolatrous "mountain." This was precisely the message of Minneapolis. In response to it, fear, pride, and self-justification stimulated personal enmity and bred injustice, as well as a wresting of Scripture in violation of the principles of the priesthood of believers.

No matter how pure, doctrine will always engender idolatry unless we together employ self-critical, paradoxical thinking to expose the trickery of our deceptive minds. Minds that unconsciously seek to gratify our desires and justify self will unwittingly exalt our opinion of Scripture above the Creator and enforce upon His Word the outlines and contours of our own experiences. Not only is self-justification instinctive to all, but the more correct the doctrine, the more perverse the ultimate betrayal!

Theological error is never so great an impediment to justification by faith as is the spiritual pride that counterfeits justification and prompts an attitude of judgment toward others. We must thus beware how we respond to those we consider self-righteous. An honest look at their weakness through the mirror of history would actually provide a strikingly accurate portrait of ourselves!

Minneapolis is but one battle in a war between justification by faith and self-justification that has raged ever since the Fall. Had Waggoner justified himself, as did Smith and Butler, he would have belied his message. Self-justification with its corresponding judgmental spirit would have counteracted the truth he proclaimed—the truth that Christ is our only righteousness. For justification by faith is not so much a theology as an *experience* in relating to Jesus. Nor is it taught so much as *shared* by a living testimony of assurance based on God's Word.

REST STOP: THE CASE OF DAN JONES

Dan T. Jones, elected General Conference secretary at the Minneapolis General Conference session, for a year and a half allied himself with those whom he perceived to be defenders of the faith. Dan opposed not only Waggoner and A. T. Jones but also W. C. and Ellen White. Convinced that the key issue was the law in Galatians, he scarcely concealed his anger that justification by faith should be used to "maneuver" the acceptance of a new, "dangerous" doctrine. For, he reasoned, "rather than reject those that were objectionable our people would be led to accept that which they could not fully endorse."

Ellen White's repeated disclaimers about her involvement in the controversy only intensified his doubts about her integrity. For with other key leaders, Dan saw in her support of Waggoner a defense of Waggoner's theological arguments. Satan cleverly tricks us into division over obscure side issues that disguise the real issues. When he finally came to his senses, Dan confessed to W. C. White:

"I had supposed . . . the law in Galatians, the theory of the covenants, etc.—were the questions at issue, and that the object . . . was to bring in those doctrines and establish them as the belief of the denomination. *I thought the doctrine of justification by faith, with which I have agreed theoretically, and with which all our leading brethren have agreed, was only a rider . . . to carry through these other things*" (*Manuscripts and Memories of Minneapolis*, p. 161; italics supplied).

Concerning his assumption that others had manipulated Mrs. White, Dan admitted: "I see that my conclusions were all without foundation, and that my surmisings were the surmisings of a carnal mind" (*ibid.*, pp. 159, 160).

The True Witness is knocking again (Rev. 3:14-21). Will we, like Dan Jones, at last listen? Some of us, in our blindness, represent Smith and Butler. Others of us, like Dan Jones, find ourselves deceived by efforts to defend the writings of Ellen White that in fact violate her testimonies.

---

[1] I recently read a copy of *Towards Righteousness by Faith: 1888 in Retrospect* (1989), five articles edited by Arthur J. Ferch and published by the South Pacific Division of Seventh-day Adventists. Some of their conclusions about Waggoner and his message reflect a theological pattern I seek to correct. Nevertheless, it is urgent that we examine views that challenge our own for helpful perspectives and/or correctives. Truth is bigger than any of us or all of us, and we cannot afford to ignore the insights of those with whom we may disagree. As time permits I shall examine the primary documents for this purpose.

Meanwhile, positively as well as negatively, the book points up the urgency of our need for the ability to think paradoxically by learning how to exercise priesthood of believers principles. I particularly appreciate the introductory chapter. Arthur N. Patrick succinctly enunciates the paradoxical elements that sparked the Minneapolis crisis-*continuity and change:*

"The crisis arose from a destructive collision between two legitimate forces that are endemic within Christianity, and thus always present within Adventism. The first force arises from *the desire to preserve traditional beliefs (continuity);* the second force derives from *the motive to respond to the onward leading of God (change)*" (p. 13; italics supplied).

I appreciate his comment that "while it is admitted that the interpretation of history involves certain risks, the attempt is appropriate in a setting where individual opinions can be honed by mature, friendly critics." I must confess, nevertheless, that tension between the two groups still persists to the point that "friendly critics" are generally restricted to "party members."

The saddest fact is that neither party really cares how the other responds. Indeed, each side expects a negative response and almost gleefully grasps it as evidence that the other side ignores truth to maintain its "proof." A true application of the principle of the priesthood of believers would make us all *"friendly* critics," however different our findings. Only when we relate to each other in this way will we be able to unite paradoxical principles in a manner to exclude error.

Most pertinent is Patrick's following observation: "It is so much easier to point out the frailties of these stalwart pioneers than to learn from their mistakes." And again: "Our accountability is greater than theirs, for the Lord has given us fresh resources to employ" (p. 21).

[2] But if *paidagōgos* is or includes the moral law, would this not mean it is no longer valid? Are tutors no longer valid when we graduate? Of course not. The Father does not keep the mature child under a slavemaster. But others will need such disciplinary instruction.

Verse 19, "till the seed should come to whom the promise was made," relates to the corporate body of God's biblical people rather than to individuals. The promise is not to "seeds," but to "Seed, which is Christ" (Gal. 3:16). The promise to His people, who formed His earthly body, comes only in and through Him. Had the Jews received Him by faith, He would have released the nation from the ritual system that merely pointed to Him and had neither power nor merit in itself.

Verse 25, on the other hand, relates to the individual Jew or Gentile who together now make up His body. "In Him," our head, the promise comes to all who receive Him by faith. Properly understood, the entire ritual was a promise-indeed, a prophecy of the Seed in whom we receive the promise. Even in Old Testament times, those to whom faith in the Messiah came found liberty by having His law written in the heart (Ps. 19:7-11; 119:92, 97).

[3] But denial of the historical context of Galatians in favor of its conceptual context could only confirm Canright in infidelity. Only God knows what would have happened had Waggoner integrated the historical context of Galatians with his Christ-centered fusion of law and grace. Had he not been asked to choose between two truths, Canright might have been stabilized by seeing the law in its true relation to grace. If he had thus triumphed over the exaltation-depression cycle imposed by his law focus, instead of destroying my grandfather Eugene Wheeler's faith by *Adventism Renounced*, he might have helped him escape his own vicious, legalistic cycle by uniting law and grace!

Priesthood of Believers: The Twofold Key to Unity

10

Before leaving Minneapolis, Ellen White related a vision concerning that General Conference session that she had received two years earlier (1886). The vision portrayed not only that session's ugly spirit but also the fact that neither side was without error:

"I was told that there there was need of great spiritual revival. . . . There was not perfection in all points on either side of the question under discussion. We must search the Scriptures for evidences of truth" (*Ellen G. White 1888 Materials*, p. 165).

Ellen White's supreme concern was never who was right, but that the church must have unity in truth. Hundreds of later references to the Minneapolis episode called for a focus upon Christ, in whose righteousness alone we stand by faith. Simultaneously she urged unity by a priesthood of believers approach to Scripture. Again and again she quoted or referred to Christ's prayer for unity in John 17.

MINNEAPOLIS CURE: VERTICAL/HORIZONTAL PRINCIPLES

Throughout the years Ellen White referred scores of times (e.g., *ibid.*, p. 199) to the spirit that prevailed at Minneapolis, which she repeatedly identified as satanic in origin. In concluding her account of the 1886 vision she urged, by contrast, a fair and honest approach:

"Let a spirit of fairness come in. Though you think his [E. J. Waggoner's] ideas upon this subject may not be sound, do not make false statements, do not mistake his words; place him in no false light; maintain the spirit of Christ; keep the commandments of God, love God supremely, and your neighbor as yourself" (*ibid.*, p. 175).

Were Smith and Butler aware that they misrepresented Waggoner's position, twisted his words, and put him in a false light? Definitely not. Without the principles represented by the priesthood of believers concept and the paradoxical thinking that they stimulate, we are all blind to one side or the other of any truth. Such blindness makes it virtually impossible to treat an opponent fairly—our minds cannot allow significance to his or her point. The Spirit of Christ and *corporate* study of His Word are foundational to unity in truth. When we do not practice such principles, our differences on crucial issues are sure to foster hard feelings. To cure that spirit and remain open to both poles of truth, we must combine the vertical and horizontal principles involved in the priesthood of believers.

God does not propose to perfect us in independence. The Holy Spirit's ministry is itself paradoxical. He ministers to all individually but perfects each in relation to the body. He gives each person insights to share with the many but at the same time corrects each individual by and through the many.

By His discipline the Spirit seeks to expose and eradicate sin's central traits, self-centeredness and pride. His discipline involves a twofold subjection. We surrender to the Spirit individually as we seek truth and purity. But we can distinguish His voice from our own self-centered impulses only when we also put ourselves in subjection to the body. The Spirit always seeks to work through the corporate body or community of faith. Such unity forces us to deep heart-searching as we probe every attitude and motive that divide us. Failure to unite both the horizontal and vertical principles we have been discussing will ultimately prove fatal to us both as individuals and as a community of faith. If, like Smith and Butler, we do not apply the horizontal principle, Satan will intercept and block our vertical channel of communication with God.

When we fail to seek unity in promoting truth, the fruits of the flesh that Ellen White identified with Minneapolis will replace the fruits of the Spirit (Gal. 5:19-26). These fruits she repeatedly identified as attitudes of judging, bitterness, jealousy, envy, self-righteousness, pharisaism, and evil surmising.

As with Butler and Smith, those who now presume to defend the testimonies while at the same time violating priesthood principles and ignoring counsel about unity are self-deceived. Their "straight testimony" is crooked. Any defense of truth not expressed in love and linked to equal commitment to unity reflects the self-justifying spirit of Minneapolis.

More urgent than technical truth is an understanding of ourselves and our attitudes toward others. If we view ourselves as we really are, we will condemn sin, especially within ourselves, but at the same time we will not judge the motives of others and will have compassion for those who err. Unless we see ourselves as Christ views us, we will be unwittingly self-righteous, as were Smith and Butler.

Moreover, regardless of whether their efforts are accepted or resisted, unless reformers share with others only what they continually apply to themselves, they will stimulate nothing but self-righteousness in those they come in contact with! We have neither the authority to proclaim truth nor the discernment to assure fidelity to the "straight testimony" except as we continually engage in penitent self-examination and remain committed to unity.

The "straight testimony" we desire to present can never truly be straight until we first humble self. If we fail to do this, we will violate the weightier matters of the law! Some in the various independent ministries have become increasingly conscious of this fact. But they need a right example from those in the church organization. Let us beware of the fear and unrecognized pride that caused the 1888 denominational leaders to declare war upon erring young men who needed encouragement and godly examples instead of censure. By decrying the mistakes Waggoner and Jones made, yet themselves failing to humbly initiate a united study of the issues, Butler and Smith only increased their own guilt.

Ironically, the younger men ultimately followed in their footsteps. It had been difficult for them to believe honest men could lay such totally false charges—that they and W. C. White manipulated Mrs. White and her writings. Yet in time they became so blind as to repeat the very same charges themselves against W. C. White. And, once again, in presumed defense of the Testimonies!

Meanwhile, a debating spirit and hostility, which Smith and Butler boldly denied they had, was the surest sign that the Holy Spirit's place had been usurped in their lives (ibid., pp. 168, 169). A message Mrs. White sent soon after Minneapolis speaks of their "remarkable blindness":

"My burden during the meeting was to present Jesus and His love before my brethren, for I saw marked evidences that many had not the spirit of Christ. . . . A different spirit had come into the experience of our brother ministers, and . . . was leavening the camp. There was, I knew, a remarkable blindness upon the minds of many, that they did not discern where the Spirit of God was" (ibid., p. 216).

The True Witness whom the church resisted in 1888 now knocks at our own door (Rev. 3:20). To remove our blindness, He seeks to direct attention to Himself.

Adventism in Conflict

After discussing an attempt to change the American constitution that if passed would "bind the consciences of all those who keep the Bible Sabbath," Ellen White described a council Satan had held to explore "how he should keep pen and voice of Seventh-day Adventists silent" (*ibid.*, p. 210). The method he and his angels agreed upon was to divide the church body. Excerpts from her report reveal a threefold burden that

(1) personal opinions of Scripture must be harmonized by corporate study of Scripture;

(2) a divisive spirit must yield to Christ's prayer for unity; and

(3) the "faith of Jesus" based upon His merits, not our works, is the only key to obedience and salvation.

One paragraph especially shows how one's spirit affects the way he or she approaches Scripture:

"We know that if all would come to the Scriptures with hearts subdued and controlled by the influence of the Spirit of God, there would be brought to the examination of the Scriptures a calm mind, free from prejudice and pride of opinion. The light from the Lord would shine upon His Word and the truth would be revealed" (*ibid.*, p. 211).

Warning against grieving the Spirit by closing the "understanding to the light which God sends," she urged "humility of mind, and [willingness] to be instructed as a child," declaring: "As Christians you have no right to entertain feelings of enmity, unkindness, and prejudice toward *Dr. Waggoner, who has presented his views in a plain, straightforward manner, as a Christian should. If he is in error,* you should, in a calm, rational, Christlike manner, seek to *show him from the Word of God where he is out of harmony* with its teachings. If you cannot do this you have no right as Christians to pick flaws, to criticize, to work in the dark, to prejudice minds with your objections. This is Satan's way of working" (*ibid.*, pp. 163, 164; italics supplied).

Thus, far from protecting his views, Ellen White welcomed a "Christlike" challenge to Waggoner, whom she did not consider entirely correct.* Calling for mutual humility in examining the Word, she showed far greater concern about attitudes and methods than about who or even what was right. *When atmosphere and process are right, the Lord can then lead us to unity in truth.*

But if our spirit in relating to each other and to the Word is wrong, Satan will divide and carry us individually into confusion and/or heresy! Until we consistently employ the horizontal principle of the priesthood of believers concept, no theology can ever bring the meaning or power of the Minneapolis message into our lives and churches. As at Minneapolis, this is our great issue today.

The second principle drawn from the vision of Satan's strategy is that a divisive spirit must yield to Christ's prayer for unity. "Satan has done his work with some success. There has been variance of feelings, and division. There has been much jealousy and evil surmising. There have been unsanctified speeches, hints, and remarks. The minds of the men who should be heart and soul at work, prepared to do mighty strokes for God at this very time, are absorbed in matters of little consequence. . . .

"Satan has been having things his own way; but the Lord has raised up men and given them a solemn message to bear to His people, to wake up the mighty men to prepare for battle, for the day of God's preparation. This message Satan sought to make of none effect. . . . At this meeting the subject of the law in Galatians was brought before the ministers" (*ibid.*, pp. 210, 211).

Ellen White repeatedly warned the church leadership that their Galatians debate was making mountains out of molehills (*ibid.*, pp. 897, 898). This does not mean that Waggoner's focus upon the faith of Jesus and Christ crucified was a "[matter] of little importance." Indeed, Christ was the mountain threatened by debate. The molehill was the law in Galatians.

Since both laws are involved in Paul's counsel in the book of Galatians, both sides were wrong on this issue that she described as of comparatively "little importance." But upon the issue of greatest importance—Christ our only righteousness—Waggoner was right in spirit and in fact. Meanwhile, those leaders who were wrong in spirit were wrong even in the principle underlying their technically correct fact! For in opposing the moral law, they opposed the very principles of grace underlying the ceremonial law.

The Minneapolis controversy had been brewing for a long time. "The enemy [had] been placing his mold on the work for years" (*ibid.*, p. 179). Shortly thereafter Ellen White alluded to the longstanding nature of the conflict as she told of standing at the bedside of her dying husband seven years earlier (1881) and "[vowing] to disappoint the enemy, to bear a constant, earnest appeal to my brethren of the cruelty of their jealousies and evil surmising which were leavening the churches" (*ibid.*, p. 178).

This brings us to the third concern in the vision portraying Satan's behind-the-scenes conference: "The faith of Jesus has been overlooked and treated in an indifferent, careless manner. It has not occupied the prominent position in which it was revealed to John. Faith in Christ as the sinner's only hope has been largely left out, not only of the discourses given but of the religious experience of very many who claim to believe the third angel's message" (*ibid.*, p. 212).

Simple trust in Christ as our sacrifice and mediating priest was Ellen White's primary burden and the key to all other issues. She, whose supreme longing was to see the church's thought leaders fall in love with Jesus and with each other, refused to let herself be drawn into the theological debate. Unfortunately, however, the church leadership did not comprehend, let alone embrace, her twofold key to unity: Christ's vertical mediation of His sacrifice in relation to the horizontal principles of the priesthood of believers.

APPEAL TO LEADERS

Today, independents and church leaders alike condemn each other's enmity while remaining blind to their own. Denominational leaders consider their strong feelings justified by the threat to unity, just as did Smith and Butler. When reproved, Butler demanded to know what else could be expected of a General Conference president! What was expected? That he model those very principles he accused Waggoner of violating. Butler's accusations reveal the standard by which he himself must be judged.

Violation of those same principles deprived him of moral authority in the whole controversy. Had Butler and Smith humbled themselves and set a right example, they would have revealed the spirit of Jesus rather than that of Satan. Whatever their errors, Ellen White would have affirmed the older pair just as she had Waggoner and Jones, who did humble themselves. Had all done so, the Spirit could have drawn them into a harmony that would have released the power of the latter rain!

We also deprive ourselves of moral authority if, in dealing with extremists, we fail to humble ourselves before God, allowing Him to be our defense. If we ignore those very same principles we charge the extremists with violating, we lose the moral high ground, confuse the issues, and drive many into the camp of the opposition. Until we demonstrate the principles of Christ Our Righteousness, allowing Him to be our defense, we will find ourselves in an ever weaker position.

As with Waggoner, some independents who have previously disregarded the principles of the priesthood of believers now long for a cooperative relationship with the church body. Some welcome every administrative decision they can use to encourage loyalty in others! Indeed, some whom we condemn as reprobates because they know not how to be honest without appearing critical have knowingly risked—and lost—significant financial support by simply trying to encourage an attitude of trust among those who have lost confidence in the organization. Meantime, such independent leaders find their own confidence tested by the Smith-Butler spirit of some pastors and leaders.

Much bewilderment reigns on both sides. We all need divine grace to escape the self-righteous spirit of Minneapolis (Laodicea)! By doing what Butler and Smith failed to do, we can greatly simplify the choices of our members. When they sense a right spirit on our part, many sincere but bewildered people will find their confidence in the church reaffirmed and strengthened.

Of course, some critics are simply on ego trips. But mutual humbling of ourselves will hasten the separation between those who in the name of reform only foster a spirit of rebellion, and the honest men and women who appear divisive but want to be loyal both to God and to church administration.

Some will require church discipline. But let us relate to them in compassion. The Lord intends that the fruitage of our mutual failures prompt mutual intercessory prayer—not mutual recrimination. May we so grasp justification by faith that we will cease to defend ourselves and, by humbling self in the dust, remove roadblocks we unwittingly have placed in the path to unity.

REST STOP: YOU'RE RIGHT: IT IS UNREALISTIC, BUT . . .

A reputable theologian responded to an early manuscript of this book in a most realistic way:

"What do you do when the conservatives and the liberals will not follow your suggestions? What should the church do when the truth is being destroyed? While I would agree with your suggestions, I think it is unrealistic to assume that all will work in the framework you have suggested."

True, not all will unite as a priesthood of believers to wrestle together for truth. But let not that failure be ours. Our destiny is at stake. Ultimately a shaking will remove all who do not earnestly enter this individual/corporate process. Meanwhile, all those who do will help to form a network of roots that must ultimately spread in all directions throughout the body.

My concern is that we respond to conflict neither by neglect nor by imposed authority, but rather by spiritual humility, seeking to hear and respond in a spirit of heart-searching that is open to truth even while reaching out compassionately to those whose hold upon truth is slipping.

If we come as close as integrity (not dignity) permits and identify with every element of valid truth that others hold, we can be instrumental in saving many whom we might otherwise cast away. But this will require tact and patience during a time when fear is often great and confidence small.

Our natural response to human impossibilities is contrary to God's patience and long-suffering toward heaven's rebels. He knew many would be infected. Yet, besides giving them every opportunity to repent, He made sure all had an adequate basis for choice before taking action. This reveals the necessity that the entire body examine truth. When discipline is necessary, let us act in humility and compassion, seeking to understand and save the disaffected and to safeguard those who may have insufficient evidence, to whom the fruits may need to become more evident.

Meanwhile, let us beware of repeating the blind zeal of the sixteenth-century Reformers who grossly violated the third pillar of their movement (the priesthood of believers). Fear of compromising Scripture led many of the Reformers to reproduce the papal error they decried. Placing more confidence in their own opinion of Scripture than the Spirit's ability to guide the body of Christ, they usurped scriptural authority and enforced their own views—at times even on pain of death.

Thus the message to Sardis (Rev. 3:1-6) announces spiritual death to this period of church history despite the life-signifying name we have given to it—the Protestant Reformation. The Reformation died aborning because its leaders insisted on their own vertical relationship to God through His Word but refused to guarantee a similar relationship to others (see chapter 5).

To maintain personal accountability to Christ, we must be subject to each other in His Word. God leads no one independently. Purity of truth is assured only by dependence upon revelation, which embraces both the principle of ultimate personal dependence upon Christ and interdependent submission to one another—in Him. Only as dependence on Him is accompanied by mutual humbling one to another can we overcome the pride and selfishness that prevent growth in truth. Truth is so internally united that ignoring either paradoxical element violates both.

The Spirit speaks directly to each person. But truth's purifying power relates more to our overcoming egocentric thinking by humbling ourselves before God and others than it does to knowledge. To teach us self-sacrificing love and humility, He subjects us one to another.

Our self-induced blindness must surrender to God's Word directly in personal study and indirectly by corporate study in the body. Our connection with heaven is valid only as personal responsibility to God blends with corporate responsibility to fellow believers.

Paradoxical thinking and the priesthood of believers are absolutely essential to each other. Without the first it is impossible to unite both the vertical and horizontal priesthood principles. Without the second it is impossible to adequately see and correct our part-truth blind spots. *Upon this twofold reform hinge all other reforms.* To undermine either principle is to reflect an unbelief that effectively destroys the authority of the Word.

If efforts toward unity do not accompany our commitment to personal faithfulness, we deny the latter and reproduce the failure that destroyed sixteenth century Protestant unity and integrity. Catholics denied both vertical and horizontal principles. To preserve the vertical, Protestants violated the horizontal aspect. The result was the same. It is impossible to be faithful to one and not the other. Until we honor both, we will never overcome our Laodicean blindness.

Paradoxically, the Spirit directs even special agents such as Waggoner and Jones to be subject to correction by the body that He has commissioned them to correct! To fail to grasp this principle is to fail to apply the prescription of the True Witness who offers to heal our self-satisfied malady. Without this we can never find healing for the disease that has so far prevented us from proclaiming the loud cry.

Let us now change lenses for a closer examination of that message as it relates to those issues that continue to divide us: atonement, perfection, and the nature of Christ. Part Three suggests paradoxical keys that I believe will someday bring us into greater unity than that which marked our beginning. As we now proceed to examine the central nervous system of our divisive issues, check to make sure your own mind brake is not stuck.

---

* Some interpretations of Scripture given by Dr. Waggoner I do not regard as correct. But I believe him to be perfectly honest in his views, and I would respect his feelings and treat him as a Christian gentleman" (*ibid.*, p. 164).

Conflict
in Relation
to Covenant Concepts

Did Ellen White Speak a Language of Law?

11

For decades both before and after 1888 Ellen White warned against legalism. Nevertheless, many have often used her writings to enforce a language of law. Did she have a legalistic bias?

The problem is not hers. It is ours. Some of us impose a language of law upon her works by focusing upon her law and obedience statements. Others ignore or deny them and impose a language of grace by concentrating upon her expressions of that other pole of truth. Or else they leave the stigma of legalism upon her by mistakenly confusing her intense commitment to God's law and our obedience to it with legalism.

None could be more committed to obedience than Christ. Moreover, as with Ellen White, many of us employ His words, in both the Gospels and in the rest of Scripture to support a language of law. Yet, He is truth in its fullness! He combined both law and grace in perfect balance.

As for Ellen White, when obedience is her text, faith is its context. When she speaks of perfection, substitutionary intercession is the background. In magnifying the law, she exalts grace. And in proclaiming grace, she establishes the law.

Indeed, Ellen White's focus was always upon Christ Himself—author and source of all truth in all its glorious balance! Such balance alone permits full emphasis on either principle without distortion or extremes. When kept in balance, one cannot be too committed either to law or to grace. For each protects the other's integrity.

By alienating law from grace it is we who betray truth's unity by pitting one list of statements against the other. Some collate endless admonitions to obedience to produce a language of law. Others form a language of grace by her numerous statements about the atoning ministry of Christ. Just as a magnet passed through sand picks up only metal, so each person finds

127

what he or she is searching for. Thus anyone may gather an impressive list of quotes to defend either truth.

Both sides claim to believe the principle that the other proclaims. But each uses its arsenal in a way that threatens the integrity of truth's other pole. To avoid this we must focus upon Christ, in whom alone both find their meaning. Seen within the framework of the cross, law and grace are one great principle of self-sacrificing love in action. But without a focus on Him it is as impossible to view both poles in perspective as it is to see both sides of a coin at the same time.

A sentimental focus upon the cross will not do. The cross is meaningless without Christ's resurrection for our justification (Rom. 4:25) and ascension as high priest to prepare us for His soon coming by a process of purifying mediation (Heb. 9:26-28; Eph. 5:25-27). To relate these principles—not merely intellectually but in personal response to Christ Himself—is to discover by experience the dynamic relationship between law and grace, in which each supports the other.

To truly exalt Christ is to magnify both aspects of His nature: law and grace. In this way only can we glorify Him (Rev. 14:7). Though recognizing that Waggoner's message was not without error, Ellen White was thrilled because he united the converse principles of law and grace by exalting Jesus, in whom alone we find truth's perfect balance. To expose just how we fracture principles she so carefully united, we now will examine back-to-back paragraphs in chapter 7 of *Steps to Christ*.

STEPS TO CHRIST SUMMARIZES MINNEAPOLIS

Ellen White's first post-1888 book set forth the paradoxical principles of Minneapolis. By splitting her unified message, we in opposite ways impose contradiction upon its polar statements. Each side sees the other's distortion, but neither recognizes its own. Conservatives emphasize obedience statements, such as the following:

"The condition of eternal life is now just what it has always been—just what it was in Paradise before the fall of our first parents—perfect obedience to the law of God, perfect righteousness. If eternal life were granted on any other condition short of this, then the happiness of the whole universe would be imperiled. The way would be open for sin, with all its train of woe and misery, to be immortalized" (p. 62).

The text says, "Perfect obedience . . . perfect righteousness"—nothing "short of this"—is "the condition of eternal life" now, just as in Eden.

But every text has a context. The next paragraph, a prize liberal passage, offers that framework:

Did Ellen White Speak a Language of Law?

"It was possible for Adam, before the fall, to form a righteous character by obedience to the law. But he failed to do this, and because of his sin our natures are fallen, and we cannot make ourselves righteous. Since we are sinful, unholy, we cannot perfectly obey a holy law. We have no righteousness of our own with which to meet the claims of the law of God. But Christ has made a way of escape for us. . . . He lived a sinless life. He died for us, and now He offers to take our sins and give us His righteousness. If you give yourself to Him, . . . for His sake you are accounted righteous. . . . You are accepted before God just as if you had not sinned" (ibid.).

Conservatives agree that God places Christ's "sinless life" and death to our credit to cover *past sins*. But, as did Smith and Butler, many restrict justification to past sins. That even Spirit-prompted obedience must be purified is considered rank heresy. Yet Ellen White urgently taught the necessity of a substitution to purify our obedience:

"Oh, that all may see that everything in obedience, in penitence, in praise and thanksgiving, must be placed upon the glowing fire of the righteousness of Christ. The fragrance of this righteousness ascends like a cloud around the mercy seat" (*Selected Messages*, book 1, p. 344).

Ellen White pleads that "*all may see* that *everything in obedience, in penitence, in praise and thanksgiving,* **must** *be placed upon the glowing fire of the righteousness of Christ*" (ibid.; italics supplied). It is urgent that we seek to obey fully. But as we do, our trust must be in His perfect obedience to meet the law's demand, not in our imperfect obedience.

"The *religious services, the prayers, the praise, the penitent confession* of sin ascend from *true believers* as incense to the heavenly sanctuary, but passing through the *corrupt channels* of humanity, they are so defiled that unless purified by blood, they can never be of value to God. . . . *Unless the Intercessor, who is at God's right hand, presents and purifies all by His righteousness, it is not acceptable* to God" (ibid.; italics supplied).

Only "His righteousness" makes our obedience "acceptable to God"! Unless we view perfection in light of this substitutionary key, which was at the heart of Minneapolis, we pervert her meaning. To use her testimonies to urge perfection without honoring Christ's mediation to purify obedience itself is to force contradiction upon paradoxical concepts that in reality form an undivided unity!

Her message was consistent. Ten years before, she had warned against "false ideas of justification" and that "Satan would work in a special manner to confuse the mind on this point. . . .

"The point which has been urged upon my mind for years is the *imputed* righteousness of Christ. I have wondered that this matter was not made the subject of discourses in our churches throughout the land, when the matter has been kept so constantly urged upon me, and I have made it the subject of nearly every discourse and talk" (*Ellen G. White 1888 Materials*, pp. 810, 811; italics supplied).

Will we accept her consistent message? If so, we must recognize the necessity of atonement for obedience: "All must be laid upon the fire of Christ's righteousness to cleanse it from its earthly odor before it rises in a cloud of fragrant incense to the great Jehovah and is accepted as a sweet savor.

"I ask, How can I present this matter as it is? The Lord Jesus imparts all the powers, all the grace, all the penitence, all the inclination, all the pardon of sins, in presenting His righteousness for man to grasp by living faith—which is also the free gift of God. If you would gather together everything that is good and holy and noble and lovely in man, and then present the subject to the angels of God as acting a part in the salvation of the human soul or in merit, the proposition would be rejected as treason" (*ibid.*, p. 816).

Christ's own perfection is the vital key to all our efforts. "Many feel that their faults of character make it impossible for them to meet the standard that Christ has erected; but all that such ones have to do is to humble themselves at every step. . . . *He adds to their work His perfection* and sufficiency, and it is accepted of the Father. We are accepted in the Beloved. The sinner's defects are covered by the perfection and fullness of the Lord Our Righteousness. *Those who with sincere will, with a contrite heart, are putting forth humble efforts to live up to the requirements of God are looked upon by the Father . . . as obedient children, and the righteousness of Christ is imputed unto them*" (*ibid.*, p. 402; italics supplied).

Is this not what liberals have been insisting? Sadly, it is not! Indeed, many consider all such "efforts to live up to the requirements of God" to be the essence of legalism. By warning against spiritual effort, neutralizing obedience, and treating perfection as heresy, they, too, force contradiction upon Ellen White. To pit either pole of truth against the other violates both principles and escalates the theological war.

THE SUBSTITUTE: OUR ONLY SURETY

Three years later, about the time she had *Steps to Christ* printed, Ellen White expressed her paradoxical principles by two terms: "covenant of grace" and "Substitute and Surety." "*Under the covenant of grace God requires from man just what he required in Eden—perfect obedience*. The believing sinner, *through his divine Substitute and Surety, renders obedience* to the law of God. Christ kept the law perfectly, and through Him the believer shall not perish, but have everlasting life" (*Signs of the Times*, Sept. 5, 1892; italics supplied).

The "covenant of grace" does not change the law, but upholds its demands, which remain the same as "in Eden—perfect obedience." It does, however, permit "the believing sinner" to meet an otherwise impossible requirement in and "through his divine Substitute and Surety."

Without God's covenant of grace provisions we would have to be absolutely perfect from the moment of justification or be lost! For the law demands perfect obedience. To be acceptable, our very obedience itself must be purified by blood. As Substitute, Christ covers even our present obedience. As Surety, He assures the future. "Christ kept the law perfectly, and through Him the believer shall not perish." We are neither declared perfect nor assured "everlasting life" because of our obedience. *Both are ours only through our Substitute and Surety, who "kept the law perfectly."*

As Substitute, He declares us perfect in Himself. And as Surety He assures "everlasting life," not upon our ability to live a sinless life, but upon continued faith in His justification. If the sacrifice covered only past sins, justification would have to provide holy flesh or be a strictly legal function. Otherwise, no one would ever have any hope.

Desmond Ford thus rightly repudiates past-only justification. But the solution is not strictly legal justification—past, present, and future—as *effected* at the cross 2,000 years ago. Forensic-only justification denies personal responsibility and reflects a "once saved, always saved" theory rooted in Augustinian predestination.[1]

Neither Ford nor Adventist liberals really want to foster predestination or the once saved, always saved theory that gave rise to forensic-only justification. They seek only to remove the anxiety felt by those who believe they must do good to be justified. And they insist upon the 1888 principle that justification must precede true obedience. We truly obey only when we are justified (reconciled) and are in Him. But strictly legal justification by faith is as contrary to the Bible and writings of Ellen White as is holy flesh.

The solution to both anxiety and legalism lies in a perfect Substitute (past/present) who, as our Surety (future), treats our commitment to obey as true obedience. Every phrase below is crucial:

"Righteousness is obedience to the law. The law demands righteousness, and this the sinner owes to the law; but he is incapable of rendering it. The only way in which he can attain to righteousness is through faith. By faith he can bring to God the merits of Christ, and the Lord places the obedience of His Son to the sinner's account. Christ's righteousness is accepted in place of man's failure, and God receives, pardons, justifies, the repentant, believing soul, treats him as though he were righteous, and loves him as He loves His own Son.

"*This is how faith is accounted righteousness; and the pardoned soul goes on from grace to grace*, from light to greater light. He can say with rejoicing, 'Not by works of righteousness which we have done, but according to his mercy he saved us, by the washing of regeneration, and renewing of the Holy Ghost; . . that being justified by his grace, we should be made heirs according to the hope of eternal life' " (*Review and Herald*, Nov. 4, 1890; cf. *Selected Messages*, book 1, p. 367; italics supplied).

We can meet the law's demand only by bringing "to God the merits of Christ." To our account He "places the obedience of His Son." But this is not merely a point in time. Nor is it primarily a book entry in heaven. To be accounted perfect, two factors must fuse: a faith that claims Christ's obedience rather than our own to satisfy the law; and an ongoing experience in justification, as "the pardoned soul goes on from grace to grace." Note again this twofold principle:

"Without the grace of Christ, the sinner is in a hopeless condition . . . , but through divine grace, supernatural power is imparted to the man, and works in mind and heart and character. It is through the impartation of the grace of Christ that sin is discerned in its hateful nature, and finally driven from the soul temple.

"It is through grace that we are brought into fellowship with Christ, to be associated with Him in the work of salvation. Faith is the condition upon which God has seen fit to promise pardon to sinners. . . . *Faith can present Christ's perfect obedience instead of the sinner's transgression and defection.* . . . The repentant soul realizes that his *justification* comes because *Christ, as his substitute and surety*, has died for him, *is his atonement and righteousness*" (*Review and Herald*, Nov. 4, 1890; italics supplied).

REST STOP: SURETY PAYMENT IS REAL PAYMENT

When I was a small boy my parents often had no money for gas. When necessary, my father would offer his prized car jack, worth far more than a few gallons of gas, as a substitute for cash, a surety that he would return to pay. Because of the jack's inherent value, the owner of the gas station never turned down this substitute. Indeed, nothing more was needed for payment. But something was required to retain possession of the valuable jack. Had my father not returned with cash, he would have lost its ownership and could no longer have used the jack as credit.

We have no merit by which to use justification's credit line. But we assure continued substitution ("jack") by gratefully choosing to obey. Upon the basis of this choice, our Surety guarantees that He, the Substitute, will pass us through the judgment and preserve us until His return (Phil. 1:6). Unless we choose to obey, however, we surrender all claim to justification.

The choice to obey—not obedience itself!—permits an honest credit claim. Obedience follows as we trust the Surety. My father could not honestly return for the jack without the exchange. Nor can we receive justification without surrendering our sinfulness for His righteousness. The substitution does not act directly upon the future. But the future is assured so long as we retain the credit line by a faith in our Surety, a faith that honors His ownership and lordship.

A lack of commitment to obey may mean we claimed justification dishonestly—like getting gas without paying but refusing to leave the jack. If so, we were never justified in the first place. Our claim was not an act of loyal faith but of disloyal presumption. Or we may have exercised true faith but forfeited justification by adopting a false assurance that we need no exchange, no continued commitment to obey.

In the latter we again become responsible for sins of the past (cf. Eze. 18:20-26). Not because Christ retracts past credit, but because of the nature of the credit line. The past is always covered by present justification—never by past justification. Christ Himself—not some mark in heavenly records—is our justification! We are justified when we are in Him and unjustified out of Him!

Nor is sin ever justified. It is the sinner that is justified, but only as he himself or she herself condemns sin, which is implicit in choosing righteousness (justification). Thus the end of those who cease to receive justification by remaining in Christ is worse than if they had not claimed justification (2 Peter 2:20-22). When we cease in reality to claim His righteousness by faith, we thereby assume responsibility for our whole self. *That means all our sin, past as surely as present.*

The record of our sin in heaven is merely a transcript of our character and the history of its development. Thus the primary function of justification is, by both our standing in Him and His personal presence in us, to care for the record of sin stored in the mind and nervous system!

---

[1] Robert Wieland answers Desmond Ford's legal, *effective* justification *at the cross* by a

"universal, legal justification at the cross that is *effective only as claimed by faith*" (*Gold Tried in the Fire*, p. 21). Knowing it would be confused with Ford's view, several years ago I wrestled with Robert Wieland over the term he used. Far from being the forensic-only doctrine, the concept he attributes to Waggoner does correct Ford's error, while it retains truth that the Plymouth Brethren abandon in their doctrine of justification at the cross—which claims a complete and final atonement in A.D. 31. In distinguishing legal justification at the cross from justification by faith, Wieland retains an *ongoing priestly atonement* based upon the *completed sacrificial atonement*.

His "universal, legal justification" refers to the Lawgiver's declaration at the cross that He paid in full the debt for all sin of every person for all time (Heb. 2:9). However, this *complete sacrificial atonement* is *mediated* to believers only as they claim it by personal exercise of faith.

To correct Ford's forensic-only justification, Arnold Wallenkampf uses the phrase "temporary universal justification" (*Justified*, p. 37). By "temporary" he seeks to avoid the confusion of Wieland's term. Both combine present justification with security in Christ for the future, but avoid a "once saved, always saved" declaration that justification covers the future.

Part Three

Loyalty: Test of True Faith

12

"When it is in the heart to obey God, when efforts are put forth to this end, Jesus accepts this disposition and effort as man's best service, and He makes up for the deficiency with His own divine merit. But He will not accept those who claim to have faith in Him and yet are disloyal to His Father's commandment" (Signs of the Times, June 16, 1890).

As indicated previously, there is a wide variety of understandings among both liberals and conservatives. We now distinguish Minneapolis conservatives from traditional conservatives, and Fordian liberals from traditional liberals. With all liberals, Minneapolis conservatives prize the above passage. Traditional conservatives see in it a threat to perfection. Since many employ it against perfection and it seems so unrepresentative of Ellen White's views, traditional conservatives sense a dishonest subterfuge behind any reference to it, and bury it under a collection of perfection quotes. Nevertheless, it is truly representative of Mrs. White's perspective, as we shall see.

"When it is in the heart to obey" refers not to a mere desire to be good but to the exercise of the will to obey. Loyalty is the litmus test of true faith that God accounts for righteousness. That He accepts heart commitment alone as true obedience both warns us against judging others (Matt. 7:1) and demands heart-searching on our part. "Examine yourselves as to whether you are in the faith. Prove yourselves. Do you not know yourselves, that Jesus Christ is in you?—unless indeed you are disqualified" (2 Cor. 13: 5, NKJV).

Many who assure themselves that Christ is within, working through them, will someday hear the terrible words "I never knew you; depart from Me, you who practice lawlessness!" (Matt. 7:23, NKJV). The problem is

135

clearly disloyalty. For the loyal are always accounted obedient. Since many "practice lawlessness" in the name of faith, we must examine our own hearts, praying: "Examine me, O Lord, and prove me; try my mind and my heart" (Ps. 26:2, NKJV).

But here we face danger. As Professor Paul Heubach used to say: "It's dangerous to think. But it's more dangerous not to think." Heart-searching can lead to a neurotic focus upon self. Without it, however, we cannot seriously claim Christ's righteousness. Unless we examine self in dependence upon Him as our "righteousness, and sanctification, and redemption," we are certain either to justify self or to intensify those neurotic patterns that invite false guilt and deepen our real guilt.

We need assurance or else guilt will undermine our commitment and prevent the exercise of faith. But valid assurance comes only from Him—not from within. Only He who reads the heart knows whether we are truly loyal. Loyalty means readiness to hear and respond to reproof by the True Witness. We think we hear Him, but few are really tuned to His warning against self-righteousness. Laodiceanism results from tuning, instead, to inner messages that unwittingly either make obedience the basis for our security or attempt to offer security by grace without obedience.

To prize Christ in a way that does not seek to be like Him in every way denies His cross. His atoning blood purifies our obedience only when we take the cross and choose to die to all sin. Thus to reject the goal of perfection is to repudiate justification. It is to make "provision for the flesh." It is to refuse to "put . . . on the Lord Jesus Christ" (Rom. 13:14), our only substitute and our sole surety.

But to deny that even our best obedience must be atoned is equally disloyal. It disclaims that Christ is our only righteousness. To limit His substitutionary ministry to the past is to repudiate His cross by an attempt to provide for Him what He died to provide for us!

Unless we are cleansed by His blood, our most obedient actions only intensify our condemnation. And any commitment to obey that does not rest upon faith in *His* obedience either leads to despair or trains us in Laodicean self-deception. In contrast to the cruel deception of external obedience that does not depend upon substitution (and is thus the essence of works-righteousness), the internal obedience of heart faith produces righteous fruit in transformed behavior.

Otherwise, all efforts to reform only deceive us into thinking that we are righteousness. But even our good behavior represents a righteousness that the True Witness rebukes. Attempts to obey without at the same time a sense that even our obedience itself must be atoned for led us into Laodiceanism in the first place. It then caused us to reject the 1888 message. It now permits us to judge harshly those who try to expose our self-deception. Meanwhile, we prevent the sealing work of imprinting the character of Christ upon us as surely as do those who deny this process by opposing perfection as legalism.

The Spirit can seal His character in our experience only as we draw ever nearer to Him in a continually deepening relationship. But unless we by faith claim His atonement for our obedience, to draw near is to invite despair because we will then more clearly recognize our own imperfection! Without His substitutionary provisions the very presence of Christ is a condemning law, as it displays a perfection we have not achieved. Indeed, to evade His guilt-producing presence, Jewish leaders crucified Him!

To maintain a sense of security or to avoid despair, we thus instinctively seek by obedient behavior to assure ourselves of a Presence from which we at the same time unconsciously shrink! And to the degree we succeed in hiding from reality we only deepen our Laodicean malady. Meanwhile, an honest despair of any perfection in self is absolutely necessary to cure our Laodicean self-justification.

Until we lose all hope in our own obedience and begin to claim His righteousness alone, all grace comes to us as law! Only as we recognize its impossible demand and fall upon Christ the Rock in despair of our old covenant self, letting Him shatter our self-delusions, can we ever rise in triumph through faith in Christ, our only righteousness (Gal. 3:22-26). *Unless a concept of Christ as our only righteousness (obedience) unites with an ever stronger commitment to obey, our very claim to believe becomes a substitute for faith, thus leaving us in a "lawless state"!* This double key alone can unite and complete the partial truths held by liberals and conservatives.

A CLOSER LOOK AT LANGUAGE-SPLITTING

We now return to *Steps to Christ*, which dramatically illustrates Ellen White's lifelong pattern of urging perfect obedience while simultaneously proclaiming Christ as our only perfection. By back-to-back paragraphs from chapter 7 we demonstrated in a previous chapter that conservatives and liberals alike fracture her paradoxes. In choosing opposite "texts," each side wars against its own context—the other's text! Her message not only requires both, but in a relationship that fully honors each.

A survey of the rest of chapter 7 will now show how alternating paragraphs continue to hold these principles in balance. Only by holding both do we deny all human merit. To belittle either denies the paradoxical principles found in the Bible just as in Ellen White. And that has constantly fueled the conflict that presently rages among Adventists.

"So we have nothing in ourselves of which to boast. We have no ground for self-exaltation. Our only ground of hope is in the righteousness of Christ imputed to us, *and* in that wrought by His Spirit working in and through us" (p. 63; italics supplied).

"Our only ground of hope" is thus neither imputed nor imparted righteousness—it is both together! Neither alone will suffice. One alone does not provide sufficient standing "ground."

"Exactly!" say conservatives, grasping this second liberal proof text for their use. "That is just what we have been saying!"

Not so! The standard position does claim both, but upon the wrong basis—a basis Desmond Ford rightly challenges. Both obedience and perfection, as truly as justification, rest upon Christ's obedience and sacrifice. But Ford's strictly legal, anti-perfection justification errs in the opposite direction. He undermines the test of genuine justification—inner commitment to obey.

Tragically, while liberals resist this Minneapolis test by denying perfection, conservatives who reject a substitutionary element in obedience (as the only way to perfection) also deny it. Any other approach to righteousness than unity of both is fraudulent presumption.

The Minneapolis key to true faith efforts toward perfection lies neither in Christ's cross nor human will alone, but in their unity. Any valid seeking of perfection requires a full commitment in response to Christ's great self-sacrifice. To remedy conservative distortion and expose liberal error, obedience texts (or contexts) must interlock with substitutionary contexts (or texts).

The third conservative text follows the second liberal text (above):

"When we speak of faith, there is a distinction that should be borne in mind. There is a kind of belief that is wholly distinct from faith. . . . Where there is not only a belief in God's Word but a submission of the will to Him; where the heart is yielded to Him, the affections fixed upon Him, there is faith—faith that works by love and purifies the soul. Through this faith the heart is renewed in the image of God. And the heart that in its unrenewed state is not subject to the law of God, neither indeed can be, now delights in its holy precepts" (*ibid.*, p. 63).

Behavioral change is clearly based upon the exercise of our will. But, liberals quickly insist, the entire focus is upon internal, nonobservable factors such as heart and affections. "Faith [not concrete obedience] . . . works by love [abstract] and purifies the soul." Behavior is thus a by-product of internal attitudes and motives. These alone determine the quality and value of obedient acts.

Nevertheless, Ellen White's obvious purpose is to certify obedient behavior. The fusion of these external and internal principles would revolutionize both liberal substitution and conservative perfection. It would open channels of communication and permit the correction of errors in both camps while preserving the truth each now defends!

The second conservative text emphasizes the will:

"More than this, Christ changes the heart. He abides in your heart by faith. You are to maintain this connection with Christ by faith and the continual surrender of your will to Him; and so long as you do this, He will work in you to will and to do according to His good pleasure. So you are able to say, 'The life which I now live in the flesh I live by the faith of the Son of God, who loved me, and gave Himself for me.' So Jesus said to His disciples, 'It is not ye that speak, but the Spirit of your Father which speaketh in you.' Then with Christ working in you, you will manifest the same spirit and do the same good works—works of righteousness, obedience" (ibid., pp. 62, 63).

Again, context is important. This passage follows the first Liberal text and explains its pronouncement that Christ's obedience must continually stand in place of the believer's in order for him or her to be "accepted before God just as if [he or she] had not sinned" (ibid.). As Waggoner insisted, far from relieving us of obedience, God's accounting us as righteous actually motivates true obedience. Only internal change based upon a divine-human relationship can produce acceptable behavior.

The secret of perfection lies not in either of the principles we have been studying alone, but in their working together: liberal substitutionary obedience and death, and conservative union of the human and divine. The two are one: Christ is Himself our only perfection. Whether in standing before God or in a life of victory, all is by virtue of Christ's life, death, and resurrection to a high priestly ministry.

The last two pages of chapter 7 continue to harmonize both principles in a way to correct our misuse of each. Note how Ellen White seeks to remedy the weaknesses produced by a perfection emphasis that does not center upon Christ or rest upon His substitutionary obedience:

"There are those who have known the pardoning love of Christ and who really desire to be children of God, yet they realize that their character is imperfect, their life faulty, and they are ready to doubt whether their hearts have been renewed by the Holy Spirit. To such I would say, Do not draw back in despair. We shall often have to bow down and weep at the feet of Jesus because of our shortcomings and mistakes, but we are not to be discouraged. Even if we are overcome by the enemy, we are not cast off, not forsaken and rejected of God. No; Christ is at the right hand of God, who also maketh intercession for us" (ibid., p. 64).

Only those who are serious about character perfection will "often . . . bow down and weep at the feet of Jesus" because of their failure. Nor without this high goal could His righteousness be so precious to them. As we come closer to Christ our (only) righteousness we ever more clearly sense our defects. But this is evidence of spiritual growth! Thus instead of causing us to "draw back in despair," it should prompt us to rejoice even more in *His* perfect obedience!

"As we come to distrust our own power, let us trust the power of our Redeemer, and we shall praise Him who is the health of our countenance.

"The closer you come to Jesus, the more faulty you will appear in your own eyes; for your vision will be clearer, and your imperfections will be seen in broad and distinct contrast to His perfect nature. This is evidence that Satan's delusions have lost their power; that the vivifying influence of the Spirit of God is arousing you" (ibid., pp. 64, 65).

True perfection involves an increasing sense of our imperfection that produces ever greater gratitude for and dependence upon substitutionary obedience—the key to becoming like Him. Any other approach to perfection only intensifies our Laodicean self-justification. Nor, in the absence of a constantly growing awareness of our need for His atoning blood to purify our obedience, can we rest assured that "Satan's delusions have lost their power."

Only as our perfection recedes into its true reality in Him will we see the salvation of the Lord. We are perfect at every imperfect step only as we join Paul in striving for a perfection we must always deny having attained (Phil. 3:9-15)—yet one that increasingly marks our character!

"No deep-seated love for Jesus can dwell in the heart that does not realize its own sinfulness. The soul that is transformed by the grace of Christ will admire His divine character; but if we do not see our own moral deformity, it is unmistakable evidence that we have not had a view of the beauty and excellence of Christ" (ibid., p. 65).

Here is a stunning paradox. "Deep-seated love for Jesus can dwell in the heart" only as we recognize our own "sinfulness"—not merely our "defects." Only the soul "transformed by the grace of Christ will admire His divine character" so as to become ever more keenly aware of its own contrasting sinfulness. Here is genuine righteousness by faith! Seeing "our own moral deformity" gives "unmistakable evidence" that we view "the beauty and excellence of Christ."

And what a great climax follows in this skillfully integrated and paradoxical chapter:

"The less we see to esteem in ourselves, the more we shall see to esteem in the infinite purity and loveliness of our Saviour. A view of our sinfulness drives us to Him who can pardon; and when the soul, realizing its helplessness, reaches out after Christ, He will reveal Himself in power. The more our sense of need drives us to Him and to the Word of God, the more exalted views we shall have of His character, and the more fully we shall reflect His image" (*ibid.*, p. 65).

Ellen White's secret of perfection is threefold: claiming Christ's perfect righteousness, recognizing our own total sinfulness, and responding to His constant offer of exchange. This, rather than celestial records, is at the heart of justification. Yes, records do reveal the process and testify to the universe that the transformation is taking place. Yet the key is not records but our continual humility before Him in receiving His personal, cleansing presence.

Had conservatives grasped this justifying-perfecting principle, we might have avoided liberal error. Only in comprehending this is there any hope of restoring the full message to sincere liberals. Only then can we give the straight testimony or proclaim the loud cry to a world perishing in split-language confusion. Meanwhile, either to deny the subtitutionary element in obedience or to repudiate perfection is to betray Ellen White's formula: earnestly seek character perfection but fix our eyes upon the Righteous One as our only source of perfection.

THE REST OF CHAPTER 7

We have seen how three pairs of key conservative and liberal texts unite in succeeding paragraphs in chapter 7 to demonstrate both the consistency of Ellen White's paradoxical balance and our own violation of that balance. A brief survey of the prior pages of the chapter will complete our review.

First, dwelling upon the unseen ministry of the Spirit as the transforming agent in producing a "new creature," Ellen White assures us that "a change will be seen in the character, the habits, the pursuits." Nevertheless, "We cannot do anything to change our hearts or to bring ourselves into harmony with God." Thus, she warns, "We must not trust at all to ourselves or our good works." Unless renewed by Him, even necessary changes in behavior are unacceptable:

"There may be an outward correctness of deportment without the renewing power of Christ. The love of influence and the desire for the esteem of others may produce a well-ordered life. Self-respect may lead us to avoid the appearance of evil. A selfish heart may perform generous actions" (*ibid.*, pp. 57, 58).

The real issue: "Who has the heart? With whom are our thoughts?" The test is whether our hearts are fixed upon Christ and our conversations dwell upon Him (p. 58) or whether our focus is upon ourselves and our own attempts at reform. He, the source of our righteousness, releases it only as we respond to His love. "Love is of God. The unconsecrated heart cannot originate or produce it. . . . In the heart renewed by divine grace, love is the principle of action. It modifies the character, governs the impulses . . ." (*ibid.*, p. 59).

Ellen White then addresses two opposite errors: conservative obedience not adequately rooted in grace, and liberal faith that denies or minimizes obedience.

"The first, already dwelt upon, is that of looking to their own works, trusting to anything they can do, to bring themselves into harmony with God. He who is trying to become holy by his own works in keeping the law, is attempting an impossibility. All that man can do without Christ is polluted with selfishness and sin. It is the grace of Christ alone, through faith, that can make us holy" (*ibid.*, pp. 59, 60).

I know no Adventist who admits to trusting works or trying to make himself or herself holy. (Many do claim this as a past, false experience, however.) But self-dependence is avoidable only when our efforts to obey are based upon complete dependence upon Christ's substitutionary obedience. Nor do liberals confess antinomianism. But their resistance to perfection speaks volumes:

"The opposite and no less dangerous error is that belief in Christ releases men from keeping the law of God; that since by faith alone we become partakers of the grace of Christ, our works have nothing to do with our redemption.

"But notice here that obedience is not a mere outward compliance, but the service of love. The law of God is an expression of His very nature; it is an embodiment of the great principle of love, and hence is the foundation of His government in heaven and earth. If our hearts are renewed in the likeness of God, if the divine love is implanted in the soul, will not the law of God be carried out in the life?" (*ibid.*, p. 60).

Thus while obedience in the unrenewed heart (old covenant dependence upon self) is really legalistic disobedience, obedience in the renewed heart (new covenant dependence on Christ) is faith in action. The new covenant expresses a love that can neither refrain from good works nor lead to legalism. Grace is the only cure for legalistic disobedience:

"He who is trying to become holy by his own works in keeping the law is attempting an impossibility. All that man can do without Christ is polluted with selfishness and sin. It is the grace of Christ alone, through faith, that can make us holy" (ibid., p. 60).

Moreover, internalized law is the only cure to antinomianism: "When the principle of love is implanted in the heart, when man is renewed after the image of Him that created him, the new covenant promise is fulfilled, 'I will put my laws into their hearts, and in their minds will I write them.' And if the law is written in the heart, will it not shape the life? Obedience—the service and allegiance of love—is the true sign of discipleship" (ibid., p. 60).

REST STOP: SIX BLIND MEN OF HINDUSTAN

It was six men of Hindustan to learning much inclined,
Who went to *see* the elephant (though all of them were blind!),
That each by observation might satisfy his mind.
The first approached the elephant and happening to fall
Against his broad and sturdy side at once began to bawl,
"Why, bless me! But the elephant is very like a *wall!*"
The second, feeling of the tusk, cried, "Ho, what have we here?
So very round and smooth and sharp? To me 'tis very clear,
This wonder of an elephant is very like a *spear!*"
The third approached the animal, and happening to take
The squirming trunk within his hands, thus boldly up he spake.
"I see," quoth he, "the elephant is very like a *snake!*"
The fourth reached out his eager hand and felt about the knee.
"What most this wondrous beast is like is very plain," quoth he.
" 'Tis clear enough, the elephant is very like a *tree!*"
The fifth, who chanced to touch the ear, said, "E'en the blindest man
Can tell what this resembles most. Deny the fact who can,
This marvel of an elephant is very like a *fan!*"
The sixth no sooner had begun about the beast to grope,
Than seizing on the swinging tail that fell within his scope.
"I see," quoth he, "the elephant is very like a *rope!*"
And so these men of Hindustan disputed loud and long,

143

Adventism in Conflict

Each in his own opinion exceeding stiff and strong.
Though each was partly in the right, and all were in the wrong.
    —John Godfrey Saxe

We laugh at the blind men who went to *see* the elephant. Neither a rope nor a wall, not even a tree, nor a spear, snake, or fan provides any true concept of an elephant. Yet in his blindness each insists that his view alone is correct. The laugh is on us, however, to any degree that we do not view truth as a whole. We are most blind toward those issues that for decades have been central in our debates. And that blindness is intensified by an almost universal use of theologically loaded Bible terms.

Part Three

Pre-Fall or Post-Fall Nature?

13

What does Paul mean by "God [sent] his Son in the likeness of sinful flesh" (Rom. 8:3)? Could Christ take real "sinful flesh" yet still remain sinless? Conservatives cry yes! Liberals indignantly reply no! Speaking for the latter, Desmond Ford insists that " 'likeness' never means 'sameness.' " "Let it be specially noted that the only passage of Scripture which uses the expression 'sinful flesh' affirms that Christ only came in 'the likeness' of such. 'Likeness' never means 'sameness.' According to Philippians 2:7, He was made 'in the likeness of men' but He was *not* just a man, but the God-man" (in *Theology in Crisis*, p. 251).

To say "He was not just a man, but the God-man" only confuses the issue. Our debate is not at all over Christ's divinity. To this, we all heartily agree. Our conflict is rather strictly over the nature of His humanity. What kind of humanity did God take? Was it only "like" but not the same as that of other human beings? Or did He take the full human heredity?*

Paul leaves no doubt that Jesus was "made of the seed of David, *according to the flesh*" (Rom. 1:3) A parallel reference, also in Romans (Rom. 4:1), to "Abraham our father, as *pertaining to the flesh*" affirms that "sinful flesh" in Romans 8:3 is the same as that of David and Abraham.

Hebrews unequivocally confirms this hereditary key. "According to the flesh" identifies Christ not only with the sinful flesh of Abraham, but with that of all humanity. "Forasmuch then as the children are partakers of flesh and blood, He also himself likewise took part of the same" (Heb. 2:14). "For assuredly He does not take hold of angels, but He takes hold of the seed of Abraham" (verse 16, literal Greek; see margin).

"Likewise also" obviously means "in the same way." And this parallels "likeness" in Romans 8:3. "He Himself *likewise also* partook of the same" "flesh and blood" (NASB) as all the children share. But Hebrews is still more emphatic. "For *assuredly* He [did] not take hold of [the nature of unfallen] angels," but took "hold of the *seed* of [fallen] Abraham." This parallels "seed of David according to the flesh" (Rom. 1:3), but goes back many generations. To rescue His family, God "had to" take hold of what the whole race had—an estranged, fleshly nature.

As Abraham took hold of Adam's fallen nature and David took hold of Abraham's, so, through the "sinful flesh" that each generation inherited from Adam, Christ took David's fallen nature. But that is not all: "He *had to be* made like His brethren in all things." "Therefore, He had to be made like His brethren in all things, that He might become a merciful and faithful high priest in things pertaining to God, to make propitiation for the sins of the people" (Heb. 2:17, NASB).

"In all things" refers specifically to biological heredity. Don't overlook the definitive "flesh and blood" of verse 14. Jesus Himself declared that "flesh and blood" (which He took) cannot inherit the kingdom (John 3: 2-5). But while "that which is born of the flesh is flesh," Christ also declares "that which is born of the Spirit [as He was] is spirit" (verse 6).

No wonder that in speaking of the "seed of David" and Abraham, Paul carefully identifies this as "according to the flesh." Thus he obviously implies a contrasting nature according to the Spirit that the children are not born with—and that can indeed inherit the kingdom.

"Likeness of sinful flesh" can thus refer only to Jesus' nature "according to the flesh." It cannot refer to His spiritual nature, or mind—which alone can defile. In taking "sinful flesh," He restored the spiritual nature of Adam before sin. Luke thus calls him "that holy thing" (Luke 1:35).

Note how the book of Hebrews confirms that in assuming a fallen physical nature, God the Son assumed a pre-Fall, spiritual nature by restoring that body, at conception, to God's will: "Therefore, when He comes into the world, He says, . . . 'A body Thou hast prepared for me.' . . . Then I said, 'Behold, I have come . . . to do Thy will, O God'" (Heb. 10:5-7, NASB).

In taking sinful flesh "to do Thy will, O God," Jesus restored that flesh as a temple of the Spirit, who implants God's law in the higher faculties of the mind. Restoring God's law (will) within "sinful flesh" at conception assured His own absolute purity—even while dramatizing His new covenant promise to write His law in our minds and hearts by the same Spirit: "And the Holy Spirit also bears witness to us; . . . I will put My laws upon their heart, and upon their mind I will write them" (Heb. 10:15, 16, NASB).

Ford is partly right, however. According to the Spirit, Christ did have a pre-Fall nature. But he wrongly threatens His humanity by denying a post-Fall nature "according to the flesh"—the "sinful flesh" received from Adam, Abraham, and David. Consider again Ford's claim: "'Likeness' never means 'sameness.' According to Philippians 2:7, He was made 'in the likeness of men,' but He was *not* just a man, but the God-man" (in *Theology in Crisis*, p. 251).

Again Ford is partly right. But that partial rightness also proves him wrong! "Likeness of sinful flesh" does have the same meaning as "likeness of men." Both identify the fleshly nature (heredity) Christ took upon His divine nature. Each declares it the same humanity as other human beings. But Hebrews 10 explains clearly that Christ gave to that "sinful flesh" a sinless, spiritual nature at conception by submitting (His) will to the Holy Spirit. Thus that which was born of the flesh was simultaneously born of the Spirit. And "that which is born of the Spirit is spirit" indeed!

But some would label the view of a sinful nature "according to the flesh" and a "sinless nature" according to the Spirit as a form of dualism (separate human natures). Is it? Not at all. No more than the union of humanity and divinity represents dualism (separate divine and human natures). The divine and human were united in one being, the God-man, having one personality.

So also in taking "sinful flesh" and surrendering it to the control of the Holy Spirit as a temple of God, there was but one thinking, functioning human organism. In taking the fallen heredity ("sinful flesh") of humanity, Jesus sanctified that flesh as an undefiled temple of God!

Conservatives and liberals both appear to affirm this paradoxical reality—only to deny either pre- or post-Fall evidence (Heb. 2; 10). To protect the one pole of truth that seems most vital, each destroys the unity of the Bible and Ellen White statements that portray both poles.

SIN PRODUCES SCHIZOPHRENIA

The Creator's plan to subject His earthly government to a being made in His own image but also part of the animal kingdom he was to rule offers a vital key to the Incarnation mystery. As a body temple, Adam provided a link between Creator and creature. Through Adam's affections, God shared Himself with His animal world. Adam's own animal nature was under the control of a large forebrain endowed with faculties of reason, judgment, and will that enabled him to commune with his Maker, think His thoughts, and represent His government to the rest of creation. Union between the higher faculties of his biological nature and the Holy Spirit made Adam a bearer of the divine presence on earth.

God designed the human nerves and emotions as an electronic guidance and communication system with an autonomic (automatic) center for routine function and a Spirit-directed central control center for rational function. With the higher faculties in conscious control, this system permitted human beings to respond meaningfully and joyfully both to their Creator and to the created world around and within them. Such a union permitted God Himself to rule over all nature.

But by rebellion, Adam short-circuited this system and triggered an emergency plan. As the Second Adam, God Himself must restore the link between heaven's self-sacrificing love and creaturely affections. Forever would He be both true God and true human!

At Creation every bodily impulse had provided meaning. But, except as interpreted by the mind, the emotions conveyed no meaning. Now separated from God, the higher faculties had neither capacity nor inclination to interpret those impulses correctly. As Eve sought meaning contrary to the Creator's will and to her own needs, so sinful humanity continues to respond to natural impulses in opposition to the Creator and to His laws of life.

Sin pertains neither to flesh nor to its behavior. Rather it is the exercise of human will in exalting self as center and director of an electrochemical system designed as a medium of Creator-creature communication. Sin dispossesses the Holy Spirit as director of the body temple. To use insights we found in the book of Galatians, this removes His jurisdiction and initiates the jurisdiction of condemning law. Faith in the Seed alone can restore the Spirit's jurisdiction, thus freeing us from that of the law.

The fruit of estrangement from God is sinful behavior. But instead of the independence they sought by cutting themselves off from their Creator, our first parents lost their capacity to govern even their own bodies. Indeed, apart from the Holy Spirit, heaven's representative, they found themselves reduced to highly intelligent but insane animals.

Since they retain certain ruling faculties, human beings imagine they are still in control of themselves. But, separated from the Holy Spirit, humanity compulsively submits to the blind impulses of the body. By animal passions and perverted human emotions that now control the higher powers, the enemy subjugates the entire being, thus forcing us to war against our Creator.

As *the* fruit of sin, such self-centered behavior involves a manipulative excitation and/or an artificial repression of the nervous system—either in perverted self-gratification or in masking the warnings of guilt and pain. The compulsion to excite or to repress one's emotions is the basis of all addictions. For addictions reflect compulsive, largely unconscious efforts to find happiness and meaning apart from the One who designed the body system for the joy of ever-increasing meaning.

To produce pleasurable sensations, the tobacco user poisons his or her entire system. The autonomic nervous system struggles to cope with the abuse caused by the deranged higher faculties that have become enslaved to the impulses of the lower organs. But to keep the system in balance, it is forced into adjustments that make it dependent upon the poisons. The body cannot recognize its self-destruction. And estranged from the Spirit, the mind suicidally misinterprets those warning signals that demand the immediate removal of the nerve stimulators or depressors, and compulsively indulges its deranged passions.

Besides physical addictions, modern addictions include novels, radio, TV, and videos. A common key to all of them is adrenaline addiction. But the supreme and master addiction is to pride.

As a boy I became addicted to novels. For years I remained under the jurisdiction of law and bore its guilt, trying desperately to quit the habit. Finally the *paidagōgos* drove me to Christ, who set me free (Gal. 3:22-25). The key to freedom—not merely from guilt but from my insane efforts to find meaning and happiness by exciting my nervous system—was a body temple restored to the Holy Spirit. In this union I discovered joy I had never imagined. True meaning available only in communion and fellowship with Christ released me from my enslavement to irrational emotions. Meanwhile, the Holy Spirit refused to permit the full demonic control over me that I had unwittingly invited through my addiction.

Except for divine intervention, the human race would forever have come under Satan's absolute domination when Adam and Eve surrendered the body temple to his manipulation. But the promise of enmity between Satan and the woman through her Seed (Gen. 3:15) assured us of divine protection and supernatural aid in returning to God's plan.

To expel Satan and rescue humanity, God must restore the divine-human dominion. In Adam's place, He Himself entered human flesh. Although subject to all the laws of heredity, He repudiated sin's right to reign in Him. With every breath He drew He expressed divine enmity against sin. The enmity against sin that the Spirit alone can instill in us is the key to our loyalty to our Elder Brother's reestablished government!

But this enmity also explains the spiritual schizophrenia in those who seek to obey but do not yield the body temple to the Spirit. The result is a losing battle with a former master who subverts by exciting those sinful desires that in the past we so assiduously cultivated! Created to control the emotions now fractured by our surrender to our bodily impulses, the mind constantly finds itself torn between the impressions of the Spirit and those of the flesh (Gal. 5:17). The only solution to this conflict is to surrender the body temple to the Spirit (verses 16, 18).

The new nature (the Spirit's directing presence in the mind) assures a continuous mental struggle between two superpowers. One seeks to manipulate our deranged faculties so as to reenslave the body to its perverted emotions. But to fully rescue and restore us, the other offers us freedom through the exercise of Spirit-directed, higher faculties. Unless we surrender to the Restorer, we will be controled to a greater or lesser extent by the destroyer.

Only as we through our higher faculties place our lower faculties under divine direction can the Spirit heal and restore our inner unity. Since He will never manipulate our emotions, healing takes time and effort. It depends upon our continued choice to remain subject to Him.

Restoration begins the moment we by faith transfer from the jurisdiction of law to the jurisdiction of the Spirit (Gal. 3:25). Yet conflict over that control continues because of the unyielding struggle between Christ and Satan over our loyalty. Satan takes advantage of a mind only programmed to evil to reduce us again to bondage by stimulating our "old" nature. And the Holy Spirit continues His commitment to our freedom by constant appeals to our conscience.

Freedom involves our continual choice to resist the instincts of degenerate faculties programmed to evil. That freedom to choose is most precious indeed. We have it only because God made His preincarnate decision to enter a human race subject to the hereditary impact of thousands of years of sin and thus to consign "sinful flesh"—our flesh—to the tomb!

CHRIST HAD NO CARNAL NATURE

Conservatives thus rightly insist on a post-Fall nature. *But those who hold that Jesus was just like us in His human nature are in error.* Exactly like us in biological inheritance? Yes! But He was very unlike us in that sin had never infected His higher, spiritual faculties. From His conception the Holy Spirit directed His body every moment!

Since He was conceived by the Spirit, some say Jesus came forth from the womb born again. But we must never equate His birth with the new birth restoration of our own bodies as temples of the Spirit. *Christ took "sinful flesh"* with its biochemical inheritance. *But He did not take our "carnal nature."*

The distinction between "sinful nature" ("sinful flesh") and "carnal nature" (sinning flesh) is the key to Romans 7 and 8. Paul uses "carnal" to identify a body controlled by its own emotions rather than the Holy Spirit. It represents the condition that required Christ to rescue us by condemning sin in the flesh—our "sinful flesh."

In contrast to "sinful flesh," which means the body itself, carnal refers to sinful experience in bondage to an egocentric mind addicted to its own emotions. Confused by hidden pride and self-deception, the carnal mind cannot resist bodily impulses (Rom. 7:14-24). Thus the higher faculties that God designed to rule the flesh have become addicted to its mindless sensations! Conversion involves dying to such carnal propensities. But since they constantly seek expression, we must continually battle those selfish impulses—impulses to which we have already trained ourselves to respond.

Christ had no programmed impulses (conscious or unconscious) to repress. Because He always acted upon the whole of truth, He was never deceived. Since the carnal propensities of sin had never fractured His physical/spiritual nature, He was never schizophrenic. He had no residue of carnal self-deception to resist.

Though damaged by sin's effects, the hereditary impulses of glands, nerves, and organs could not contaminate His spiritual nature. His hatred of sin was absolute and His love for God supreme, unmodified by any impulse within—even in response to the most fierce temptations from without.

Christ "condemned sin in the flesh" (Rom. 8:3). In total dependence upon the Spirit, He reinstated heaven's government and thus brought "sinful flesh" into absolute subjection. The highest evidence of restored dominion was His absolute rule over His own lower nature. By a life that "condemned sin in the flesh" He ever held total victory over sin! He could boldly declare: "The prince of this world is coming. He has no hold on me" (John 14;30, NIV). Thus Paul exclaims: "For what the law could not do in that it was weak through the flesh, God did by sending His own Son *in the likeness of sinful flesh*, on account of sin: *He condemned sin in . . . [sinful] flesh, that the righteous requirement of the law might be fulfilled in us who do not walk according to the flesh but according to the Spirit*" (Rom. 8:3, 4, NKJV).

Christ condemned sin where it exhibited its power—in "sinful flesh." But this did not contaminate Him, because sin is not a physical entity. Sin involves reason and choice that have turned from Spirit-dependence to depend on feelings, emotions, and passions. Though these were designed to be controlled by reason and will, such control is impossible except under the Holy Spirit's guidance.

"According to the flesh," estranged human beings can serve only the impulses of their perverted glands, nerves, and organs, which, with a self-centered mental microchip, form an ultimate computer through which Satan plays his evil games of destruction. But a victorious Second Adam restored the body temple. He not only lived a perfect life; *He restored heaven's government in our flesh. Now He offers us the key to our lost kingdom! Restoration of that dominion begins with control over our impulses.*

From infancy the Spirit continually restricts and restrains the evil agencies that attack us. But to receive His freeing power, we must be born again (John 3:3-6). Even then, though the new birth produces a new nature, our minds retain their old mental files programmed by carnal instincts.

But Christ did not have this problem! It is only us who must daily war against a cultivated, carnal nature that always seeks to reenslave us. Only by remaining on the cross in daily death to self can we avoid the spiritual schizophrenia that haunts us with a carnality we unconsciously seek to retain—even while we try desperately to free ourselves from its deadly effects!

FLESH CAN NEITHER SIN NOR FORCE ONE TO SIN

Since the physical and the spiritual fuse in one nature, with each affecting the other, some insist that neither can be infected without infecting the other. This may seem true on the surface. Yet sin relates not to the body but to the mind. The flesh defiles only as a self-centered mind becomes enslaved to its impulses. "Listen and understand," Christ admonished the Pharisees. "It is not what goes into the mouth that defiles a person, but it is what comes out of the mouth that defiles" (Matt. 15:11, NRSV).

The mind, not the flesh, determines sin and its defilement. The flesh cannot defile the mind. But the mind defiles both itself and "sinful flesh" by subservience to its impulses. Paul labels this "in the flesh," in contrast to "in the Spirit" (Rom. 8:9-14).

"For *those who live according to the flesh set their minds on the things of the flesh*, but *those who live according to the Spirit set their minds on the things of the Spirit*. To set the mind on the flesh is death, but to set the mind on the Spirit is life and peace. For this reason *the mind that is set on the flesh is hostile to God*; it does not submit to God's law—indeed it cannot, and *those who are in the flesh cannot please God*" (verses 5-8, NRSV).

"In the flesh" means to "live according to the flesh," with minds set "on the things of the flesh" and thus in captivity to emotions produced by "sinful flesh." Thus, "in the flesh" must not be confused with in "sinful flesh." Even those "in the Spirit" remain in "sinful flesh." But though possessing carnal propensities that they must resist, those freed from "the law of sin and death" by "the law of the Spirit of life" (verse 2) are no longer "in the flesh."

That is, they cease to be "carnal." They are no longer ruled by "things of the flesh." Nevertheless, those who are "born again" do not cease to have the "carnal nature" they acquired while "in the flesh."

Christ, by contrast, was never "in the flesh." The higher faculties of that Holy One, conceived of the Spirit, "made of a woman," in all respects "made under the law," never surrendered to the fleshly impulses of the lower nature—as have the faculties of every other child of Adam!

To fulfill every moral precept, our Substitute subjected Himself to the law of heredity by which all other human beings have been betrayed into sin. Christ's perfect obedience thus gives us the right to "receive the adoption of sons." Moreover, to confirm the gospel that the ritual law portrays and to demonstrate the principles by which we receive His grace, He also perfectly fulfilled the typical law's requirements (Gal. 4:4, 5).

Yet, to the behaviorally oriented Pharisees, Jesus appeared to violate the moral law by Sabbathbreaking and the ceremonial law by putting His hands upon lepers and the dead, etc. In fact, however, Jesus not only demonstrated true Sabbath observance, He deepened our insight into the ritual law, whose twofold function was to warn of sin's uncleanness and to dramatize how God cleanses from guilt and sin's contaminating presence. Had He violated either law, He could not have become our substitute or surety.

But while the Jewish leaders' reaction testifies to our inability to perceive paradoxical truth except by the aid of the Holy Spirit, His apparent violation actually portrays the Creator's purpose. God had designed the prohibition against touching lepers and the dead—both symbols of sin—to teach us that sin defiles all sinners upon contact. Evil from without awakens evil from within the mind. But no evil from without could awaken evil within Jesus. For no evil lurked within the pure mind of the One who took "sinful flesh" to subject it wholly to God's law!

To demonstrate both His sinlessness and His power over sin and evil, Christ publicly placed His hands upon the dead and upon lepers. Had He not been perfectly sinless, this would have violated the law. But the sinless One had still another lesson to teach. "Sinful flesh" could not defile a mind fully directed by the Spirit to condemn "sin in the flesh" (Rom. 8:3) by subjecting it to the control of Spirit-directed higher faculties.

Adventism in Conflict

Christ thus signaled His incarnate purpose to so purify and restore temples depraved by carnal minds that evil from without will ultimately cease to awaken evil from within (verse 4). This is the issue of perfection. Before ceasing His mediation, Christ leads us through such an experience of death to self that evil from without ceases to awaken evil from within. Triumph over pride and every other motive that might prompt sin is to result from beholding Christ crucified, our substitute and surety (2 Cor. 3:18).

THE FUNCTION OF ADJECTIVES AND NOUNS

Adjectives modify nouns but cannot endow them with characteristics of which they are innately incapable. A "wicked blow" cannot mean sin was in the blow—which may have been struck by an animal, a falling limb, etc. Nor can "sinful flesh" mean actual sin in the flesh. For flesh cannot sin.

Indeed, animals also have "sinful flesh." For their flesh bears the effects of sin. Yet, without higher faculties, animals do not sin. The adjective "sinful" only refers to the impact of sin upon the flesh. Failing to grasp this principle, Desmond Ford has confused "*sinful* flesh" with "*sinning* flesh"—which involves the process of sin.

The impulses of depraved flesh may stimulate human beings to sin. But they are not in themselves sin. Nor can they enforce sin upon a mind not already self-deceived. Sin has its seat in egocentric thoughts and motives. Except by distorted minds, resulting from alienation from the Holy Spirit, the flesh could never produce egocentric motives.

Augustine's doctrine of original sin, based upon a false concept of sin's nature, has caused great confusion. The doctrine presumes that God imputes Adam's sin and guilt by divine decree to all his descendants. While no Adventist liberal that I know of restricts substitutionary atonement to a few divinely preelected as he did, they do obscure the role and function of the will.

They are right, however, in declaring a radical, sinful inheritance. But sin is no more an essence independent of the mind than it is primarily a behavioral act. Nor was the original sin imputed by God. It was imparted by Adam! Sin relates to our independence from our only source of righteousness. The real original sin was the surrender of reason and will to irrational impulses and appetites by rejecting the Holy Spirit's role as director of the body temple. Separated from God, even right behavior reflects that original sin and is in God's sight sinful.

So subversive is our nature that we hide sin within ourselves that we readily expose in others. But we never truly recognize sin's reality until we grasp its pervasive presence in us. The cause is indeed the original sin! As head of the human family, Adam surrendered to Satan authority to rule our body. Thus even our earliest impulses center on self.

Liberals rightly oppose any focus upon behavior that obscures the seat of sin in attitudes and motives. But then they stop short. Having identified guilt with the mind rather than behavior, they betray their vital principle by next identifying sin with mindless nature—sinful flesh. Which is worse—to locate the seat of sin in behavior that at the very least involves the exercise of will, or to identify sin with nature, something we have no choice over?

Spiritual guilt is neither matter nor a genetic essence divinely passed from parent to child. It involves moral responsibility for alienation from God (James 4:17) and is determined by motives.

An Anchorage snow plowman was horrified in 1957 to see blood and flesh spray from his machine. But neither God nor the Alaska court charged him with murdering two children playing in a snow house they had tunneled into the very snow it was his job to remove.

A true doctrine of original sin must relate to the loss of dominion in our separation from God, rather than divine imputation of sin and guilt. To restore that dominion, Christ took "sinful flesh" that had for millennia been subject to demonic harassment and manipulation via emotions. As the new head of humanity He reversed Adam's decision. By His preincarnate choice He returned reason and will, the governing center in man's nature, to the Spirit's direction. Then, by the Spirit's presence and power, He as man daily denied the demon-control that Adam had invited and that had warped the "sinful flesh" through millennia of degeneration (The Desire of Ages, pp. 34-38, 49). Thus He demonstrated that neither Satan nor sin has any legitimate authority or power over mind or body.

Sin is insanity. It exists not through sinful flesh per se, but by self-deception. The flesh has no consciousness by which to interpret its feelings. In craving indulgence, a carnal mind deceives itself by attributing good to evil; it rationalizes its submission to its uncontrolled impulses. Conversion, on the other hand, involves death to the flesh by denying the perverted cravings of a depraved mind. The new human being rejects the control of emotion over the mind.

We cease to be carnal and become spiritual when emotions and impulses that once dominated the enslaved mind now come under the rulership of a Spirit-directed reason and will. One is thus spiritual only as, by the Holy Spirit, the rational faculties regain control of the fleshly impulses.

But, as noted above, the spiritual man or woman not only retains the sinful flesh that Jesus took, he or she must continue to diligently battle against cultivated, carnal habit patterns that Jesus did not take and never had!

Rest Stop: Preparing for a Wrap-up

Liberals and conservatives both sometimes seem to express the paradoxical conclusion we have reached above. Why, then, do they circumvent the otherwise obvious? Because each view of Christ's nature is required by a corresponding concept of righteousness by faith. This, in turn, is determined by conflicting views of perfection. Blinded by split-truth thinking, neither dares to acknowledge the other's truth. To do this would threaten their position for or against perfection.

To defend perfection, conservatives compulsively deny a pre-Fall nature. On the other hand, to deny perfection, liberals repudiate a post-Fall nature. But in so doing, each invalidates justification, which rests upon the fulness of a threefold atonement!

The Passover depicted a complete sacrificial atonement that must validate a two-phase, heavenly atonement, one typified by the holy place, the other by the Most Holy Place. Pentecost initiated the continual atonement in the holy place. The Day of Atonement in the Most Holy Place portrayed a final atonement that will bring continual atoning to an end.

To oppose perfection, liberals emphasize a finished atonement on the cross but invalidate the entire heavenly ministry by repudiating a final atonement. But to defend a final atonement perfection, which brings the continual atonement to an end shortly before Christ's return, conservatives invalidate a completed sacrificial atonement—upon which the entire heavenly ministry rests.

Thus, to defend perfection, one threatens justification's sacrificial base, while to repudiate perfection, the other reduces justification to its legal base. Nevertheless, when understood in the light of the threefold atonement, perfection, now the underlying cause and perpetuator of our divisions, actually offers us a key to unity.

---

* Desmond Ford answers by calling Jesus "the immaculate Man" (in *Theology in Crisis*, p. 254). This view differs from the Roman Catholic concept of the immaculate conception only in that Jesus alone, and not Mary, is declared to be conceived immaculately. The implications concerning Christ's nature are the same either way. Ford asserts:

"It is not true to say that Christ's [body] was born of Mary in the way that water passes through a pipe assuming nothing from the substance of the pipe, but it is true to say that the substance of Mary was moulded into a perfect nature for our Lord just as in the beginning the Holy Spirit took chaos and made a perfect world" (*ibid.*, p. 255).

Could it be that the nature of Christ is really no closer to Mary's (and thus to ours) than the relationship of "chaos" to the "perfect world" created from it? Is that scriptural? Not at all! To say that the biological "substance of Mary was moulded into a perfect nature" independent of the laws of heredity is to contradict the Scriptures, including the book of Romans, directly.

Part Three

Perfection, Source of Conflict: Key to Unity 14

I believe that honorable debate over the concept of perfection has become impossible in the Seventh-day Adventist Church. Each side of the issue makes the other "an offender for a word." Each reacts like a mother bear protecting her cubs. And for the same reason. Each sees in the other a threat to the church family. Both caricature each other's position and misrepresent their statements while haranguing them from within the safety of their own ideological community.

The opposing camps freely use the Bible and the writings of Ellen White with little attention to context. They narrow terms that bear a variety of concepts to fit a one-sided view. Having thus imposed opposite meanings on the terms, the sides employ the same vocabulary to speak two very different languages.

If only either side would honor context and try to hear the heartbeat and grasp the legitimate concerns of the other! But each contemptuously avoids comprehending the other position for fear of confusion. Nor can either afford to understand. This would risk the sharpness and force of their one-sided arguments in which persuasion depends on misrepresenting the other position.

Each camp quickly exposes the misuse and error in the other, but neither party recognizes its own error. Yet God ordains that this unending impasse should challenge us to paradoxical thinking as we seek to honor valid principles on both sides. For each is essential to the validity and balance of the other.

PERFECT: MANY AND DIVERSE MEANINGS

The King James Version translates as perfect 10 Hebrew and five Greek roots, each with a range of meanings. Two Hebrew roots provide nearly 70 percent of all the Old Testament occurrences. In the New Testament three

Greek roots account for more than 90 percent. The conservative idea of perfection is not primary, however, in a single one of the five root words. "Perfect" is the definition listed last for *teleios*, which accounts for two thirds of all New Testament KJV occurrences. And even this is not a separate listing. It is merely an extension of the idea of completeness. Lexicon and concordance definitions simply do not imply sinlessness. And few scriptural references in context could possibly suggest this.[1]

In Philippians 3 Paul uses *teleios* in three distinct ways in a space of only eight verses. Conservatives are interested only in the first of these, which liberals are careful to avoid: "Not that I have already attained, or am already perfected; but I press on, that I may lay hold of that for which Christ Jesus has also laid hold of me. Brethren, I do not count myself to have apprehended; but one thing I do, forgetting those things which are behind and reaching forward to those things which are ahead, I press toward the goal for the prize of the upward call of God in Christ Jesus" (Phil. 3:12-14, NKJV).

Any idea of a perfection for which Christ "laid hold of" Paul, as a "goal" to "press toward," can only embarrass liberals, to whom the goal is abhorrent and the striving is offensive. They emphasize the second usage of *teleios* in the very next verse, to which conservatives give scant attention: "Then as many as *(are) perfect [teleioi]*, let be of this mind. . . . Yet (as) to *where we have reached*, (let us) walk to the same rule, (being) of the same mind" (verses 15, 16, Green's Greek Interlinear).

Perfect obviously has very different meanings.[2] The key to perfection in Philippians 3:15 (NKJV has "mature") is *in Christ. In Him* they and he had already reached the goal and were perfect. Yet he urges them to imitate his example and to seek a perfection they are still far from achieving. The context of the passage relates this perfection to the mind of Christ.

The "perfect" (mature) are to be "of this mind" and "walk to the same rule, being of the same mind" (verses 15, 16). Paul introduces "this mind" in Philippians 2:5: "Let *this mind* be in you, which was also in Christ Jesus." Three stages in humility characterize "this mind" (verses 6-8):

1. He came down by divesting Himself of the exercise of divine prerogatives of power, glory, and honor in equality and fellowship with the Father.

2. He came down to this wicked world as a lowly servant in fallen nature.

3. He reached the ultimate stage of self-denial by obedience even to the cross, suffering the pangs of eternal death.

No wonder Paul denies having attained this level of perfection. Immediately before referring to "this mind," he repudiates his own righteousness, claiming Christ's righteousness alone:

"But indeed I also count all things loss for the excellence of the knowledge of Christ Jesus my Lord, for whom I have suffered the loss of all things, and count them as rubbish, that I may gain Christ and be found in Him, not having my own righteousness, which is from the law [that is obedience to His law], but that which is through faith in Christ, the righteousness which is from God by faith; that I may know Him and the power of His resurrection, and the fellowship of His sufferings, being conformed to His death [which we see above is death to self] . . ." (Phil. 3:8-10, NKJV).

This is the perfection that Paul denies having achieved (verses 12-14)—that of Christ's perfection of humility and self-abnegation in leaving a position of equality with His Father to suffer for a perverted race that arrogantly rejected and despised Him (Phil. 2:5-8). But it is the perfect we are to seek. Paul urges us to copy his example. With him we must strive, press forward, and reach forth unto "this mind." Yet we are to rest assured all the while that we are also accounted perfect so long as we too repudiate our own righteousness and seek the perfection set "before" us (Phil. 3:15-17; cf. verse 9 and Phil. 2:5).

CHRIST'S CHARACTER TO BE PERFECTLY REVEALED

"Christ is waiting with longing desire for the manifestation of Himself in His church. When the character of Christ shall be perfectly reproduced in His people, then He will come to claim them as His own" (*Christ's Object Lessons*, p. 69).

Nearly half a century of disappointment in myself and the church has elapsed since I first claimed this promise. But I still believe. I now know as I could not then, however, that its fulfillment as I first understood it is impossible. The victory is His, not ours. And it must be received in defeat! Nor is its primary focus upon individual attainment, but upon "the church," His "people." We have long delayed its fulfillment by viewing perfection primarily as an individual attainment *rather than* a corporate experience in the body of Christ (see Eph. 5:27).

Of course, individual experience is involved. But perfection cannot occur in isolation. Independence accentuates human selfishness and breeds egocentricity. To counteract that egocentricity, we must humble ourselves one to another within the body. Only by practicing true priesthood of believer principles can we lay the ax to the root of the tree—pride and self-centeredness.

Conservatives cherish and even idolize perfection. Liberals deny and even hate it. Nevertheless, as our focus shifts from ourselves to Christ as our only righteousness, a true doctrine of perfection will emerge to unite us. We will then mutually confess that our intense defense of, and resistance to, perfection have alike been part-truth misrepresentations.

Liberals are right in that sin's infection is too deep for human beings to overcome while in mortal flesh. But they wrongly deny God's purpose and provisions, upon which conservatives focus: "Higher than the highest human thought can reach is God's ideal for His children. Godliness—Godlikeness—is the goal *to be reached*" (*Education*, p. 18; italics supplied).

The book of Galatians bids us transfer from obedience under law to a higher righteousness by faith in His promises. But our independence is deep-seated. Like the iceberg, it is mostly invisible. God can do in and for us what He promises only as we despair of ourselves accomplishing it through our own efforts to obey, however intense they might be. He cannot finish His work in the world or in our hearts until we recognize its absolute impossibility—but believe it anyway! Yet, paradoxically, ours is a vital role.

God's ideal for us will never be reached without our cooperation. For the human will alone can trigger that divine power that ever awaits our faith demand. In disillusionment with self we must trust fully and only in Him to do in and through us what we ourselves can never do.

But this will require a very different approach than now fuels our perfection debate. The primary issue is to have "the mind of Christ" by a union of the human and the divine. Shortly before his *telos* references (Phil. 3:12-15), Paul offers a profound clue to what he has in mind.

"Let this mind be in you which was also in Christ Jesus, who, being in the form of God, did not consider it robbery to be equal with God, but made Himself of no reputation, taking the form of a servant, and coming in the likeness of men. And being found in appearance as a man, He humbled Himself and became obedient to the point of death, even the death of the cross" (Phil. 2:5-8, NKJV).

To receive this mind of self-denial requires a sense of the vast contrast between the purity of His humility and unselfishness and the corruption of ours. We must respond to His mind by allowing it to expose our pride and selfishness. Each of us must continually claim His righteousness and cease to focus neurotically upon ourselves—upon either our victories or our defeats.

OVERCOMING SELF-DECEPTION AND SELF-RIGHTEOUSNESS

When not yet 2, our daughter liked to stand on tiptoe before the sink and turn on the water. One day I turned it off, telling her no! Noticing as

I left that she lagged behind, I stepped into the next room to watch her behavior through an air vent between the rooms.

Walking cautiously to the door, Leanne slowly closed it and gave it a little push to latch it. Then, looking back over her shoulder, she moved quietly to the sink. With eyes fixed anxiously on the door to make sure I was not around, she raised her hand, slowly stretched up, and turned on the water. The lesson she then received was to help her overcome the deceitful, disobedient, carnal nature I had bequeathed to her at birth—a carnal (self-centered) nature that Christ never had.

From infancy we develop a system of self-deception that affects virtually our every motive. The Holy Spirit does not enforce His desires, but directs our minds so as to restore our dominion through the exercise of our own will. But progress in "undeception" is slow. It requires our increasing readiness for a deepening exposure of our maze of hidden self-deception.

In response to the Spirit's divine revealing of our true condition, we must continually choose to die to a deceitful self. But to avoid the pain of such exposure, our human nature instinctively reacts in self-justification. It wants to deny what the Spirit uncovers. Converted believers thus have not one but two natures—natures that fight each other. For the new nature to remain whole, the old, carnal nature must be continually deactivated by death to the old self. Healing cannot be complete until converse principles of truth unite continuously, not merely in our minds, but also in the whole life.

Our own efforts to perfect our behavior can never transform a proud, self-centered mind. The greater our apparent success as we try, the more self-righteous we become. "O wretched beings that we are, who shall deliver us from such bodies of death?" (see Rom. 7:24).

Healing ("wholing"), by uniting truth's converse principles in mind and experience, requires both the ministry of our High Priest in heaven's temple and His Spirit's ministry in our earthly, body temples. But our willingness to take the cross determines the effectiveness of that combined ministry. And it is presented to us in God's exposure of our inherent self-deception.

Undeception requires our continuing choice to accept and have the mind of Christ. As we seek to experience His mind we must ever claim the perfection of our Substitute and Surety. Nevertheless, with Paul, we must seek that level of perfection for which Christ has called us (Phil. 3: 12-14). Ellen White provides three keys to this perfection: (1) Its purpose must be to honor God; (2) It requires divine subduing—only God can accomplish it; and (3) It must take place within the church.

Perfection, Source of Conflict: Key to Unity

The very intensity of our church's long debate reflects the importance of perfection. The more vital a subject, the more divisive its potential. God permits an ever greater intensification of the theological conflict in order to confront us with the urgency of probing its issues in greater depth so that we may discover truths' inner balance.

Our behavior must be transformed. But the change must begin from within or it only deceives us and blocks true perfection. The first principle of change is to focus upon His honor:

"The church, endowed with the righteousness of Christ, is His depositary, in which the riches of His mercy, His grace, and His love, are to appear in full and final display. *Christ looks upon His people in their purity and perfection, as the reward of His humiliation, and the supplement of His glory*—Christ, the great center, from whom radiates all glory" (*The Desire of Ages*, p. 680; italics supplied. For the meaning of "depositary," see *Ellen G. White 1888 Materials*, p. 778). (Note: Also review this quotation in relation to point 3.)

Until we grasp this first key—*the honor of God*—we will only pervert the perfection we so ardently seek. Indeed, our broadside condemnation of liberals dishonors Him. In their insistence that our righteousness is always and only in Christ; that we are declared perfectly righteous the moment we come to Him; and that to seek any other perfection is treason against Christ and His cross, liberals hold a vital key to the perfection Ellen White advocated:

"If you would gather together everything that is good and holy and noble and lovely in man, and then present the subject to the angels of God as acting a part in the salvation of the human soul or in merit, the proposition would be rejected as treason" (*Ellen G. White 1888 Materials*, p. 816).

The language of law employed by many conservatives blocks this substitutionary principle and prevents the integration of its numerous Bible and Ellen White expressions with those of obedience. We will never recover from a language of law so long as we are motivated largely by fear and compulsion to combat liberalism—that motivational glue that bonds so many different kinds of conservatives who would otherwise find it hard to get along with each other.

Unfortunately, however, without paradoxical principles, liberals use their own key to deny perfection instead of coming to understand it better. Instead of using it to shed light upon perfection, they lock it up and put it off limits. The conflict is unresolvable so long as we focus upon only one side of truth or the other.

Christ's coming is delayed until we reflect His character. Commitment to His restored image is essential to our continued growth in grace. But perfection is required neither to be saved nor to remain saved! Its *purpose never has been nor ever will be our salvation. Rather it is God's glory!* We are saved by the righteousness of our Substitute alone. And we retain salvation only by faith in Him as our surety.

Indeed, Christ, our only righteousness, assumes responsibility for our perfection (1 Cor. 1:30; Phil. 1:6; Jude 24). Why, then, does He call for perfection? Answer: to glorify God: "The very image of God is to be reproduced in humanity. The honor of God, the honor of Christ, is involved in the perfection of the character of His people" (*The Desire of Ages*, p. 671).

When we see perfection for what it is—continuous, unqualified commitment to honor and glorify God—the focus shifts from self to Him. How sad when our efforts to become perfect wind up fostering that self-centeredness that underlies all sin! As liberals well know, to believe behavioral perfection is necessary to salvation robs us of the very perfection sought. For it shifts the focus away from Him to ourselves and to our own behavior. Only as we accept perfection in Him—now and always—can we overcome this common neurosis.

Our responsibility lies in our unreserved cooperation with the Spirit in exposing the roots of sin that keep sending forth shoots we vainly cut down. But this requires continual death to self. We must refuse to defend self but, rather, trust wholly to the defense of His righteousness.

SECOND KEY: PERFECTION REQUIRES DIVINE SUBDUING

But since this is humanly impossible, perfection requires divine intervention. *The Holy Spirit must both expose and subdue us:* "Through the Scriptures the Holy Spirit speaks to the mind, and impresses truth upon the heart. Thus He exposes error, and expels it from the soul. It is by the Spirit of truth, working through the Word of God, that Christ subdues His chosen people to Himself" (*ibid.*, p. 671).

By His Spirit and Word Christ exposes our error. But it always requires our consent and cooperation. Unless we at every step choose to undergo this process of exposure, His efforts will either intensify our self-righteousness or produce despair. Despair is in some ways safer, for it might prompt us to look to Christ. Because of our unrecognized self-protection, it may be necessary for Him to publicly expose the sin we have so carefully hidden (rationalized). The most difficult sins to expose and expel are motives relating to good behavior. Only by the Spirit can we recognize and overcome our resistance to His subduing efforts:

Perfection, Source of Conflict: Key to Unity

"The Spirit was to be given as a regenerating agent, and without this the sacrifice of Christ would have been of no avail. . . . Sin could be resisted and overcome only through the mighty agency of the Third Person of the Godhead, who would come with . . . the fullness of divine power. . . . It is by the Spirit that the heart is made pure. Through the Spirit the believer becomes a partaker of the divine nature. *Christ has given His Spirit as a divine power* to overcome all hereditary and cultivated tendencies to evil, and *to impress His own character upon His church*" (*ibid.*; italics supplied).

This introduces our third key. Perfection in the last days cannot be achieved in isolation from the body or community of faith. Christ is "to impress His own character upon His *church*," a process that requires a corporate experience.

THIRD KEY: PERFECTION TAKES PLACE IN THE CHURCH

Our efforts toward perfection often disguise rather than expose the root of sin. When we concentrate primarily on changes in our own behavior, the mind centers upon self. This tends to stimulate ever greater independence from a church that seemingly resists reform. Isolation may appear to be the only solution. But nothing more certainly precludes perfection than pride's handmaid—independence!

Christ is to "impress His own character upon His *church*"—not merely upon pure individuals. For this He is willing to wait. Those who, because of the church's serious defects, would perfect their own characters apart from the body are attempting the impossible. They unwittingly substitute their own obedience for Christ's righteousness.

But, you say, "The majority of the church will never be subdued. The real church is spiritual, made up of the truly faithful." I agree with the statement but heartily disagree with the implied failure of Christ's prayer for unity in His visible, church militant. Only those who in faith join in His intercession to that end can participate in the triumph that will come in answer to His mediatorial prayer:

"The *prayer of Christ* to His Father, contained in the seventeenth chapter of John, *is to be our creed*. It shows us that our difference and disunion are dishonoring to God" (*Selected Messages*, book 3, p. 21; italics supplied).

In contrast, it is increasingly common to denounce the visible church and apply all prophecies of triumph to an invisible church—within which such accusers inevitably include themselves. At the same time they exclude all who do not concur with their theology or meet their behavioral expectations. This involves a twisting of words so as to deny Christ's message. Ellen White gave numerous assurances that distinctly pertain to the organized church. The first given below bears close examination:

Adventism in Conflict

"*The church* may appear as about to fall, but it does not fall. It *remains*, while *the sinners* in Zion *will be sifted out*—the chaff separated from the precious wheat. This is a terrible ordeal, but nevertheless it must take place. None but those who have been overcoming by the blood of the Lamb and the word of their testimony will be found with the loyal and true, without spot or stain of sin, without guile in their mouths. We must be divested of our self-righteousness and arrayed in the righteousness of Christ" (*ibid.*, book 2, p. 380; italics supplied).

"Sinners in Zion [are] sifted out [of the church]—the chaff separated from the precious wheat." This refutes all those claims that the church is now merely a spiritual body. The chaff, false members of the visible church, have never been part of the invisible church. Thus they can only be shaken out of the visible church, which "remains" or continues in existence. *True believers* do not separate from it. In the "terrible ordeal" that "must take place" so much chaff is blown away, however, that the church visible appears "about to fall."

"None but those who have been overcoming *by the blood of the Lamb* . . . will be found with the loyal and true." Only as we commit ourselves to complete obedience will we be overcomers. But this must be "by the blood of the Lamb," recognizing that even obedience "*must be laid upon the fire of Christ's righteousness to cleanse it from its earthly odor*" (Ellen G. White 1888 Materials, p. 816; cf. *Selected Messages*, book 1, p. 344).

Only thus can we be "divested of our self-righteousness and arrayed in the righteousness of Christ." Without this vital principle our ineffective efforts for perfection only stimulate a self-righteousness that fuels liberal animosity against perfection as the perceived cause of legalism! Indeed, though their conclusion is wrong, such legalistic fruit is now evident in a growing separatist movement that defies God's counsel and nullifies His plan for perfecting "His church":

"I know the Lord loves *His church*. It *is not to be disorganized or broken up into independent atoms*. There is not the least consistency in this; there is not the least evidence that such a thing will be. *Those who heed this false message and try to leaven others will be deceived and prepared to receive advanced delusions, and they will come to nought.*

"There is in some members of the church, pride, self-sufficiency, stubborn unbelief. . . . But that will not blot out the church that it will not exist. Let both tares and wheat grow together until the harvest. Then it is *the angels that do the work of separation.* . . .

"God hath a church, and Christ hath declared, 'The gates of hell shall not prevail against it'" (*ibid.*, book 2, pp. 68, 69; italics supplied).

Perfection, Source of Conflict: Key to Unity

God clearly has a visible church that contains tares as well as wheat. But notwithstanding the tares, the gates of hell shall not prevail against it! The tares remain within until the angels remove them at the harvest. Those who listen to the siren song of separatism need to consider such testimonies that characterized Ellen White's writings until the end of her life. But we all must also heed those solemn warnings of divine judgment given at the same time.

Some collect judgment warnings like a magnet and ignore or diminish the assurances—even feel angry if you remind them of their existence. Others focus upon the assurances and respond angrily to calls to repentance. We need both assurances and warnings—not merely one or the other! Paradoxical principles require that neither nullify the other.

From its inception, apostasy, misrepresentation, and dissension within God's visible church have tarnished His name and denied His power. The Redeemer's glory rests upon His success in perfecting and uniting His church. Thus Ellen White responded to 1888 by consistent pleas for unity. The war with Satan can only be won as Christ's prayer for His church is realized.

No one can have a part in answering that prayer who does not unite a quest for perfection with intercessory prayer for and practical commitment to that unity. Ellen White, after quoting from Christ's high priestly prayer, concludes: "Thus in the language of one who has divine authority, Christ gives His elect church into the Father's arms. As a consecrated high priest He intercedes for His people" (*The Desire of Ages*, p. 680).

To fulfill His intercessory prayer, Christ continues to delay His coming. Through unity alone can the church glorify Him in loud cry, latter rain power. His prayer must be fulfilled in final atonement (at-one-ment) before He can cease His mediation—the very purpose of the Most Holy Place ministry. Meanwhile, we must not despair because of the evil we see in the church:

"While the Lord brings into the church those who are truly converted, Satan at the same time brings persons who are not converted into its fellowship. While Chirst is sowing the good seed, Satan is sowing the tares. There are two opposing influences continually exerted on the members of the church. One influence is working for the purification of the church, and the other for the corrupting of the people of God. . . .

"And *all our zeal will not be successful in making the church militant as pure as the church triumphant*" (*Review and Herald*, Sept. 5, 1893; italics supplied).

No reform efforts will ever make "the church militant as pure as the church triumphant." Moreover, while Christ enrolls the truly converted,

Satan sows his tares in the church. The separation that those who would be the self-proclaimed guardians of the writings of Ellen White call for will not take place until the harvest: "Then it is the angels [not disaffected members] that *do the work of separation*" (*Selected Messages*, book 2, p. 69; italics supplied).

"The time is not far distant when the test will come to every soul. The mark of the beast will be urged upon us. . . . *In this time the gold will be separated from the dross in the church*" (*Testimonies*, vol. 5, p. 81; italics supplied).

Until the mark of the beast is enforced (by Sunday laws), dross will mingle with gold "*in the church.*" Only then will it be removed. Thus those now calling for separation choose to be removed as dross even before the angels are prepared to do their work of separation. But we all do well to note the following warning: "All who assume the ornaments of the sanctuary, but are not clothed with Christ's righteousness, will appear in the shame of their own nakedness" (*ibid.*).

To truly love Christ is to seek to be like Him. Thus the problem is not in seeking perfection—but in a perfectionistic focus that fosters a self-righteous independence that competes with the cross, the only thing that can make us acceptable to God.

Those who assume "the ornaments of the sanctuary [holiness], but are not clothed with Christ's righteousness." unwittingly seek their own perfection. They do not depend upon His righteousness to purify even their obedience. No matter how beautiful their ornaments of behavior, they "will appear in the shame of their own nakedness." Such self-righteousness stimulates "the sophistry of men" who promote separation in the name of those testimonies that actually warn against it.

"*No advice or sanction is given in the Word of God* to those who believe the third angel's message to lead them *to suppose that they can draw apart.* This you may settle with yourselves forever. It is the devising of unsanctified minds that would encourage a state of disunion. The sophistry of men may appear right in their own eyes, but it is not truth and righteousness" (*Selected Messages*, book 3, p. 21).

Only "the devising of unsanctified minds" "would encourage a state of disunion." "*Settle with yourselves forever*" that God's Word does not sanction—let alone advise—anyone to draw apart from the church body.

In their attempt to explain away such emphatic divine counsel, separationists imitate the very liberal rationalization they condemn. Instead of judging them, however, let us learn the lesson God would teach us by them. It is His atoning desire to use both their accusations and their rationalizing to expose and cleanse us. For the process of perfection involves our co-operation with the Spirit in exposing our own self-deception so that He can lead us to confession and victory over self-justification.

Both sides of the conflict employ the same self-protective techniques. One shields self by denying perfection. The other seeks perfection by withdrawing from the very body in which God plans to perfect us. Any focus upon behavior rather than upon Christ our righteousness counterfeits the only righteousness God will honor. The tragedy of our four-decade-long conflict over perfection is that it stimulates both sides to intensified misrepresentation of God's character.

If only liberals had led us out of the wilderness in which our Smith-Butler language of law bound us. Had they only retained a Waggoner-Jones commitment to the restored image of God in man. But, like Canright, they opened their eyes to recognize legalism but closed them to truth formerly held. Meanwhile, conservatives who see no necessity that our most perfect obedience remain under the blood unwittingly confirm the liberal opposition to perfection.

---

[1] Forty-seven of 68 Old Testament uses of perfection come from two roots. Observe carefully how these and three primary Greek roots are defined by *Strong's Exhaustive Concordance*:

"*Shalam* (17): to be safe (in mind, body, or estate); fig. to be (cause, make) completed; by implication, to be friendly; by extension, to reciprocate (in various applications):—make amends, (make an end, finish full, give again, make good, (re) pay (again), (make) (to) (be at) peace (able), that is perfect, perform, (make) prosper (ous), recompense, etc."

"*Tamam* (30): to complete, in a good or bad sense, lit. or fig., trans. or intrans. (as follows):—accomplish, cease, be clean [pass]ed, consume, have done, (come to an, have an, make an) end, fail, come to the full, be all gone, be all here, be (make) perfect, be spent, etc."

"*Teleios* (39 [of 60]): complete (in various applications of labor, growth, mental and moral character, etc.); neut (as noun with 3588) completeness:—of age, man, perfect."

Sixteen of the remaining 21 come from two Greek roots. "*Katartizo* (9): to complete thoroughly, to repair (lit. or fig.) or adjust:—fit frame, mend, (make) perfect (ly join together), prepare, restore." (Acribos (7): means exact understanding; see Acts 18:26; 23:15, 20).

[2] In verse 19 *telos* refers to the "end" of the wicked—their destruction as "enemies of the cross."

Final At-one-ment

15

"The Saviour was deeply anxious for His disciples to understand for what purpose His divinity was united to humanity. He came to the world to display the glory of God. . . . Jesus revealed no qualities, and exercised no powers, that men may not have through faith in Him. His perfect humanity is that which all His followers may possess, if they will be in subjection to God as He was" (The Desire of Ages, p. 664).

Ellen G. White does not say Christ had no advantage over us, as many assume. If He did not, He would have been enslaved by the "sinful flesh" He took. Rather, she says He "revealed no qualities, and exercised no powers, *that men may not have through faith in Him.*" By faith we claim His advantages as ours. To do so honestly, we must learn to be subject to Him, as He was to His Father. This means that His supreme motive—to glorify God—must become our own supreme motive.

When our salvation is the primary motive, however, perfection centers on self. Thus we not only implicitly deny the righteousness Christ has already bestowed upon us, but we also unconsciously resist His mind of humility by which alone we are perfected. Perfection involves claiming His righteousness in turning from self "to display the glory of God." Here is the experience Christ longed that His disciples share as they by faith realized who He really was—God in human flesh. "Christ was seeking to lead them from their low condition of faith to the experience they might receive if they truly realized what He was—God in human flesh" (*ibid.*).

A PEOPLE NOT YET READY

The raw nerve in our debate over the nature of Christ and perfection is the seal of God. Only those who perceive God's incarnate purpose will the Spirit be able to lead from a defeating "low condition of faith" to victory through union with God. That experience is the purpose of Christ's final atonement just before He leaves His post of intercession at the mercy seat. It was the primary issue in Ellen White's earliest visions concerning the seal of God in the preparation of His people for probation's close before Christ returns (see *Early Writings*, pp. 13-20, 36-38). In 1888 she refers to the 1844 disappointment:

"But the people were not yet ready to meet their Lord. There was still a work of preparation to be accomplished *for* them. Light was to be given, directing their minds to the temple of God in heaven; and as they should by faith follow their High Priest in His ministration there, new duties would be revealed. *Another message of warning and instruction was to be given to the church*" (*The Great Controversy*, pp. 424, 425; italics supplied).

What could this mean? That these early Adventists were not yet ready for Christ to come? After all, who today reveals greater evidence of perfection than those men and women who displayed such love that many of them gave all they had to the cause? But a special work of perfection (at-one-ment) had to be done *for* them that could not be done *by* them. The phrase "another message of warning and instruction" refers to the third angel's judgment announcement. "New duties" relate to the newly revealed concept of the Most Holy Place ministry.

As God set before them a deeper purpose for the Sabbath and gave to them a health reform message, this was to open to them a depth of meaning to His warning against the beast and his image. It would open to them the necessity for a special work of atonement—a perfecting that only God can do *for* us! Nevertheless, that divine work requires our active cooperation in performing the new duties involved. The most important of these is to cooperate in His final atonement by allowing the Spirit to expose our corrupt self—a self that imposes a kind of creature worship (of self) that, if not overcome, will result in worship of the prophetic beast.

The issue is Creator worship versus a creature worship that centers upon self. Our task is to overcome pride, independence, and self-centeredness, traits that perfectionism actually intensifies! (The term *perfectionism*, when properly used, does not mean belief in the goal of perfection, but a primary focus upon perfection.) In any case, pride and independence are so aligned with self-righteousness that their removal will take time and require submission to fiery discipline:

"Says the prophet: 'Who may abide the day of his coming? and who shall stand when he appeareth? for he is like a refiner's fire, and like fullers' soap: and he shall sit as a refiner and purifier of silver: and he shall purify the sons of Levi, and purge them as gold and silver, that they may offer unto the Lord an offering in righteousness' " (ibid., p. 425).

To call God's people out of spiritual Babylon with loud cry, latter rain power, God's last-day spiritual priesthood must have victory over pride, the taproot of Babylon's apostasy.

"Those who are living upon the earth when the intercession of Christ shall cease in the sanctuary above are to stand in the sight of a holy God without a mediator. Their robes must be spotless, their characters must be *purified from sin by the blood of sprinkling. Through the grace of God and their own diligent effort*, they must be conquerors in the battle with evil. While the investigative judgment is going forward in heaven, while the sins of the penitent believers are being removed from the sanctuary, there is a special work of purification, of putting away of sin, among God's people upon earth. This work is more clearly presented in the messages of Revelation 14" (ibid.).

Note that purification from sin is a work done *for* us by "the blood of sprinkling." Self cannot overcome self. But for the Spirit to accomplish it for us, our focus must be upon Christ and His atoning ministry rather than upon the perfection of our own behavior. Yet our role is active as well as passive. We are saved only by claiming Christ's righteousness at the beginning, during, and to the close of our conflict with evil. But such a claim requires our unqualified commitment to obey. To be "conquerors in the battle with evil," divine and human effort must combine ("the grace of God and their own diligent effort").

"When this work shall have been accomplished, the followers of Christ will be ready for His appearing. 'Then shall the offering of Judah and Jerusalem be pleasant unto the Lord. . . .' Then the *church* which our Lord at His coming is to receive to Himself will be 'a glorious church, not having spot, or wrinkle, or any such thing' " (ibid.; italics supplied).

The above quotes reveal the error many make of restricting perfection just to victory over every known sin. The Philadelphians met that objective. For weeks they "for the most part laid aside" worldly business and "examined every thought and emotion . . . , as if upon [their] deathbeds." But they were not yet ready (Life Sketches, p. 56). As did Smith and Butler, many conservatives unwittingly belittle perfection by their very focus upon it. They do not grasp the principles underlying final atonement—an atonement that Christ alone can effect. But He will do it only with our full cooperation as He uncovers the hidden pride and independence that characterize our self-centeredness.

The Minneapolis conflict was between an old guard's perfection by obedience through God's grace, and the message that *Christ our righteousness alone can prepare us for the seal of God—with our cooperation.* Do they at first glance seem the same thing? Let me assure you that they are not!

Both concepts call for obedience. But the first is based upon active faith in God's power and human ability to respond. In the latter, passive faith (a total self-distrust that relies upon Him alone) stimulates our active faith and motivates obedience. Both call for cooperation. But one assumes an inherent ability to obey perfectly—by God's help, of course. The other recognizes that sin has so deeply infected our wills that even our obedience requires atonement.

The 1888 leadership thought they saw an antinomian threat to obedience and denial of perfection in the idea of passive dependence upon atonement and the necessity that even our obedience must be atoned. Far from denying obedience and perfection, however, the call was for the full restoration of the body temple to the Spirit's control. This means cooperation with His work of exposing every element of that self-deception that drives us to seek our security and salvation through our own obedience! The most serious form of self-deception we struggle with relates to our interpretation of Matthew 5:48.

"BE YE THEREFORE PERFECT"

Conservatives have seriously damaged the cause of perfection by the way they use their key perfection text: "Be ye *therefore* perfect [*teleioi*], even as your Father which is in heaven is perfect [*teleios*]." Indeed, the Liberal movement arose as an attempt to correct our claim that Jesus here demands a perfection in us corresponding to that of His Father. Such an interpretation totally ignores the text's context.

Jesus is here teaching that internal obedience rather than external behavior characterizes His kingdom. He contrasts His Father's love in caring for the evil and the good with that of those scribal perfectionists whose motive was reward. To bring this contrast to a sharp climax, He enjoins: "Be, therefore, perfect, as your heavenly Father is perfect."

Luke's briefer account puts "merciful" (*oiktirmones*) in Christ's mouth rather than "perfect" (*teleios*): "Be merciful, just as your Father is merciful" (Luke 6:36, NIV).

Oiktirmones occurs six times in the New Testament. James 5:11 declares: "The Lord is very pitiful, and of tender *oiktirmown*." Hebrews 10:28 says of those who violated the law of Moses that they "died without *oiktirmown*." Two passages refer to "bowels of *oiktirmown*." The remaining two reflect similar usage. (Romans 12:1 refers to "the *oiktirmown* of God.") None of the six passages employing the word even remotely suggests sinlessness!

Nor does Young in his definition of *teleios* include perfect. It is simply "ended, complete." Strong also begins with complete, but the idea of maturity dominates a complex definition that includes the sense of perfect. But even then it comes last, and only in relation to "full age."

To understand Christ's message we must harmonize both accounts. That is not difficult. For Matthew's summary signal, "therefore," immediately follows Jesus' statement that the Father sends rain on the "just and the unjust." This virtually demands the idea of "mercy."

In Luke, "Be merciful, just as your Father is merciful" follows Christ's statement that "the Most High is kind to the unthankful and evil." Things equal to the same thing are equal to each other. Compare each clause in Matthew to its corresponding clause in Luke.

"But I say unto you, Love your enemies, bless them that curse you, do good to them that hate you, . . . that ye may be the children of your Father which is in heaven: for he maketh his sun to rise on the evil and on the good, and sendeth rain on the just and on the unjust. For if ye love them that love you, what reward have ye? do not even the publicans do the same? . . . Be ye therefore *teleioi*, even as your Father which is in heaven is *teleios*" (Matt. 5:44-48).

"For if ye love them which love you, what thank have ye? for sinners also love those that love them. . . . But love ye your enemies and do good, and lend, hoping for nothing again; . . . and ye *shall be the children of the Highest: for he is kind unto the unthankful and to the evil*. Be ye therefore *oiktirmones*, as your Father also is *oiktirmones*" (Luke 6:32-36).

Though each clause in Luke differs in wording and in order, there is an exact parallel in thought. This reminds us that in divine revelation it is not the words but the message that is inspired.

Neither Gospel says anything about sinlessness. Nor does either bid us to strive to equal the Father's perfection. Christ's sole purpose has been to warn against a Pharisaic focus upon behavioral perfection or withdrawing from others, as some Jews did from the Gentiles or their fellow Jews who did not seem as religiously scrupulous as the Pharisees were. Each Gospel faithfully summarizes this by a command for us to seek perfection by copying His compassion.

Both Gospels have the same meaning. Luke simply quotes Jesus as bidding us to reflect God's merciful attitude (*oiktirmones*) even toward evil persons. In context Matthew's *teleios* has the same meaning, but refers to that spiritual maturity that must underlie true mercy.

UNSELFISH LOVE: PERFECTION'S KEY TO CHRIST'S KINGDOM

To test this conclusion, we now examine the progression in Matthew 5-7. The Beatitudes offer a preamble to the constitution of Christ's government. The rest of the Sermon on the Mount outlines and illustrates the principles of His kingdom. After presenting the conditions of happiness that all true citizens are to enjoy, Jesus turns to the scribes and Pharisees who react in anger to His omission of any reference to law and obedience and, in essence, insists to them, "You think My principles will destroy the law and the prophets. But you are very wrong. Indeed, I came to help you grasp their true, spiritual meaning" (Matt. 5:17, paraphrase).

Next, speaking to the multitude, Jesus emphatically declares, "Unless your righteousness exceeds the righteousness of these perfectionists whose compulsion is to insist upon strict obedience to the law, you will in no way enter My kingdom of love and grace" (verse 20, paraphrase).

By a series of "You have heard the scribes say . . . , but let Me explain the principle," Jesus shows why their legalistic bias will not pass the entry requirements of His kingdom. He then illustrates those requirements by a family analogy: illegitimate children have no right of inheritance. And what is the test of legitimacy? True children will bear their Father's characteristic of self-renouncing love: "That you may be children of your Father in heaven; for he makes his sun rise on the evil and on the good, and sends rain on the righteous and on the unrighteous" (verse 45, NRSV). Be therefore *teleioi* [not by copying scribal obsession with obeying every letter of the law, but] by copying your Father's kind of *teleios*—in loving even your enemies!

"Be ye therefore perfect" thus concludes Christ's contrast between Pharisee perfectionism and His Father's compassion. This, in turn, provides the basis for the rest of the sermon.

The next verses warn against religious hypocrites who (contrary to their Father's character) trumpet their large contributions. Declaring that His followers should give their alms in secret, He also warns them not to parade their own righteousness in long public prayers. Giving a sample of a modest prayer, Jesus urges forgiveness. But this scandalized the Pharisees, who saw it as accommodating sin! Then warning against hypocrisy in public fasting, Jesus concludes by pronouncing judgment upon all who do not live out in their relationships to others the principles He has just enunciated.

Adventism in Conflict

On the night of His betrayal Jesus reiterated the primary principle of His kingdom: "By this shall all men know that ye are my disciples [children of My Father], if you have love one to another" (John 13:35). Two days before, He had declared love to be the test of all obedience (Matt. 22:36-40). Decades later the apostle Paul defined love as "the fulfilling of the law" (Rom. 13:10).

Too long have we used Matthew 5:48 to urge the very perfectionism ("sectarianism," see below) against which it warns. Our misinterpretation does not strengthen the evidence for His final atonement cleansing. Indeed, by reversing Christ's repudiation of religious perfectionism, our traditional approach only undermines that concept. Matthew 5:48 declares how we are to seek perfection *(teleios)*—by a Christian maturity revealed in compassion.

The same concern for context and harmony of principles must also characterize our approach to all biblical and Ellen White references to perfection. Whatever their specific context, the Sermon on the Mount provides the general principle for all of them. Our heavenly Father's compassion is the model (unselfish love) that we must imitate in seeking perfection of character.*

"He has also given the Holy Spirit as a sufficient power to overcome all hereditary and cultivated tendencies to evil, and to impress His own character upon the human agent. . . . Love is not simply an impulse . . . ; it is a living principle, a permanent power. . . . Our affection for one another springs from our common relation to God. . . . 'And above all things put on charity (love), which is the bond of perfectness.' *Will we consider that this pure, unselfish love, one toward another, is the bond of perfectness in character?" (Ellen G. White 1888 Materials*, pp. 1508-1510; italics supplied).

The above question is increasingly urgent in light of Christ's longing to complete (perfect) His Day of At-one-ment, sanctuary cleansing. The following section probes this issue.

Final At-one-ment Versus Sectarianism

Unless we behold Christ crucified, our only source of righteousness, our claims to perfection by grace through faith will be as deceptive as were those of Smith and Butler. All attempts to become perfect instantly shift our attention from our Substitute and His ministry as our surety to our own spiritual performance. Rather than expressing its mediatorial provision and power, our obedience thus actually competes with the cross!

"It is through faith in His *name* that we are saved. We are complete in Him. Jesus will not sanction *sectarianism* or a *legal religion*, which is so prevalent even among those who claim to believe present truth. Christ and His *righteousness* is our only hope" (*ibid.*, p. 453).

To be "complete *in Him*" results not from our perfect behavior, but from *His* perfect life and sacrifice, which *He accounts* to all who in faith accept Him as substitute and surety.

Nothing so stimulates a neurotic focus upon self as does perfectionism—that is, commitment to absolute sinlessness in order to be saved in the judgment. The inevitable result is a "legal religion" such as stimulated the 1888 rebellion against "Christ and His righteousness."

But what is "*sectarianism* or a legal *religion*" which "Jesus will not sanction"? Webster defines *sectarianism* as: "adherence to the interest of a sect rather than to those requiring wider sympathies." Obviously this applies to those who now withdraw their sympathies from the church. But Ellen White here links sectarianism to Smith and Butler. Even as denominational leaders, they withdrew their sympathies from the broader good and formed a party of opposition to defend their "legal religion."

Sectarianism would include any focus upon doctrine or perfection that detracts from Christ Our Righteousness. Its inevitable results are despair and/or a lowering of the law's internal requirement to permit self-satisfaction, etc. Concerning the latter ("self-idolatry"), Ellen White wrote:

"They do not see that their *spirit at Minneapolis* was not the spirit of Jesus Christ. . . . They justify their course in everything. . . . *Faith* in Christ alone can destroy selfishness and *self-idolatry* in the human soul" (*ibid.*, p. 468).

Note that the true formula for perfection is removal of "self-idolatry" by "faith in Christ *alone*." Anything less than the destruction of self-idolatry, the root of all sinful behavior, simply cuts the tops off while leaving behind sin's roots. However much we may insist that it is by grace and through faith, a focus upon behavior sabotages God's purpose that we fully remove "self-idolatry"!

Sectarianism is a self-righteous approach to the gospel. The bottom line is an exaltation of ourselves above those we perceive as less righteous. Such behavior gives credence to the protests many have made against our claim to be the remnant. Unless we are humbled by a sense of our own need, we cannot escape self-exaltation and a false remnant concept that would ultimately identify us with the remnant of Babylon, whose chief characteristic is pride (Isa. 14:22), rather than of the true Israel (Isa. 10:20-22).

Four years after her sectarian warning, Ellen White compared Australia to Minneapolis, asserting: "Satan has insinuated his awful, deceiving suggestions, and *they have believed a falsehood*" (*ibid.*, p. 1220). The Australian believers were "under the specious training of Satan, until the meshes of his net have entangled these souls in *self-conscious righteousness*" (*ibid.*, p. 1219; italics supplied).

There can be no more fearful state than "self-conscious righteousness." But it is the only alternative to despair for many of those whose focus is upon perfection. Such a "legal religion" prevents our continuing toward completeness "in Him." Anyone who tries to overcome Laodiceanism by perfect behavior is like a driver who, discovering the bridge is out, steps on the accelerator rather than the brake!

Our only cure is in Jesus' straight testimony to Laodicea: "Come to Me for faith that works by love and purifies the soul. Receive My righteousness and ask Me to anoint your eyes, that you may see hidden motives and renounce any thought of preparing for the judgment by perfecting your own obedience—which itself must be purified by My atoning blood."

"Do we then make void perfection by grace? By no means! Yea, we establish perfection by a focus upon Him in Whom we, by faith, are perfect even as we seek perfection."

ELIJAH, A TYPE OF TRANSLATION PERFECTION

The experience of Elijah, the type of those who will be translated, must guide our understanding of the sealing process. To ignore him as type or to impose legal implications upon Matthew 5:48 is to exalt opinion above revelation. To view Matthew 5:48 in light of the biblical type of those who will be translated would dramatically change how we seek to give the straight testimony! We dare not distort God's plan of perfection that alone must prepare us to give His last message of mercy—a message demonstrating "His character of love" (*Christ's Object Lessons*, p. 415).

Elijah reveals how God Himself assumes responsibility for preparing for translation all those who thus remain *in Him*. He first trained Elijah to depend on Him for every necessity. Protecting him from his enemies, He demonstrated His power over pagan gods.

Elijah's obedience was uncompromising. His behavior was correct. But he was not yet ready for translation. He had not yet faced the full reality of a self-idolatry so hidden as to be impossible to discern. The insane impulses that drove him to run for his life finally exposed his true nature and condition. He who faithfully faced death threats from the king ran in terror from the queen.

To expose the root of those hidden motives that could not otherwise be discerned, God now permitted the full force of those trials that He had until then moderated. He alone could expose Elijah's self-centeredness without destroying His prophet. He who will not allow any temptation we are not yet able to bear (1 Cor. 10:13) prepared Elijah for a translation that the prophet was in danger of thinking he had already qualified for. Without such divine intervention in forcing a refocus upon God, Elijah's very victory would have prevented him from receiving translation perfection. (That perfection must be received—it cannot be achieved.) A similar false sense of righteousness tempts all who stand firmly against evil. We are safe only as we claim the incense of Christ's righteousness—even for our most perfect obedience.

Elijah did not have to flee. He might have recognized the root of sin in his very terror—might have turned to God in faith. But God works in all things for the good of His people. The prophet's running away dramatized our own utter inability to prepare ourselves for translation. As probationary time nears its end, God intends to use our sense of weakness and our own inability to complete the refining process to expose and remove the last vestiges of dross.

All who are translated must first fully realize the necessity of a purer righteousness than the most perfect obedience can provide. But not until we face the Sunday law will God allow the ultimate test, a test that will destroy and remove us from God's people if we are not ready. Meantime, as He did with Elijah, He teaches us through carefully controlled tests and circumstances to depend upon Him for all our necessities, even for life itself.

"In Elijah we see the *natural* elements of his character revealed amid the *spiritual* life, *commingling together in strange confusion*; the grace of God and the impulses and passions of the natural man, each striving for the supremacy. The human is being tried in the furnace and the dross is revealed, impurity is brought to the surface, but the trial of Elijah is a scene that all heaven was looking upon . . . with deep solicitude. The fine gold appears in his character, the dross is lost sight of and consumed. This must be our individual experience" (*Ellen G. White 1888 Materials*, p. 490; italics supplied).

"Natural elements . . . commingling together in strange confusion" "amid the spiritual life"! Ellen White here gives us insight into the process of attaining translation perfection. This paradox must warn us against all false attempts to achieve perfection, attempts that will result in despair or—worse yet—in the assumption that we are without sin because we are not aware of any sinful behavior. This very assumption nourishes hidden self-righteousness into full-blown counterfeit "self-conscious righteousness."

Truth is paradoxical. Unless converse truths unite, the result is either to reject perfection or to foster a "*sectarianism or a legal religion*" that "Jesus will not sanction" (*ibid.*, p. 453).

Adventism in Conflict

If there was a "commingling together in strange confusion; the grace of God and the human impulses and passions of the natural man" that Elijah—the prefigure of those who will be translated—could not perceive, can we safely assume we attain to a purer obedience? His surrender to fear at the very height of victory warns against the danger of placing our obedience in competition with Christ's righteousness!

---

* One of the very few Bible references to perfection that can honestly be used in support of preparation for the seal of God (Phil. 3:12-14) in its full context (verses 1-11) also provides the same urgent warning against perfectionism!

Part Three

Pulling Things Together   16

A twofold purpose has driven this book: to uplift Christ, the Truth, as our sole source of righteousness; and to demonstrate a twofold violation on our part that delays the loud cry. Despite the fact that God has divinely attested our doctrinal pillars, we still fracture the truth of each one by unwittingly subordinating one or the other of its two poles because we do not adequately unite the vertical and horizontal dimensions of the priesthood of believers. Even when we unite them in theory, we often fracture them in practice. To overcome this universal problem, we must learn to unite our personal, dependent relationship to Christ as head of the body with a proper interdependent relationship to one another within that body, the church.

Paradoxical thinking and the priesthood of believers are mutually interdependent. One cannot function without the other. We cannot recognize how we constantly shatter truth's poles until we first submit to one another in the Lord and through His Word. Nor is a true priesthood of believers possible unless we seek to harmonize the apparent contradictions in every truth. For this alone provides the necessary basis for recognizing the integrity of those whose view of truth may conflict with our own.

As tension builds in conflict between the two poles of truth, we begin to fear both confusion and compromise and instinctively withdraw from those who disagree with us to the safety of those who already affirm our position. But paradoxical thinking is the real key to resolving confusion. And it has nothing in common with compromise. Indeed it does not tolerate compromise.

It simply seeks to bring the whole Word to bear upon any issue, recognizing the Creator's balancing principles within all life, each of which must be carefully cherished. Paradoxical thinking acknowledges that each pole of a specific truth has a peculiar function that must not be compromised by the other.

Yet I say "simply," not "merely." Paradoxical thinking is not just balancing and unifying the various principles. That is impossible for fallen human beings. No matter how balanced our theory or how determinedly we try to harmonize the principles, this is impossible when self is at stake! Thus, an earnest plea for the Holy Spirit's guidance is prerequisite to all paradoxical thinking.

But even seeking the Spirit's guidance does not automatically assure balance. We must cultivate self-distrust as the basis for true faith. It is instinctive to trust our own judgment and to distrust any who differ with us. Yet, to any degree we trust our own judgment, to that degree we fail to trust the Word. God's plan is thus to so expose self and faulty judgment that we dare not trust self any longer.

The priesthood of believers has two functions to perform. Negatively, God intends that as we see our own imbalance and unwillingness to face reality in others, we will then recognize our own need for humble heart-searching to discover hidden resistance to truth within ourselves.

Positively, He intends that we listen carefully to those with whom we differ so that we may discern any biblical principle to which we have until then been at least partially blind.

But I do not call for compromise of principle. Far from it. I ask you to refuse to surrender any principle you now hold. Guard it as with your life even while you seek its converse principle, a principle that God ordains to provide the parameters necessary to preserve the integrity of that truth you now defend!

To compromise any truth is to violate one's own integrity. And integrity is more precious than life itself. But true integrity rests upon something higher than conscientious opinion. It must be based upon the Word—the whole Word. We prove the genuineness of our integrity by our willingness to "hear the Word of the Lord" from whomever God uses to clarify it—even if that person is in other ways in error. The ultimate test is to hear that Word when it confronts our own sincere concept of truth.

But two fears block that hearing. Consciously, we fear the pollution of a Laodicean church, while unconsciouly we dread the exposure of self.

"Knowing" that thought leaders are in error and sure that they will not humbly listen, but will try to turn us away from the cherished truth, we feel compelled to excuse ourselves from the horizontal principle of the priesthood of believers, just as did both J. H. and E. J. Waggoner when they sought to proclaim righteousness by faith. Their history and ours both proclaim their serious error. They were too blind to see that the very disease they feared in others was already within themselves, seeking to enforce confidence in self and to move them to set aside divine instruction from the very One they sought to proclaim.

A secret fear of having his pride exposed united with his conscious fear to drive J. H. Waggoner to refuse to honor the practice of priesthood of believers even after the church leadership agreed with his primary emphasis. Because he refused to confront the latter fear, he was never able to recognize pride as the motivating power behind the first fear.

To maintain his self-confidence, he clung to his technical error as if to precious truth! More seriously, he reduced Christ Our Righteousness to a mere theory that became a substitute for the real thing.

Thankfully, E. J. Waggoner accepted reproof, humbled himself, and clearly acknowledged that pride had driven him to violate the principles of the priesthood of believers. Having thus recognized pride and set self aside, he was able to lift up Christ to the rest of the church.

LAODICEA: HOPE LIES ONLY IN DIVINE JUDGMENT

The Laodicean state (Rev. 3:14-17) that gave birth to and perpetuates our conflict is peculiar neither to Adventism nor to our age. We feel comparatively rich and increased with goods because we fail to recognize that we have cut ourselves off from our true Head (verse 20). Thus we follow our own impulses while assuming that He is still guiding us. As with Smith and Butler, we are sure our attacks upon each other are Spirit-directed, when it is quite another spirit that is actually in charge! This will cease only as we submit to His twofold discipline that He administers both by His Word and through His body, the church.

Meanwhile, the True Witness warns us that we have deceived ourselves into thinking that we are spiritually competent to judge each other. There are only two kinds of justification: self-justification (in self-deception) and justification by faith. To experience the true, we must "buy" His righteousness (verse 18). But the only exchange He will accept is the total surrender of self.

Self-justification comes from a mind so fractured by sin that we hide from reality, just as did our first parents. From infancy we rationalize truth to affirm our opinions and desires and to justify our behavior. To assure our rightness, we must emphasize those aspects of truth that seem to support our own perspectives. Thus we convince ourselves and often others that we have an integrity that the True Witness warns us that we in actual fact lack. Moreover, having discredited truth by using it to enforce error, we use the part-truth error we have cultivated as the measure by which to determine truth itself. And the rule by which to judge others!

Truth is reality. But to focus upon a single pole of any specific part of truth denies the whole of reality. Nor are we aware how we subtly shift out of focus those elements of truth that challenge our opinions or threaten our security. Unconscious motives always influence our behavior far more than does conscious reason. Hidden drives ever seek to protect us from any alignment of truth's poles that would expose our self-deception and lay bare our nakedness. Thus we instinctively invite those aspects of truth that seem to affirm our opinions and habit patterns and thus preserve our sense of security.

Meanwhile, those hiding from one pole of truth call forth the indignation of those who flee the opposite pole. Each side places the spotlight on that from which the other hides! Neither can tolerate the other's threat to unmask their error and expose their self-justification.

Our only hope lies in the judgment of the True Witness to Laodicea. He not only diagnoses the disease that has so far prevented us from proclaiming Him in the latter rain power of the loud cry—He prescribes its cure. His straight testimony seeks to expose our nakedness. He longs to restore the divine covering lost in Eden and never fully recovered because of human self-justification.

PEOPLE IN JUDGMENT TO BECOME JUSTIFIED PEOPLE

Our spiritual healing depends upon the threefold prescription offered by the True Witness (Rev. 3:18). The symbolic gold tried in the fire is faith that works by love. Only the love He instills by His faith-evoking sacrifice can remove our self-centeredness. In response to His self-sacrifice, we come to abhor our own self-righteousness and surrender our spiritual rags in exchange for the white raiment of His perfect righteousness. This alone truly covers our spiritual nakedness and removes the shame of our delusive self-satisfaction. But our ability to recognize our condition and seek His righteousness depends upon that symbolic eyesalve that the Holy Spirit provides as our repentance deepens.

Had Adam and Eve been able to repent fully, God might have been able to restore to them the spiritual covering of the light of truth. But this required a full realization of the terrible nature of sin, something that only the Incarnation, life, and death of Christ could portray. Even then, only the evidence of centuries of spiritual failure could prove humanity incapable of the depth of repentance it must experience to remove the root of its self-justification.

Genesis 3 presents several lessons for us to consider. Adam tried to transfer blame for his sins to Eve and her Creator. Eve fingered the serpent and its Creator. Before Christ can return, He must forever break the power of sin to perpetuate such defensive reactions. The perfection He requires lies only in His righteousness. But the price is nothing more nor less than absolute surrender of self-righteousness!

That is why a true understanding and acceptance of the concept of the priesthood of believers is so important. We each see self-deception in others that we cannot discern in ourselves. Moreover, we all see some truths clearly to which others remain blinded by their own self-defensiveness.

Unless we learn to think paradoxically, any recognition of another's self-defense will only confirm our own false sense of comparative righteousness. Paradoxical thinking not only requires that I seek to understand the opposite side of those principles I consider vital, it also demands that I recognize in the blindness of others a symptom of my own spiritual eye disease. It means choosing to seek and to destroy every idol that might obstruct my own vision. Indeed, that is the purpose of the message to Laodicea.

Two Greek words join to form the name Laodicea. *Laŏs* means people, while *dikaiŏs* may indicate righteousness, justification, justice, or judgment. Thus it refers to people in judgment, or judgment-hour people.

In context, however, *laŏs dikaiŏs* indicates a *self-righteous people under God's judgment*. But the significance ultimately intended is *a justified people!* The True Witness warns an unrighteous (*adikŏs*) people living during the judgment hour that they stand condemned for self-righteousenss, but offers them His own righteousness (*dikaiŏs*).

Christ our judge appeals to us to accept His role as Substitute before He must pass His eternal sentence of justice (*dikaiŏs*). Indeed, before His im*manent decree*—"*He that is unjust or unrighteous, let him remain adi-kŏn*"—He offers to justify (*dikaiow*) His people so that He can justly proclaim of them: "He that is *dikaiŏs* let him remain *dikaion* forever" (see Rev. 22:11).

WAKE-UP CALL: APOSTASY, HERESY, AND SEPARATIONISM

After a century and a half of unwitting self-justification, our only hope lies in a divine wake-up call. The problem is that we have long ago turned down our spiritual hearing aids to avoid His loving voice because it threatens our homemade security.

But the Amen (Rev. 3:14) will not plead in vain. *He will be heard.* To raise the volume, He permits apostasy, heresy, and separationism to strike the church! All three problems will intensify until each person either accepts His call to repentance or severs himself or herself from the Head and separates from His body. Unfortunately, all who persist in judging others and defending themselves will be shaken out!

The problem itself is not new. Delay in the judgment hour makes the difference. Because we continue to be deaf to the Faithful Witness who calls us into judgment, He continues to release His protection, thus permitting the intensifying problems that shake the church to arouse us to reexamine His straight testimony, which liberals openly resist and that we conservatives publicly seek to proclaim but distort because we miss its true application.

Unfortunately, in confusing the symptoms for the disease itself, we ourselves avoid the straight testimony by blaming liberals for our lukewarmness (verse 16). Our failure to accept the indictment of verse 17 results in our frantic efforts to manipulate the symptoms—in desperate attempts to become spiritually hot! Thus a zeal magnified by a focus upon behavior masks our disease and intensifies a self-justifying, judgmental spirit.

Our only hope lies in distinguishing the disease from its symptoms. Instead of justifying ourselves because we are lukewarm, we must recognize and acknowledge that we are lukewarm because we *justify* ourselves. That we persist in resisting the Holy Spirit's efforts to engender a true zeal that does not evoke self-righteousness.

The prescription of verse 18 will indeed cure our symptoms, but only when we apply it to the disease itself. Otherwise we, at best, only exchange one spiritual symptom for another. The purpose of the true and faithful Witness is to cure our self-righteousness. To save us from its eternal consequence, He lovingly exposes our disease (verse 19).

TIME TO TAKE OUR MINNEAPOLIS PRESCRIPTION

After more than a century, is it not high time to take the Minneapolis-Laodicean prescription? That prescription is not a new (or old) theology. It is a loud cry: "Behold your God" and freely receive His righteousness. Ellen White perceptively says of it:

"This message was to bring more prominently before the world the uplifted Saviour, the sacrifice for the sins of the whole world. It presented justification through faith in the Surety; it invited the people to receive the righteousness of Christ, which is manifest in obedience to all the commandments of God.

"Many had lost sight of Jesus. They needed to have their eyes directed to His divine person, His merits, and His changeless love for the human family. . . . This is the message that God commanded to be given to the world. It is the third angel's message, which is to be proclaimed with a loud voice, and attended with the outpouring of His Spirit" (*Testimonies to Ministers*, pp. 91, 92).

She sharply and repeatedly reproved church leaders for their harsh, condemnatory spirit in violating the principles of the priesthood of believers. Again and again she urged them to seek unity by prayerfully searching the Scriptures together. During the 1888 session she warned:

"Brethren, God has most precious light for His people. I call it not new light; but oh, it is strangely new to many. . . . Be careful how you oppose the precious truths of which you now have so little knowledge. . . . I saw an angel of God inquiring of these men who have educated themselves as debaters, 'How many prayers have you offered?'" (*Ellen G. White 1888 Materials*, pp. 140, 141).

Indeed, she commended Jesus' prayer for unity as their creed. Thus we must always combine our search for and defense of truth with the desire for and effort toward unity. Unity in searching Scripture would lead to paradoxical unity between grace and law, the principles of each serving as the proper context for the other. While at Minneapolis, Ellen White exclaimed:

"I see the beauty of truth in the presentation of the righteousness of Christ in relation to the law as the doctor has placed it before us. . . . That which has been presented harmonizes perfectly with the light which God has been pleased to give me during all the years of my experience. If our ministering brethren would accept the doctrine which has been presented so clearly—the righteousness of Christ in connection with the law—and I know they need to accept this, their prejudices would not have a controlling power, and the people would be fed with their portion of meat in due season" (*ibid.*, p. 164).

Of course the church leadership believed in both law and grace. But, refusing to retain the tension, they subordinated grace to law in hostile opposition to both the message and the messengers of 1888. Their most serious offense was in violating the very principles of the priesthood of believers that they reprimanded the younger men for spurning. The higher the office, the greater the responsibility to foster these principles by personal example.

Practice of these principles was and is our most urgent need. It is not even safe to think that beholding Christ could be more urgent. For we cannot behold the true Christ while remaining defensively independent of one another within the same body.

For the past century the church has urged its members to behold Christ. But the wounds and bruises incurred by the infighting between the advocates of opposite poles of truth remain unhealed. The test of our love for

Adventism in Conflict

Jesus lies not merely in a *passion for truth* but in *compassion for one another* and an intense commitment to unity through a priesthood of believers approach to Scripture. Each must honor the other, seek to hear and understand just what that other is saying, and strive for unity in the Word.

But once again, while the priesthood of believer principles are essential to paradoxical thinking, paradoxical thinking is just as necessary in priesthood principles. Unless we are willing to examine those principles that on the face of it seem to threaten our own particular concept of truth—indeed, until we seek to grasp truths opposite to those that seem so urgent to us—we will never be able to really implement the processes behind the concept of the priesthood of believers. Even then, such principles require that we behold Christ crucified before they will work at all. The cross alone can break the heart. It produces such a hatred of sin and its proud root that it repudiates self's unlawful authority to dictate our religious experience.

Adventism to Triumph as It Began—By Priesthood Principles

Our movement was born as Adventist pioneers deliberately focused upon the principles they held in common even while honestly and corporately seeking to resolve significant differences by the light of Scripture. The important thing was to distinguish major from minor issues and to allow as much latitude of viewpoint as possible on all nonstrategic points. Then, as now, it was difficult for individuals to perceive when their own burden was not major. But when conflicts arose, the leaders stopped the discussion for a time of heart-searching and prayer. Those unwilling to submit to such priesthood of believer principles separated from the body and ceased to have any significant influence in it.

Already by 1854, however, a key leader, J. H. Waggoner, set aside the principles of the priesthood of believers. True, the leadership may not have readily affirmed his view, but to violate the principle while proclaiming vital truth shows a lack of faith in our heavenly Captain. It also does more than anything else to retard that truth. By this and a majoring in the minors that resulted from the debates that he stimulated, J. H. Waggoner blocked his own message. The fact that Christ is our only righteousness, to be received only by faith, thus lost much of its impact.

Three decades later God called Waggoner's son, E. J. Waggoner, to proclaim the same principles. That he followed in his father's erring footsteps speaks eloquently of the universal nature of the problem. He had greater reason to fear rejection because of the feelings that still lingered toward his father. But that was even greater reason not to violate priesthood principles. For that, rather than his father's theology, was what burned in the minds of the old pioneers!

Had E. J. Waggoner continued to violate priesthood principles, as did his father, he could not have lifted up Christ as he did at Minneapolis. Nor would he have had the opportunity.

When will we learn the lesson that the violent opposition of Smith and Butler, earnest men sincerely committed to protecting the pillars of truth, also offers to teach us? Not until we discover and keep in mind that unconscious motives drive both conscious reason and unconscious fears. That lesson must someday penetrate us deeply. We all tend to be one-sided in our thinking and need a priesthood of believers process to correct our errors and hone our truths.

But this can come only through deep heart-searching in commitment to such priesthood of believer prinicples and a determination to know the other side of truth—even when it hurts. It requires a continual choice to die to self, which can only happen as we train our eyes and hearts to focus upon Christ crucified and cooperate with Him in His final, atoning ministry.

Theological issues, meanwhile, are not nearly so crucial as our motives and attitudes in relating to each other. That does not mean that any issue of truth is unimportant, however. We must train ourselves to constantly unite truth in our own minds and hearts by the spirit of truth. As we do, things that most divide us now will become links in a common chain to bind us together. In this hope I now summarize the three theological issues examined in chapters 11 to 15.

My purpose in treating atonement, the nature of Christ, and perfection was not to solve all the issues in our conflicts over them, but to illustrate some principles that will permit us to honestly confront the issues together. The actual working through will take time and require that each one of us stand for principles as we see them, but at the same time remaining deliberately open to valid principles held by others.

CHRISTOLOGY, PERFECTION, AND ATONEMENT

At Minneapolis the Holy Spirit sought to focus our minds upon Christ by a twofold process: the priesthood of believers that seeks a *unity of truth* that will in turn provide the *unity in truth* for which Christ prayed in John 17. This alone will permit the message once proclaimed at Minneapolis again to go forth in loud cry power! As I review the principles of Christology covered above, I remind you that uplifting Christ as we unite in studying His Word is far more important than any answers I might suggest.

Adventism in Conflict

Was Jesus our example or our substitute? Yes! Yes! Did He take the nature of man before or after sin? Yes! Yes! Was He the same as we are or in some way different? Yes! Yes! Can we by His example fully overcome all sin or must our obedience be atoned? Yes! Yes! Did Christ make a full atonement at the cross or does atonement really take place in the heavenly sanctuary? Again, Yes! Yes!

No, I do not suggest compromise. The Bible and Ellen White both testify to each element of all the pairs. Indeed, paradoxical principles offer the only way to avoid compromising one side or another of any divinely revealed truth.

The Incarnation is a great mystery we can never fully understand. Nor are we required to grasp how the opposite poles unite. But we must honor both, permitting neither to make the other of none effect as we seek the keys to their ultimate unity.

If Jesus were not our example, we could have no true concept of perfection nor any basis for seeking it. Unfortunately, our failure to recognize the nature of that example and our inability to grasp the relationship between example and substitute often flaws our search for perfection. Unless Christ is substitute, first and last, any focus upon Him as example is certain to stimulate legalism.

Structurally we seem *almost united* on the nature of Christ, while at the same time it severely divides us! If only we could share our convictions with one another nondefensively in an atmosphere of trust in the Holy Spirit and in mutual commitment to His Word, we might soon be in essential unity. We all agree to His perfect character and also to a fallen nature. Our debate over what this means is heated, however, by issues of atonement and perfection.

The books of Romans and Hebrews clearly teach that Christ took the same biological heredity every child of Adam inherits. Hebrews 10 explains that in becoming man, the Son of God restored the body He took as a temple of the Holy Spirit, forever and only to seek and to do His Father's will.

Since sin and guilt relate to the mind and the mind controls the body, by surrendering to the Holy Spirit in His incarnation, Christ broke the chain of sin (alienation from God). He thus always distinguished the voice of the Holy Spirit from those emotional impulses that have otherwise deceived the entire human race. Though the same in biological substance and glandular function, Jesus was thus very different from us. He was never deceived by evil. Nor did He in any way develop a carnal nature that resisted the Holy Spirit because of its subjection to emotions and passions.

The real block to our unity on the nature of Christ is its impact upon the issue of perfection. A paradoxical understanding of that nature, however, would also correct the errors on both sides regarding perfection and the atonement. Perfection is a vital doctrine. But it must be perceived in light of a *distinction* between *the fallen nature Christ took* upon His pure, divine nature and *the carnal nature every human cultivates* from infancy, a nature that Christ, our atonement, never assumed!

The complete union with God that Christ restored at His incarnation is the goal of the final atonement. But because of a carnal nature, our obedience at every step must be purified by the merits of Christ's perfect obedience and sacrifice. To this end atonement falls into three stages: (1) a full and complete atoning sacrifice at the cross followed by (2) a continual, atoning ministry in the holy place in applying the blood of His sacrifice ultimately terminated by (3) a final atonement in the Most Holy Place, which fully effects the at-one-ing sacrifice.

As but one of a priesthood of believers, I welcome any challenge that might correct or throw greater light upon any facet of these fundamental truths. We may not know how to unite some or all of these opposite poles of truth. But unless we seek to do so, we lack a real love for truth and do not have the commitment to grow in its life-giving principles.

We find the greatest insights into the balance of truth within the most mysterious paradoxes. Becoming familiar with the paradoxical patterns characteristic of all truth will stimulate us to seek the balancing principles within every issue. And it will also make us more understanding and compassionate toward those who differ with us. Honoring their pole of truth, we will first kindly affirm it and then seek to show its unity with our converse truth.

Finally, paradoxical thinking will teach us to retain the tension that must always to some degree exist in our minds because we cannot fully fathom even the simplest truth. Thus we will be led to love and treat respectfully even our strongest opponent. As we each set before others an example of how to honestly seek unity through God's Word as we bow in faith before truth's mysteries, Christ will fulfill in us His own request in prayer to His Father that we might be one in Him, as He is one with the Father.

When that happens, the glad cry will ring throughout every country in the world: "Babylon is fallen. Her power to hold her captives is broken. Behold your God and go free—free from fear, free from guilt, and free from the bonds of sin. Free at last to rejoice ever and only in the Lord our righteousness!"

Ellen White on Salvation

A CHRONOLOGICAL STUDY Woodrow W. Whidden II helps reconstruct exactly what Ellen White believed on the complex issue of salvation. He provides a historical perspective, showing how certain aspects of Mrs. White's teachings on justification and perfection flourished at different times. Hardcover, 160 pages. US$14.95, Cdn$21.70.

Handbook for Bible Study

A guide to understanding, teaching, and preaching the Word of God. Includes reproducible worksheets for contextual, cultural, structural, verbal, theological, and homiletical analysis. By Lee J. Gugliotto. Hardcover, 432 pages. US$39.95, Cdn$57.95.

How to Teach the Bible With Power

Christ-centered principles and strategies help you make the Bible relevant and exciting to any age group at home, school, or church. By Charles H. Betz. Paper, 144 pages. US$7.95, Cdn$11.55.
